ERIN JEFFERIES

PRONE TO VIOLENCE

Hamlyn Paperbacks

PRONE TO VIOLENCE
ISBN 0 600 20551 7

First published in Great Britain 1982
by Hamlyn Paperbacks
2nd printing 1982
Copyright © 1982 by Erin Pizzey & Jeff Shapiro

Hamlyn Paperbacks are published by
The Hamlyn Publishing Group Ltd.,
Astronaut House,
Feltham, Middlesex, England.

Printed and bound in Great Britain by
Cox & Wyman Ltd, Reading

The events and incidents referred to in this book are based on the authors' personal experience and information given to them. The names of the persons referred to in the text work have been altered, and all reasonable steps have been taken to ensure that they are not identifiable.

This book is sold subject to the condition that it shall not, by way of trade or otherwise, be lent, re-sold, hired out, or otherwise circulated without the publisher's prior consent in any form of binding or cover other than that in which it is published and without a similar condition including this condition being imposed on the subsequent purchaser.

DEDICATION

This book is dedicated to all the staff who were working with Erin in 1976, in particular to Anne Ashby who has been her friend and colleague for ten years and who is now the Director of Chiswick Family Rescue. With her capable hands she will guide this new project according to her own ideals and vision. We both wish her every success. Also to David Astor and Lord Goodman who have done so much for battered women and their children. Our thanks go, too, to John Pontin, and to the J.T. Group in Bristol, who have made it possible for our work to continue in this country.

Last but not least we would like to express with this Dedication our appreciation for all the hours of work put into Women's Aid by David Morris and Alan Cohen.

Separately we would like to give our thanks to our publisher's editor Peter Lavery for all his help.

CONTENTS

Authors' Preface 7
Introduction 9
Chapter One: *The way we see it* 15
Chapter Two: *Is it love or is it addiction?* 35
Chapter Three: *Children of violence* 58
Chapter Four: *Till death us do part* 92
Chapter Five: *Which way now?* 135
Chapter Six: *Is it all in the chemicals?* 166
Appendix A: 1976 - 1977 Report from Chiswick Women's Aid *184*
Appendix B: Observations on violence-prone families (*New Society* article, 1981) *221*
Appendix C: Client's brief for an ideal refuge for problem families *229*
Appendix D: Wife-torture in England (taken from a report by Frances Power Cobbe, 1878) *238*

AUTHORS' PREFACE

The premise of our work is that every baby needs to feel love and happiness. A baby will bond these instinctive feelings to whatever people and situations are available. It is the birthright of every child to be surrounded by nurturing and loving parents in an atmosphere of peace. In a non-violent family, a child grows up in such an atmosphere, and then, working from the secure base of being loved, will develop an independent and choosing self that is able to recreate happy love both in future relationships and with its own children. In a violent family, however, this birthright to love and peace is betrayed, because from the moment of conception the child lives in a world where emotional and physical pain and danger are always present. The child then bonds to pain. This bonding becomes an addiction to pain. The child then cannot grow to form an independent self, because he or she is slave to this addiction. Throughout life, the person then recreates situations of violence and pain, for those situations stir the only feelings of love and satisfaction the person has ever known.

Whether the children of violent families learn to find satisfaction through the inflicting or the receiving of emotional and physical pain, the violence that these people live on is merely an expression of pain. The role of the caring community is to undo this fundamental betrayal of people who have been emotionally disabled by their violent childhoods. By creating a loving environment in which deep internal work can be done to help violence-prone people to understand and to overcome their addiction to pain, these people can then learn to trust and be happy in *love* instead of pain.*

This book records ten years of work in such a community, along with the techniques and insights gained through these years. Erin had worked for eight years before she started working together with Jeff — for an additional two years.

The book is therefore written in the style of Erin's personal narrative, up to the point where the 'I' becomes 'we'. We two will be going off to America, where we plan to write books on the subjects of incest, psychopaths, and middle-class violence. The work now continues in Britain through Women's Aid Ltd, which runs a house in Bristol.

The Authors
19 February 1982

---

*Our understanding of the chemical basis for the addiction to pain is discussed in Chapter Six.

INTRODUCTION

The idea of a meeting place for women and their children grew out of my disastrous brush with a local group of the newly emergent Women's Movement in 1971. I was then feeling lonely and isolated, with two small children to care for, and a husband frequently away. When I first began to read the articles that other women were writing, I felt they were writing about me. It was certainly a liberation to find I was not the only woman who could not knit or sew, and that there were other women out there who shared my pathological hatred of housework. I began to look out for our nearest group.

Unfortunately that group, in particular, seemed to be more concerned with world politics than with my day-to-day problems, like how to cope on my own with two children, two dogs and a cat — for the loneliness was sometimes dreadful. Luckily I did meet some women like myself who wanted not only to bring up their children properly at home, but also to use their energies and talents in improving our community life, so that we would no longer feel so cut off and isolated that we lived our lives on valium. Therefore we left it to the women's group to decide the solution for world problems, and got on with the more immediate task of finding a place where mothers could meet each other and bring their children.

So with two of my friends I began to scout round Hounslow for a little house to use as a women's centre. Eventually Hounslow Council wrote to me about No. 2 Belmont Terrace, and I collected the keys. When I first opened the door, I burst into tears — it was derelict. But it was ours! By now our group had grown quite large, and we determinedly got on with the work. Harry Ferrer, our plumber, showed us how to fit pipes and mend washers, and we completely renovated the building until one day it was ready for occupation.

Mothers living locally began to call by on their way to and from school. They would stop in for a chat or to share a problem with us. Gradually we all pooled our knowledge and began to learn the complex Social Security laws. We discovered that many women would come to see us who could not face anything as authoritarian-seeming as a town-hall or a Social Services department. We had created a very happy little community of people from all walks of life, who knew that any time they were lonely or in need of company they just had to go down to No. 2 Belmont Terrace, and someone was almost sure to be there to talk to. And even when no one was there, it was still a warm, welcoming place to take your kids. Then home did not seem so much like a prison.

All this changed the day the first battered woman walked through the front door and showed me her bruises. 'No one will help me,' she said. Those words took me back to a time in my own childhood when no one would help *me* — as I begged them to bury my mother because my father refused to. 'I will help you,' I promised her, and refuge was born.

Within weeks there were at least forty mothers and children packed into four tiny rooms. Fortunately for me, our predicament was high-lighted in a small piece written by a journalist for the *Observer*. After that a man called by one day and, sitting himself down on a mattress, asked me what I most needed. 'A new house,' I told him. 'Go and find it,' he said. I did. This man was Neville Vincent, the Managing Director of Bovis Ltd. In November 1974 we acquired a much larger house in Chiswick High Road. However, we were still not out of the woods. Even as we moved in, our numbers were already too great. We were still officially overcrowded. Because at that time there was nowhere else for women to run to, I insisted that no one should ever be turned away. As a result, although we were legally allowed to house only thirty-six residents, our numbers sometimes went as high as one hundred and fifty mothers and children. My colleague Anne Ashby agreed with me over the 'open door' principle, and we enshrined it in our policy that the door would remain open day and night. This, of course, created an unbearable tension between ourselves and our local Borough, who quite rightly were worried by the overcrowding, the ensuing health hazard, and the possibility of fire. On 29 April 1976 the Borough first took me to court for overcrowding.

Just before I was to appear in the Acton Magistrates' Court, I was invited to tour America with Tina, Nikki, and Annie, who were working with me at the time. I was genuinely startled and moved that anyone should consider that we had anything valuable to offer, so I accepted at once. We flew into New York on 12 March 1976, and visited sixteen other cities to raise funds for new refuges springing up all over the USA. I remember that I was particularly interested in finding if anyone else had come to similar conclusions on why some people actually *choose* violent relationships — which is the major theme of this book. But in response I mostly met again the hostility of those people who insisted that all women were simply victims of male oppression.

It seems to me that America's Women's Movement is much more broadly based than its British counterpart. It was with members of the National Organisation of Women that we had the best dialogues — at seminars and meetings where people wanted to share a sense of bewilderment arising from the fact that now there were established refuges, so many women seemed to be merely using them like revolving doors. They would come to the refuges when the level of violence got too much, only to return to their violent men for another few weeks, and then come back to the refuges again for help.

Some of the refuges dealt with this problem by allowing such women three visits only. As they explained to me, this rule meant that the staff could concentrate their efforts on the women who *genuinely* wanted to get out of violent relationships. But they knew, just as we did, that if you wanted to do effective work in a refuge, the problems attached to women who seemed unable to stay away from violence would have to be fully explored sooner or later.

Our trip ended with a lunch of honour in Washington DC,

sponsored by Congresswoman Lindy Boggs and Congressman Newton Steer. As I stood to give my speech in a lovely room surrounded by members of Congress on Capitol Hill, it was hard not to feel bitter that back home, within a few weeks, I would be facing charges in an English court for carrying out the refuge work I was now describing to a supportive audience.

Thanks to a brilliant manoeuvre on the part of our barrister Stephen Sedly and David Ormondy, a public health adviser, the Acton Magistrates' Court found me not guilty of overcrowding. The good news was followed immediately by bad news. Hounslow appealed, and got ready to take me to the High Court in the Strand.

During this time, through a series of fortuitous events, we managed to persuade the reluctant civil servants to give us a grant of £2,000 a month. This generosity could have had something to do with the threat of our group arranging a sit-in outside 10 Downing Street. We numbered about one hundred and twenty mothers and children, and we were already well known for our immediate ability to get on the streets with our placards and demand action where necessary. We had received a reassuring letter saying that our application for a grant would be considered. However, we heard nothing for several months, and it was not until October 1974, the day before the publication of my book *Scream Quietly or the Neighbours Will Hear*, that a cheque arrived by taxi, with a letter from the Department of Health and Social Security.

Meanwhile, during the Conservatives' period in office, I had been encouraged by Sir Keith Joseph to apply for an Urban Aid Grant of £10,000 a year. The Urban Aid scheme was a very new idea in those days. Hounslow had many other schemes to put forward to the Government, but due to local pressure and the continued support of a local Labour councillor, Jim Duffy, they did put my scheme in. To their surprise and my amusement, it was granted. By this time, help came from another direction. David Astor had resigned from the *Observer* and offered me his services. He brought with him the kindly and powerful figure of Lord Goodman. Now, at least, Anne Ashby and I were no longer on our own.

We had a curious mixture of dedicated staff and volunteers. We scoured London, taking possession of empty houses belonging to other boroughs which refused to take financial responsibility for their own families, who turned up on our doorstep. We took these houses over by night, to create new communities for such additional families. By the time of the court cases, Chiswick Women's Aid had established twenty-two squats, and had also acquired the Palm Court Hotel (forty-five private suites), three Greater London Council properties, and a large vicarage in Bristol. Even so, at our main refuge we had to erect large garden sheds in the backyard to cope with the overflow of one hundred and fifty mothers and children living in the house.

As the case in the High Court approached, the battle lines were set, but I was no longer powerless, or fighting in a vacuum. We had Lord Goodman on our side, and I felt very much more confident. In the late spring of 1976, Hounslow took me to the High Court, where I was found guilty of the charge of overcrowding. We appealed this decision, and the matter went to the House of Lords in March 1977. There the five Law Lords reluctantly found me guilty, and I returned to Acton Magistrates' Court for sentencing.

During this time, and responding to so much publicity, other groups had formed to take up the idea of refuge for women and children. Many comprised good, loving people, both men and women, who sincerely wanted to help, but there were also the usual faces seen around all social movements, and I was wary enough to stay clear of their politics. I never saw Women's Aid as a movement that was hostile to men, but The National Federation, which quickly formed, made it quite clear that men were the enemy. This view totally rejected our own philosophy — which cannot be encapsulated in a political theory, but which recognises that the basis of the problem is a human one: violence occurs in both men and women. That is not a politically fashionable view in certain quarters, and, indeed, for them we were outcasts from the very beginning because we had always employed male workers at our Refuge — and we also ran a special house for the men of the problem families who sought our help.

The civil servants, who hated our open-door policy as much as they hated our evidence of the mistreatment of problem families by the various State-run agencies, saw their opportunity to get rid of us. They removed our grant on the grounds that we were not a national organisation, even though we had been officially declared so by the Charity Commissioners and our mothers and children came from all over Britain. They handed the grant to the National Federation instead. At about the same time, Hounslow Council voted to remove our Urban Aid Grant, thus hoping to starve us into submission. Fortunately, they did not know that I had been given a sum of £50,000 by an anonymous well-wisher, which I had tucked away in bonds for just such an occasion. Those staff that could afford to all gave up their meagre salaries. Most of us were volunteers, so that presented little problem, and we soldiered on.

The final court case was my sentencing at the Acton Magistrates' Court on 6 October 1977. The following February, in response to a letter from one of our mothers, the Queen intervened and saved the Refuge.* The war was over, and the rest is history. This book is not about the politics of survival for pressure groups, because that is a whole book in itself. This book is about the problem families and my (and later Jeff's) work with them. *Scream Quietly or the Neighbours Will Hear* is about *how* people are violent. *Infernal Child*, my autobiography, is about *how* a violent childhood affects children. *Prone to Violence* is a book about *why* people are violent. In these pages we can all recognise parts of ourselves, and hopefully, in gaining understanding, we can learn compassion, and in turn help to persuade our society to refrain from further brutalising already brutalised people.

---

*The court sentencing and the letter from Buckingham Palace (quoted in full) are described in Chapter Five.

Chapter One

THE WAY WE SEE IT

Coming out of the courtroom on to the front steps, after the first trial at Acton Magistrates' Court, I gazed over a sea of well-loved faces — mothers and children I had not seen for years. But what moved me most were the gaps there, which should have been filled by the smiling faces of women I knew who had died. They should have been there with us — there was no justifiable reason for them to be dead. For they, too, had been 'refugees' in our care. But unlike many of our women who, once free, had chosen to leave their violent relationships for ever, these women had chosen to go back, thereby forfeiting their lives.

I could now see Sue beaming at me, holding up her small daughter. She had been married to a very violent man, whose chief boast was that he had bitten off another man's nose in a fight. They were married when she was very young, but once she had come to us for help, she had no further thought of returning to him. She was an enormous help in the refuge, very practical and full of fun. Eventually, she moved to a house we acquired in the south-east of England.

Julia should have been standing next to Sue, as the two had been such good friends. But Julia was dead. She was one of those who went back. In those days I did not know enough about violent relationships to recognise her addiction and to help her as I could now.

In my first book about refuge, *Scream Quietly or the Neighbours Will Hear* (1974), I wrote about our battered grandmother, whom we all loved. We called her 'Nan', and she was seventy-eight years old. There I wrote: 'She sits in our chaos of mums and kids, her face covered by wrinkles and a black eye.' She's dead now — as a result of a brutal kicking by her own son, who was himself the casualty of her marriage to her violent stockbroker husband. And I grieved for her, too, that day.

Another gap in the ranks was Sandy, whose face was dreadfully scarred from a car accident. She was left so distraught by her disfiguration that she had to be moved to a mental hospital to recover not only physically but also mentally from her accident. There she met James, her violent lover. After leaving the hospital, they lived together and had a baby. Then James became so cruel and abusive to Sandy that she fled to us for refuge — and he soon went off with another woman. Yet Sandy could not bear to be deprived of this extremely violent man — 'The only man who makes me feel alive,' she would say. She took her own life the night before she was due to move into a brand-new flat.

Rachel, mother of five lively children, insisted on moving back into her own house when she had obtained her injunction against her husband, knowing full well that he became almost a lunatic when he was angry. She died the same night she moved back home — he stabbed her to death. And their children joined the thousands of other kids in care who have little hope of being adopted or fostered, but will sit in children's homes like little time-bombs primed to explode into our streets years later, with the enormous likelihood of recreating the violent living patterns of their parents.

That poses the crucial question, the main theme of this book: why did all these particular women choose to return to their violent and often deadly relationships? We can all chart moments in our lives when suddenly we need to face a truth that we have hitherto been avoiding. In my own case, I had been avoiding *this* particular question for years. For me that moment, standing on those steps, crystallized a train of thought that had been nagging at me for months previously.

For the first few years, my colleague Anne Ashby and I were the only permanent members of Chiswick Women's Aid who worked full-time. Volunteers and well-meaning people came and went, many disapproving of our policy of never turning women away, because this policy brought about overcrowding and unhygienic conditions. But then, having lived in the Middle East and travelled extensively,

Anne and I did not share the normal middle-class repugnance for anything less than suburban standards of tidiness, cleanliness and comfort. In those days we relied very much on each other for moral support; and, of course, some of the mothers coming in for help became close personal friends.

A vivid lesson from those times was to recognise the anger and hostility shown us by certain people who would claim that 'women like to be beaten', or that they somehow 'deserve it'. This simplistic attitude served only to condone the terrible acts of violence committed under the covering excuse of 'You make your bed so you must lie in it'. In other words, that women who were victims of violent partners were largely responsible for their own regrettable situations, and could not deserve much sympathy.

I remember particularly such views being thrown at me one evening when several couples who worked in the caring agencies were gathered together for a barbecue party. The men there seemed determined to argue that many women deserved what they got. There was clearly no room for rational argument. Yet again, I could sense an invisible barrier erected between my own experience — which was then very recent in terms of my work — and their professional frustration with often difficult and recalcitrant clients who had been turning up in their offices for many years complaining about violence, only to go back to it again and again. Those professionals with me that evening could, of course, quote chapter and verse of the dreadful deeds, the unspeakable delinquency, the manipulative techniques, and the promiscuity of the women they counselled. In those early days I did not have the solid basis of knowledge and experience to answer the challenges so often thrown at me. All I could say was that it just was not that simple. For it was not a case of either liking or not liking violent behaviour; it was much more complicated than that — and some day I hoped to understand it better. But the people there were so frustrated and angry that the evening degenerated into a slanging match.

In those days it was too dangerous to attempt to share my discoveries in this field, because it was hard enough to gain public acceptance even for the idea that *battered* wives needed refuge. To discuss the notion that some women were actually *prone to violence*, and returned to violent relationships again and again, would only have served to alienate the public from these women who were in genuine need of help.*

By that time I had read a paper entitled 'Wife-Torture in England'* published in 1878 by Frances Power Cobbe. The paper was an impassioned plea to Parliament to do something to help the women and children of this country. She was promised by Parliament that a select committee would be set up, and further action would be taken. I was depressed to learn that after her select committee sat and reported, the whole subject was swept under the carpet again, to be forgotten — just as in our case.

I, too, had sat in the House of Commons, when Jack Ashley, MP, was begging consideration for the lives of such women and children. In June 1973 he put forward a Private Member's Bill which asked a minister representing the Department of Health and Social Security what they would do for battered wives. The hour was late and I, sitting with our mothers in the gallery, looked anxiously down to the floor of the House, where Jack Ashley addressed an almost empty room. The only other people there were the ministers from the DHSS and the House officials. Jack Ashley commented that if the discussion had been about dogs instead of about women and children, the House would have been full.

The subject was debated in Parliament on 17 July 1973, and it was decided that a select committee of MPs should be set up to investigate. The select committee met in the House of Commons during the summer of the following year, and one of our wives told her personal story of abuse — the first woman in history to give evidence to a select committee. This committee agreed that one refuge should be established per every 100,000 people living in Britain. A Parliamentary committee, however, has only the power to recommend, and

---

*In the course of reading this book, it is essential to understand the differentiation between our use of the words *battered* and *violence-prone*. For us, a *battered* person is the innocent victim of *another* person's violence; a *violence-prone* person is the victim of their *own* addiction to violence.

*Extracts appear in Appendix D.

no power to enforce its recommendations. Their recommendation was never put into practice.

We faced the terrible certainty that if our Refuge was allowed to go under through legal pressures due to overcrowding, and if the public was conned into believing that something was being done for these families, when it was not, then the whole campaign would sink without trace again.

To my amazement, nobody seemed to genuinely want to find out why violent people treat each other the way they do. Furthermore, I could not give my personal support to the accepted political solutions based on the notion that violence was a strictly working-class problem, and therefore a purely economic issue: the political line maintaining that men hit women because they were frustrated by their jobs, their poor housing, and their lack of money. I had seen enough middle-class women in trouble to convince me that doctors, dentists, solicitors, and Members of Parliament also indulged in bouts of violence against their women and children in sufficient numbers to make that argument invalid. In fact emotional violence is extremely common in middle-class and upper-class families, and just as damaging as physical violence.

Officialdom suggested that the solutions were to be found in other socialist, or communist, countries. But reports from Russia showed otherwise, for marital violence is a major Russian problem. And China dealt with the problem by proclaiming wife-beating a crime punishable with the death penalty. They obviously had no answer for the root causes, either.

Even if it was too inflammatory to hold public discussions on family violence, I did have by this time a large and dedicated staff. Though it included some paid members, the majority of us volunteered our services for nothing. Apart from our daily work at the Refuge, we spent many weekends together sharing our experiences of the families that came to us. We soon realised that we had much more first-hand knowledge of these families than did any of the other social agencies, because the mothers and children lived with us in our Refuge as one large family. Indeed, most of our families had already been involved with social agencies, who very rarely seemed to have fully understood their true background. Time and again, when called to a case-conference to discuss a family, we would find that, although it had been on their books for years, each agency saw only fragmented aspects of the family situation. I was often reminded of the old Chinese story about the sages who all felt bits of a huge animal in a darkened shed. After they came out they began lengthy discussions about a leg or the tail or an ear, but not one of them grasped the fact that the whole was an elephant.

During our staff seminars, we came to realise that we were catering to two very different needs in our Refuge. The first involved women like Sue who, for one reason or another, had married men who turned out to be violent. Once offered an opportunity to escape this situation, they would take it gratefully and leave, never to return to the violence. These we tend to call the genuine 'battered wives'. The second involved the type of woman unable to stay away from violence, however much she claimed she wanted to. She seemed doomed either to return to her violent partner eventually, or, having given him up, to move rapidly on to another violent man.

Our growing awareness of these two distinct problems culminated in a report that we sent to the Department of Health and Social Security in the summer of 1977. For the first time, I wrote down some of the conclusions I had reached, and the report was based on 377 mothers with 745 children who had passed through the Chiswick Refuge between May 1976 and May 1977. It was a mammoth task to record and chart the details and the origins of all these families. Seven members of staff voluntarily went into seclusion in my house until the job was done.

The introduction to that report reads:

> In 1971 Chiswick Women's Aid was originally conceived as a safe refuge for women and children on the run from violent relationships. It was at this point that the phrase 'battered wives' was coined. However, in the course of the last five and a half years one of the conclusions we have come to is that a more apt description of the families involved would be 'violence prone'. That is to say, that the members of these families have a tendency to be attracted to violent relationships or are themselves violent. We see

the term 'battered wives' as too simplistic. We do not claim that this description fits all our families or indeed all women who find themselves in a violent relationship. But what we do claim is the majority of families who come to Chiswick are in such a state of confusion and despair, having fallen through the net of all caring social agencies, that to be offered accommodation in homeless family units, bed and breakfast or temporary hostel accommodation is an unrealistic solution. What they need is for society to understand that the chaos, anarchy and drama of the violent relationships which they have lived through has created within them a special urge to continually relive the excitement of what they have left behind. The dramas in their relationships seem endless and in these conflagrations chaos reigns. Children in such a situation feel the ebb and flow of fear and excitement. Soon they grow from terrified unwilling spectators to active manipulators in the family war. These are the violence-prone adults of tomorrow. These families have failed to build the structures necessary to provide the community with law-abiding citizens. Instead we have a percentage of the population whose drive stems from fear, flight and rage which appear to produce puzzling symptoms of addiction.

In everyday life the emotions of fear, rage and flight cause the adrenalin to flow through the body, preparing it urgently for action. Most human beings rarely need this sort of protection. Our families have lived at this level of excitement for many, many years and when deprived of excitement tend to re-create hazardous situations which bring back the thrill of the moment of 'adrenalin high'. Racing drivers, mountaineers, test pilots, occasions of war are acceptable high-adrenalin pursuits, and it is our job to get our families to be aware of their addiction and the catastrophes they create for themselves and their children. It is also our job to realise that these families have largely been abandoned by the caring agencies who have tried valiantly over the years to find solutions to their problems. What we offer is to accept the damage and lack of inner structure that causes them to fail again and again and to try and re-integrate their disordered personalities to where they can leave our care having learned satisfactory methods of making relationships and standards of child care and home-making that enables them to exist happily within the community. Of course, often we fail but we have achieved sufficient success to hopefully attract funds to continue our work. One major hurdle is to get the Government to accept that these families urgently need help of a special nature and using techniques that we have developed over the years that we have been running, based on some 5,000 women and children who have passed through our hands. (This paper is quoted in Appendix A).

We were all naive enough to believe that the powers-that-be would study our evidence carefully, and perhaps accept that we had something to say. But, after weeks of waiting, the first response was merely an acknowledgement that the report had arrived. After that there was silence. It seemed that any money allotted for research by the DHSS would be given to groups prepared to spend it on safe, comfortable solutions. Again no one wanted to hear the uncomfortable truth. And that truth was that there are so many thousands of violence-prone people, born and raised in violence, who know no other lifestyle except to terrorise and mutilate each other or any innocent victim who comes into their circle.

Not only were we dealing with some of the most violent men in the country, on our very doorstep – which we expected would happen as soon as we began to offer refuge – but we had some equally violent women on the inside, too. Other refuges had careful screening measures built into their selection procedures, so that they could avoid these families. Gradually we made constructive links with good refuges who would take our 'battered wives', and in turn would send us their 'violence prone' women. It had become obvious in our struggle that any funding for our operation seemed unlikely to come from the statutory bodies. We had put our finger inadvertently on an official sore spot.

These families we cared so passionately about were truly 'dustbin' families. Their behaviour and lifestyle were so chaotic and derelict that, in the past, the solution had always been to break them up and disperse them. It is extraordinary to think that until the 1940s pregnant women were still giving birth in local workhouses, where their babies were forcibly taken into care. As soon as they were old enough, those children were shipped out to the colonies for farmwork and general labour. They were chiefly sent to Canada, New Zealand and Australia, where there was no black population to be bullied into serving the white man. The unwritten policy was definitely *dispersal*.

Within the last twenty years such overseas dispersal became more difficult, and therefore institutions were becoming packed with inmates — so another strategy came into being. This brought about the creation of 'ghettoes' where such 'dustbin' families could breed and swarm. For instance the White City Estate was built in London, and still the New Towns are growing all over the country. However, with the advent of mass communication and investigative journalism, embarrassing questions were raised about hungry and ragged children. And the ghettoes were growing so big that their violence threatened to spill over into the other, 'respectable' parts of our cities. Attempts were made to improve housing conditions. Architects and planners built huge estates that would look good from the outside but were sited well away from the cities. The Glasgow Gorbals were torn down. Families were exiled all over England.

The idea was that if you separated these huge and brawling families from each other, you would somehow reduce the level of violence and criminal behaviour in our society. But the planners reckoned without the tenacity of these problem families. For every house in a New Town that a hopeful social worker filled, another was abandoned as a supposedly resettled family quietly packed its bags and fled for the big cities.

By stumbling across the plight of battered wives who were trapped for lack of an escape route and needed support, we had also uncovered the widescale traffic of a far greater number of adults and children who were being continually passed like parcels from one social agency to another. No wonder we received so little co-operation in our efforts. A huge machine seemed to build on the misery of these helpless people. Traditionally the women took refuge in mental hospitals, the men in prisons, and the children went 'into care'. But some were now coming to Women's Aid, where, for the first time, they were made to feel welcome, and where we recorded the abysmal treatment they had suffered from the very people ostensibly trained and paid to care for them.

All would have been well if we had agreed to stick to the traditional concept of 'battered wives'. Certainly it would have made life a lot easier for myself and the people with me. But those who had worked with me for several years shared the frustrations I felt, and witnessed the often horrific circumstances of the women and children who came in a never-ceasing tide through the door. The frequent newspaper stories about the various attempts to close the Refuge helped to give us a credibility among the women who came to us. They felt that we were 'against' the law and were therefore 'on their side'. Because of this attitude, the women felt it was possible to communicate to us the often unspeakable occurrences in their families — not only the grievous acts of violence, but also the incest and the sexual abuse.

Time and again we would contact a family's social-worker to ask how such abuses could occur for so many years without some constructive and caring intervention from the social services, only to be told that 'the file on that family is closed'. This comfortable euphemism meant that they could no longer cope. Individual social workers would certainly express their own anger at the system that trapped them and rendered them impotent. Many of the most caring of them would leave after a few years, because the strain was telling on them and they found the role of Pontius Pilate unbearable, tired of handing their cases over to be crucified.

I remember once pointing out to a small group from the north of England that though Hitler was internationally condemned for trying to exterminate the Jews, we ourselves had a similar programme being carried out against our 'problem families'. The agencies even used words like 'dispersal' and 'natural wastage' in this context. But here, instead of it being six million Jews seen as a threat to the nation, we had an equally large number of people who were considered antisocial and intractable and were quietly being destroyed. The horrifying fact is that nothing at all was being done to help them. There was absolutely no concept of care involving any attempt to rehabilitate them or to understand why they behaved the way they did.

In most cases, the true crime these people had committed was merely to be born into an emotionally disabled family — taking on damage they would carry with them all their lives. Had these families been physically disabled, the various caring agencies would not only have tried to help but would have succeeded, since the care of the physically disabled is well understood. The tragedy of our time is that we have almost completely ignored the inner world of the *emotionally* disabled. Particularly in Britain, we prefer to believe that a few pills and a stern warning from a magistrate are all that is required to encourage a recalcitrant teenager to mend his or her ways. The magistrates are oblivious to the fact that most of these disabled families have no understanding of what they are talking about. You do not ask a paraplegic to get up and run a race, but somehow we expect people who have never had a chance to learn even the basic rules of living in our society, still to follow all society's complex rules, both written and unwritten. If they fail, we have jails, mental hospitals, children's homes and borstals set aside to receive them. Apart from a few such institutions run by enlightened people, these places do nothing to help.

Poppy was a classic example of a no-chance child. She was found on a railway station in a carrier-bag when she was two weeks old. I remember looking at her and thinking to myself that *this* is what actually happens to those little abandoned babies who feature in the newspapers from time to time. Usually the hospital gives the baby a name, and well-wishers send in presents, moved by the infant's plight. Having sent off their donations or a piece of knitting, they assume — as I did for many years — that the enormous sums contributed in taxes every year will ensure that this desolate little scrap is cared for and will have a future in which the sorry pattern is not repeated.

Certainly, Poppy was cared for physically. She was taken

from the hospital and put into a children's home. She remained there until she was five, and then was fostered. However, by that time she was far too disturbed to settle. She was a very pretty little girl, and the foster-parents tried hard, but she continually screamed and spat and soiled herself. She was used to living in a large group of children, with all the noise and commotion that went on in the daily routine of a children's home. She was absolutely terrified of the physical intimacy of family life, and was particularly frightened by the man of the family. She had never known any men in her little life — and had only seen them as distant figures on visiting day. She was soon returned to the home.

Poppy constantly asked about her mother — and was told differing stories. She received no cards at Christmas. No visits. Nobody. The staff at her children's home were sympathetic, but nothing could make up for the absence of any family contact. Even the most deprived of her friends had some memory — or even some record in a social service office — which gave them a twig of their own history to grasp at.

By the time Poppy was eight, the school said she was out of control. She fought in the school playground, not only with the girls but with the boys, too. This probably brought the only admiration she ever received in those days — that she was as tough as any of them. She began a pattern of being moved every so often, when she had finally driven even the most caring of the staff to distraction. In some of the homes she was beaten, in some molested — once by a milkman. By the time she was thirteen she was having sexual intercourse with boys at school. She was known as an 'easy ride', but that did not worry her. In her unit for disturbed adolescents, intercourse was the normal exchange rate for affection. Most of the children had been sexually abused when very young, and were therefore sexually aware from a very early age.

Poppy was pregnant at fifteen, and had her baby just before her sixteenth birthday. She had the child in hospital, and was sent to a mother-and-baby home that, as a rule, kept its clients for only six weeks. They actually kept her there for three months, because they were so worried about her. She was determined to keep the baby, and treated it like a doll. It was a girl, and she called it Mary. During the day she would push the child round the streets and pass the time by shop-lifting. The pram was a great help in this, and she would come back with a hoard of knick-knacks. She knew this was considered wrong, because all her life she had been pinching things she wanted and was every so often caught and punished. But, then, she had always been supplied with the day-to-day things of life in various children's homes, so having and spending money was just not part of her upbringing. Thus she was never required to save money for a pair of shoes; if they were needed she was taken to a shop and they were bought for her.

After the mother-and-baby home, yet another social worker arranged a small flat where, with the help of the social security grant, she was set up with the bare essentials. After the birth of her baby, Poppy felt prompted to ask about her own mother yet again, since she noticed her baby had a birth certificate. Admittedly it was the short form, because Poppy could not say for sure who the child's father was, but she realised she had never seen her own birth certificate. The social worker promised to check. For the first twenty-four hours in the flat, Poppy enjoyed herself. She was not a bad mother in that she was not liable to hit Mary, because she was so used to hearing children crying for hours on end that the noise did not irritate her. The problem was that she just blocked it out if she was watching television or had some other distraction. Because this was the first time Poppy had been away from institutional care, she had no inner structures to carry her through the day, and the health visitor became concerned. There was no one to get her up, no compulsion to have breakfast, lunch, tea, or dinner, no rota for cleaning, no time for lights out, nothing. Just undreamed-of, unlimited freedom.

The first freedom was the freedom to sleep all day. Meanwhile the baby was being neglected. She lay all day in her cot unwashed, hungry and screaming. Finally she didn't even bother to cry much any longer. The health visitor called a case conference, and it was decided to send in a home-help. At that juncture, however, Poppy met John outside a pub. He seemed very understanding, and would hold the baby affectionately. He was living in a hostel after falling out with his father, who was a violent brute. All John wanted was a home and a family — something he'd never properly had. He had spent some time in borstal for stealing cars and such. Poppy felt she had found a kindred castaway, and John moved in by the weekend.

The social worker decided that Poppy now had a supportive relationship, so no home-help was necessary. Also she could now safely tell her about the business of being abandoned in a carrier-bag. She explained it all very thoroughly, unaware that most of what she said was going straight over Poppy's head. Street language consists of very short sentences; anything longer goes unheard. But Poppy did hear the bit about the carrier-bag. The social worker was actually a very kind woman, and she had gone to the trouble of looking up back copies of newspapers and securing a picture of a three-week-old Poppy. Finally she left Poppy and John together, hoping he would comfort her.

That piece of news completely shattered Poppy. She had always imagined that her parents were killed in an accident. Even in her most lonely, punished moments, when all the world seemed united against her, she had kept this golden fantasy that her mother and her father had loved her passionately but, because of the car crash which left her an orphan, she was now alone in the world. After seeing *Tarzan*, she would even fantasise that she had been born in the jungle, and was stolen away from her parents by wicked white hunters. Never, never had she suspected that she was merely abandoned at a railway station. John did the best he could. He was not very good at sympathy, but he did know about pills which keep you happy. So far, Poppy had kept off drugs and alcohol; she had got most of her kicks stealing and fighting. But as John had a ready supply, and with this dreadful sense of rejection inside her, she blotted out nearly a year of her life.

Most of that year she spent drunk and violent. The health visitor arranged to get the baby into a day nursery, but Mary was now silent and withdrawn. Still Poppy did not hit Mary; she just ignored her. John was really much better in dealing with the child, as he had come from a large family, and he did at least see that Mary was fed and changed. But both of them were unable to refrain from yelling and screaming at each other. Poppy had no idea of how to take care of herself or a baby — and even less of an immature and aggressive man. Their rows were monumental. Soon he began to smash up the flat when he felt pushed beyond endurance. Angry neighbours began to complain.

Then Poppy became pregnant again, and that seemed to calm her down. They promised each other that they would try harder. The health visitor reported that things were looking better. The neighbours even began to talk to Poppy again. John got a job, but Poppy could not cope alone all day. She had never before in her whole life had any time *alone*. The mere thought of it terrified her. In care, one is occupied all the time, if not by the staff, then by other children. There is no time to develop inner resources. Aloneness is then not a creative time for self-expression; indeed it is a disturbing and fruitless condition when there is no training for it. Poppy doped herself with pills and lager all day, and then staggered back with Mary from the nursery to try and cook an edible meal. This was a difficult task because she had never been expected to cook before. Shopping for food was out of her experience. So they tended to live on tins and packet food, following virtually the same menu as a children's home.

The new baby was a boy. It was an easy birth, with John present. He was thrilled, and wanted Poppy to breast-feed the child. She declined, but she was really very pleased with the baby, and far less uncertain because she had done all this bit before. For the birth, Mary had been taken into care for two weeks, but when Poppy returned to the flat with baby Sam, her relationship with Mary became very different. In the past Poppy was largely able to ignore her, but Mary was now an active toddler, and Poppy had a new-born child to cope with. With the trial of having to be a mother to two tiny children, Poppy began to crack up. She and John began to have serious fights again. All her rage and frustration would erupt from her, and he had almost no ability to hold his temper. All the men of his family beat their wives as a matter of course. Soon Poppy was seen badly bruised by the health visitor.

The baby seemed to thrive. He put on weight and smiled, probably because he knew he was wanted by both parents. Even if they had no conception at all of responsibility, they both still wanted him. Mary did not thrive, however; she grew thinner and more withdrawn. The almost nightly fights outside the bedroom door shook her little heart; and then she ached for her mother, whose sobs and screams she could hear so clearly, followed by the dreadful sounds of crashing and falling. The neighbours starting complaining again and a petition was sent to the local housing department. The Social Services began to think seriously about receiving Mary into care, but unless a child is actually physically harmed, magistrates tend to find in favour of the parents.

The Social Services were so worried about Mary that they did not realise she at least expressed *normal* feelings of fear. If only they had been trained to recognise the budding psychopath. Already, at nine months, so cut off from any of the emotions roused by the warring couple, Sam would watch furniture fly and blood flow, and clap his little hands, his eyes alight with excitement. The social worker believed Sam to be a happy enough baby, for he had been a wanted child. We have found, however, that in a disturbed and violent household, where screaming and hitting is commonplace, a healthy child will show signs of distress. It is the disturbed child who seems to cope well in such a family — all too well.*

In truth Poppy had never much enjoyed sex. To her it had always been a means of attracting men. She had tolerated John's sexual demands in the early days because she did enjoy the feeling of his need for her. Then as soon as she was pregnant she had told him to lay off. Once the baby was born, she grudgingly let him make love to her again, but she began to taunt him sexually. This started a disastrous series of rows, in which he accused her of being a whore and a lesbian, and she retaliated by saying that she had no choice but to look elsewhere because he was not enough to satisfy her. It was at this stage that she first arrived at Chiswick Women's Aid, covered in bruises from a violent fight. She also had a torn cervix because he had held her down and thrust a milk bottle

---

*We believe that Sam's adjustment to his violent family situation was a result of his growing addiction to pain, as explained in Chapter Six.

up inside her.

It took Poppy about two days to settle in. During her first interview, she played the outraged battered victim. Many of the women in the community, who had not been sexually abused, were appalled at her descriptions. By the time Poppy had enthusiastically described the role of carrots, cucumbers, marrows and various household utensils in her sex life, I could see the brigade of 'heavy' mothers in the room looking at each other. I interviewed Poppy again that afternoon. She was still swearing by the Virgin Mary and on her babies' lives that she would never go near John again — she who only lived for peace.

That night she went out with a few of the other mothers, and the next day she appeared in the house meeting with six stitches in her head. It seemed they had all gone to the Palais for a drink and a dance, and this man had said something unacceptable to Poppy, who was forced to defend her honour in a fight. At some point in the proceedings she was hit over the head.

It was early days yet for Poppy. We needed to give her time to get to know us before we tackled her problem of only being able to express herself violently.

She very soon started a friendship with our house-father, Mike Dunne. She then made an incredibly aggressive approach to him, but we realised it was the only way she knew. I was easy for her to cope with because I represented a mother figure. Even if she had never had a real mother, she had experience of various surrogate mother figures during her life in homes, who had cuddled her occasionally. But Mike was a completely unknown quantity. She only knew how to present herself sexually, and when that failed to elicit a response from him, she was very angry. She had offered herself, all she had to offer, and he was rejecting her. Mike would talk to her about her children, about herself, about anything she wished, but that only confused her. How could you have a relationship with a man who did not fancy you?

She took to getting drunk as a skunk at lunchtime, then rolling into the sitting-room and trying to pick a fight with him. Fortunately, Mike is a big Irish lad and has played a lot of rugby. He would manage to fend off the worst of the attack, and then would hold her gently until she subsided. In the beginning, she would relax for just a few minutes, enjoying the child/parent situation, but then she would push him away and reel over to me. She would bury herself in my arms for a while, and then lurch back to attack him. We both recognised that in these moments she was working out a very deep internal conflict, and that it was necessary for her to be allowed to act out her awful pain.

The staff talked it all through among themselves, and with her, and the play staff took over the care of her children during the day. Several of our older mothers would take care of the children during the nights, because Poppy was so exhausted after these bouts. Soon it became a daily routine. Poppy would burst in, the other mothers would clear out, then she would go for Mike. Mike would patiently defend himself from harm, and hold her when he felt it appropriate, and then she would turn to me and I would hug her hard. The first breakthrough came one day when she collapsed in a heap on a mattress beside the fireplace. (This was where I tended to sit but it was also where sleeping babies were laid.) There she curled up in a foetal position and put her thumb in her mouth. I stroked her head and Mike sat down beside us. As she slept, we looked at her face, and for the first time she seemed peaceful. When she woke up she stretched and smiled, first at me and then at Mike. It was the kind of small miracle that most of our work is based on.

From that time on, she would quarrel with Mike if she felt like it, but she never again needed to physically attack him. She had learned it was perfectly OK merely to argue with him. She soon made her own friends in the community, and became much loved by the play staff.

We had a particularly gifted group of men and women working with us, and they helped young Mary to show her fears in her drawings and paintings. Sam so much enjoyed being kissed and cuddled that he bit and scratched the staff enthusiastically in return, because that was what he had seen the only people in his early life do to each other. He assumed that was how you expressed pleasure. His pleasure and pain were already crossed, so it would take a lot of skilled therapeutic work to help him back to normal.

Meanwhile, although we were pleased with the family's progress we were less happy with the contribution of the Social Services. Poppy needed at least two years of care in a large loving community, where she would not only be emotionally nurtured but also taught physical skills that would enable her to live a useful and happy life in the outside world. The health visitor could see that immediately, but the social worker seemed obsessed with John and his situation. Of course, in those cases where a genuine relationship has been formed between two people, the answer must be to work with both of them. However, the truth here was that Poppy saw John, just as he saw her — as an available port in the storm. Neither of them shared anything with each other except their violence, which Poppy was seriously attempting to give up.

We could offer John time with the male staff, but at that point we did not have a residential house for men. John, however, was not willing to make use of any help we had to offer. We were asking him to come to terms with his own violent behaviour, but he far preferred the social worker's strategy, which was to ask the Housing Department to give them a new flat. My heart sank when I heard that the Department were backing John's application. John telephoned Poppy constantly with details of the new property. With the help of the social worker, he put in for a large grant for new furniture.

As much as Poppy recognised that she still needed months of real hard work on herself and her children, she could not resist the temptation to 'play house'. We talked with John a long time, pointing out the very real danger they would both face if she reverted to her past behaviour patterns, and if he continued to drink and became violent. It was no use.

They were like small children playing at Christmas with the social worker acting as Santa Claus — a not unusual role. Poppy's flat allocation came through. She went to see it, and was delighted. As soon as the furniture grant came through and the cooker was connected, they were gone. A few weeks later we had a phone-call from Poppy: predictably, John had been drinking again. She was torn by conflicting emotions. Part of her wanted the reality of our community and the badly needed day-to-day support, but the other side of her had already plugged into a violent lifestyle again. I had one final hysterical phone-call from her. After a particularly violent fight that lasted most of the night, the police were called in. Poppy was taken to hospital, and she lost her children, for they were both taken into permanent care. The last I heard, she had left John, but had moved on to another violent relationship.

Poppy's story is only unusual in that she was found as an infant in a railway station. The rest of her case history is classic, and exemplifies the live traffic in human misery that takes place in all Western countries, where a multimillion-pound machinery has been created out of 'caring'. Not only did Women's Aid, for all those years, take in these very damaged and often dangerous families, and learn to understand and to care for them, but also we found that everywhere we turned for help or support, we encountered open hostility. It is easy to obscure the truth with a series of court cases over how many bodies a building should hold, but the reality lies in the hundreds of case histories we have gathered.

Sometimes it seems that nobody wants to hear about these families. There are no votes to be won by supporting or helping them. For they cannot be easily claimed to be innocent victims of others' aggression. They are not grateful or gentle. Their children are usually dirty, often violent, and frequently in trouble with the police. They are what they are because they were born with no chance.

Western societies have failed to understand how to care for a damaged family. This is because 'The Family' has always been seen almost as a religious concept, and therefore sacred and untouchable. In the days of the large extended family, sheer size and numbers gave individual members escape-routes. But with the increasing separation of the extended family into nuclear families we have created a dangerous lifestyle for ourselves, because this limited family is the primary socialising agency in a child's life. *Emotionally disabled parents create emotionally disabled children.*

Chapter Two

IS IT LOVE OR IS IT ADDICTION?

Olga sat by the window in the small office* of the Refuge. The prosecution for overcrowding had recently been successful, and though we had won at Acton Magistrates' Court on a technicality, we had lost at the High Court. We were given leave to apply to the House of Lords. The numbers in the Refuge were still well over the limit: most days we averaged seventy to eighty mothers and their children in only nine rooms. The conditions were chaotic, but this chaos, I was beginning to realise, contributed to the feeling of excitement in the community.

As I looked at Olga I thought to myself that if we had closed the door, she would now be one of the ones on the outside. She had a badly scarred face, but must have been a very attractive woman before she had been repeatedly beaten. Now there were ledges of scar-tissue over her eyes, and her nose was a curious shape. But when she smiled, her face lit up with such life that everyone around her relaxed and smiled at each other. She had come to us, she said, because she was in fear of her life from her boyfriend Jim. I soon knew this was no exaggeration, because the day after she arrived I had a phone-call from her local police inspector asking if she was there. Jim had yet again reported her missing, and the inspector was worried because he considered Jim so dangerous that he was prepared to order his men to dig up their back garden if she could not be found. 'He *will* kill her,' the Inspector warned, 'if she doesn't stay away from him.'

He sounded genuinely concerned about her. We chatted

---

*The little room referred to throughout the text as the 'office' was in fact normally used as a bedroom, and apart from housing the filing systems was never actually used as a formal office in the usual sense of the word.

for a while and I tried to explain to him that Olga did not 'like' what was happening to her, nor did she 'deserve it', but she was bound to Jim by forces that she could not understand. He listened to me very patiently, then after I had finished he asked if I had any idea how much she had cost the local taxpayers. Apparently, he explained, every social agency in that small city had been channelling its energies into the Olga/Jim relationship for twenty years. I could believe it. Here again was a situation I had come to recognise in most of the families that came to us.

By this time I was beginning to feel sure that behind a woman's attraction to the drama and excitement of a violent lifestyle, there must be an even more compelling need to go back to a particular man. Olga's four children had been taken into care years ago, so that could not be claimed as the reason for her not leaving him. Subsequently I sat down with her, and we talked for two and a half hours. When we finished, I had a much clearer picture of why she put herself in a position to be abused. She had never made the connection for herself, because no one had bothered to delve back far enough into her childhood. To be fair to all the people who had tried to deal with Olga she was capable of putting up such a smokescreen of demands and drama that it would be difficult for anyone to comprehend or handle the situation. Usually, when she demanded help, her unsuspecting helpers would soon find themselves drawn into a life-and-death battle between Olga and Jim.

Olga was born in Scotland. Her grandfather was a Bible-thumping Puritan bigot. The family lived in a small village, and Olga's mother was the only girl in a large family of boys. The beatings, always for religious reasons, did not spare her. The leather strap hung behind the door, both at home and at school. By the time she attended school, she was well used to the pain of it across her legs and buttocks. If Olga's mother was alive today, she would probably be able to describe the moment when she first realised that, on the knife-edge of pain, it is possible to experience the sickly, evil glimmer of pleasure.

When pain and pleasure become inextricably mixed in early childhood, as they did in the case of Olga's mother, the result is a badly abused and abusing human being. By the time Olga's mother was sixteen, she was sexually involved with a local lout who got her pregnant. Olga was the result of that union. The horror and outrage of her family were expressed in a series of beatings, which, though physically crippling, had become by now such a normal pattern of family life that they were the prime method of communication. Olga was born the only illegitimate child in the village. Her grandfather, who raged weekly from the pulpit of the local church, refused to let her be christened. She grew up with no friends: an outcast, a pariah. The only message she received from all corners of her little world was 'It would have been better if you were never born'. That message, so often repeated by her mother, formed the bedrock of Olga's personality. She should never have existed. Her existence was an offence against her community, her family, her mother and most terrifying of all, her God.

Olga too, was regularly beaten in this God-fearing family. And she does remember the first moments when pain evolved into pleasure. She was five, she thinks, and her mother removed her knickers and made her bend over her knee. She had not done anything very bad, so she was being smacked by hand, rather than strapped with the tawse. As usual, she felt a tremendous sense of fear and anxiety before bending over, but the difference this time was that as the pain in its crescendo reached its highest pitch, she suddenly felt a warm surge of tingling pleasure suffusing her whole body.

Olga was amazed and dreadfully embarrassed. Soon she began to look for that pleasure in further beatings. So she would definitely provoke her mother, and that was not difficult. She would fight at school until they whipped her and blood ran down her legs. 'The Devil's in her,' the teachers would tell her mother. Her uncles mostly lived at home. Two, she remembers, were silent and withdrawn. The other three were noisy and violent, and one of them often tried to molest her.

Olga's life was well documented by countless agencies by the time she ended up in my office, but this discussion of her need for pain to find pleasure was not something she had ever talked to anyone about before. That sense of shame and embarrassment had stayed with her all her life. She had not even discussed it with Jim. In our time together, we began to look at her life from a completely different perspective. By this time, I had sat through hundreds of interviews with women who described the same feelings. It was becoming clear to me that the difference between a non-violent woman and a violent woman is that a non-violent woman can get into a relationship with a man who is violent, and love the man but hate his violence. A violence-prone woman will look for a violent man with whom she will hate the man but cling to his violence.

By the time Olga met Jim, she was climaxing in pain. Sexual intercourse was meaningless to her. Jim was, quite simply, the most extreme, the most violent man she had ever met. 'He will kill me', she would say to me, and the awful prospect of her death would cause her face to glow. 'How will he kill you?' I would ask her. 'Like this,' she would say, putting her hands round her throat and squeezing her neck until her face became bloated and her eyes bulged.

Usually, Olga would stay with us for just three or four days, and then would go back to her own battleground. Months later she would be back on the doorstep again — thinner, with more bruises, and more stories. Then we would sit together and talk through this terrible addiction. By now, I refused to allow her to use the word 'love' in the context of this hideous sexual abuse. Again and again, we would go back to two central issues: her death-wish, a goal set for her by her rejecting family and community; and her addiction to pain, learned from her early childhood.

As I write Olga's story down, I hear from Scotland that she has left Jim again after being stabbed by him. No doubt, we shall see her at some point. She and Jim cannot live with each other, but they cannot live without each other. They are two badly abused and assaulted human beings endlessly acting out their past damage. It won't stop until one or other of them gets killed. The remaining partner will then look for another violent relationship, and it will all start over again. It was painful to listen to Olga, for I knew that listening was probably all I could do. It was almost too late for her to change.

At least Olga's children were safe, and they no longer lived in the constant torment of her and Jim's life together — they were already in care. I found it far more painful listening to Rose, because she still had her children with her. Her children had no choice but to experience and witness the violence that Rose was addicted to. Violence-prone men and women, though conditioned to need violent relationships, can still choose to leave their abusive relationships. Their children, however, have no say, no choice. They are indeed the innocent victims of violence.

Rose came into the Refuge like a tremendous whirlwind. She was tall and dark, with what we call 'adrenalin-high eyes'. They were so filled with energy they transfixed anyone who met her. She had two very active little boys in tow (she had left her little girl at her mother's). She launched into details of how her husband had sodomised her in front of the children. As she talked, the boys both nodded like two little old men watching yet another horror movie. I sent them out of the room. 'They see it all anyway', she said, uncomprehending. 'I know they do,' I replied, 'but your first lesson from me is that it isn't all right to fight and fuck in front of children.'

In our first interview she wanted to show me a picture of her dad. My heart sank. Countless times had I seen those brutal, sexually abusing men, standing proudly in the family photographs. Clustered around him were the children; at the back of the photo was the wispy mouse of her mother, worn and thin. Clutching him by the hand with an unmistakable air of possessiveness was our Rose. Within a few minutes, Rose raised her skirt to show me the faint white scars that latticed her legs. He was a huge handsome man, her father, and something of an expert with a thin cane, which he used on all the children, but mainly on his favourite daughter. Rose explained that when she got out of a hot bath the scars still flared again; and she said it all with such force. The sexual change she experienced while talking about him now brought her whole body alive.

She did not get married until after her father died. Then she met a man, Ron, who 'reminded' her of dad. Of course, that was a disaster: he was not her father, and was not sufficiently violent to satisfy her need for pain. Rose was dreadfully hard work for us because she had been brought up half-saint, half-whore. Yet this happens to so many women, particularly Catholic women: they are beaten and molested at home, then expected to attend church every Sunday. No outsider would ever have guessed that Rose was anything other than a devoted wife and mother. She was always immaculately dressed, and her children were little models in public.

Once they were settled in the Refuge, however, the children soon took over. Rose's method of control had been to beat them into good behaviour, so once her boys discovered that there was no hitting of children permitted in the Refuge, they went wild. Fortunately the play staff already knew well that battered children addicted to pain will provoke and provoke, waiting for the release of tension which a thumping brings. So the staff were trained to reverse the process. They would grasp the shrieking, struggling child firmly but gently until the child calmed down and discovered the, often first-time, pleasure of being held and caressed. Rose was amazed at our concept of child-care; she would beat her children when they were out of line, as a matter of course. I had some American stickers reading 'People are not for hitting, and children are people too,' which I used to stick on kids' jumpers to remind our battering mothers that they must learn other ways of communication with their children.

We found Rose a model member of the community during the day, but once the staff went home, Rose went out to play. Unfortunately Rose's games were extremely dangerous, particularly if she had a lot to drink. Her pattern was to begin an evening in the pub by attracting men to her table. Then, after a lot of good-natured sexual joking around, she would start drinking shorts which grew larger and larger as the men filled her glass. She usually wore very low-cut dresses and short skirts to display her excellent figure. One of her frequent acts was then to dance her version of the can-can on the table, with no knickers on. Although this was much enjoyed by the attendant men, the manager would inevitably try and stop her. Thereupon a fight ensued, with Rose joining in. The next morning a hungover Rose would sit in the offce completely denying any responsibility. It was a totally unprovoked attack by the pub manager upon her innocent person. 'Holy Mary, mother of God, would I tell a lie?' she would say to me.

The truth is she was not lying, and I learned that years ago. People from emotionally disabled families have no permanent reality. In order to develop a stable and permanent reality for a central reference point in your relationship to the world about you, you must have permanent and stable parenting, at least until you are five. Rose's life, like so many others, was a sequence of events that occurred chaotically and made no impression on her memory. Memory can only exist when there is a structure to hang it on. Our problem families have no permanent structures to their lives. Instead their lives are dictated by violent events, and they organise their living around cataclysmic eruptions.

Getting Rose to share our view of what really happened during her binges necessitated seeing that other women were with her to tell her the next day about the event. Though it was painful for her to accept the side of herself she so deeply hated, she came to understand that we loved her anyway. The hours previously spent in social workers' offices had only succeeded in making her feel more lonely and isolated. She fooled everyone so completely that she had no one to turn to. The only person she did not fool was her husband, who knew both sides of her and was hopelessly addicted to her violence.

Ron's mother had been a forceful, emotional, ebullient woman. She had died when he was about ten, and Ron went into a children's home. Her death was an act of betrayal, as far as he was concerned. Like so many other mothers, she had made her son Ron into her fairy prince. Bored with her husband, who was wedded to the television set and to his friends at the pub, she turned to Ron for companionship and spoiled him. Meanwhile his two sisters, who were second-class citizens in their mother's eyes, were expected to help her clean and cook. It was the sort of family life you could expect to find behind millions of front doors. The boy, gradually taking over the role of head of the family, was encouraged by his mother but resented by his father. Her sudden death left Ron outraged: his grief and fury at her leaving him went deep into his heart. At times his rage was murderous, but he learned to suppress its visible outburst at his children's home. Instead he learned to channel that rage into controlling his environment. He was fastidiously neat: by keeping everything ordered, he could order his rage. His great fear was that one day he might erupt, and then he would avenge himself for his mother's death and would totally explode with his rage.

At the children's home he was not particularly badly treated, but rather largely ignored. Eventually he went on to qualify as an engineer, and proved himself a regular and hard-working man. When he met Rose at a friend's house, it was love at first sight. What actually happened was that Rose, afraid of her own chaos, was attracted to Ron's apparent order. She also sensed his potentially murderous rage, and this attracted her sexually. Ron, with his need to order chaos to contain his rage, was attracted to all that Rose flaunted. When he was near her, he felt alive for the first time since his mother died. He was hooked. He could not wait to marry her. For Rose he was a good prospect: he earned good money, and they were able to buy their own house.

Rose was extremely extravagant, and she soon had the place looking like a palace, with most of the buying done on hire-purchase. Ron had to do a lot of overtime to keep up. Sexually he found himself completely enthralled. He had very little experience of sex because his children's home was for boys only. He was shy anyway with only a few unsatisfactory affairs behind him. For the first two years of marriage, things were not too bad. Rose was sexually very demanding and sometimes this frightened him; occasionally he wondered if she was acting out some dramatic part in a film. She also worried him when they were out drinking with friends, because she would sometimes change and become raucous and suggestive.

The first time they had a serious fight was when Rose told Ron that one of his friends had suggested she run away with him. The pain of that moment linked into the pain of his 'betrayal' by his mother. At the time he kept quiet because they were in the pub, but when they got home he was shaking with rage. They were hardly into the hall before he lashed out and sent her sprawling. But Rose had also been drinking, and got to her feet and began to scream at him. A dreadful torrent of filthy abuse poured from her mouth. Then the two of them suddenly stopped: he shocked by his physical attack; she snapped back into her wife-and-mother role. But the honeymoon was over, and everything started to go from bad to worse.

Rose became pregnant soon after this event, which meant she had to give up her job at a betting shop. But while she had the excitement of laughing and teasing with the customers, she could at least channel a lot of her enormous energy into her work. Once tied to home with a small baby, she went into a deeper depression. Actually, it was the fact of being trapped at home with a man who could not understand her or her needs that finally, after her second child, started off the pattern of picking up the children and running.

The children had become used to the fighting and screaming and crying. At times the older boy tried to protect his mother by throwing himself at his father, flailing at him with his little thin arms. He became hyper-active and violent at school. He could not contain the surges of hatred he felt towards his father. He could not understand why his mother would continually leave and run off to friends' houses, only to come back again. Over the six years of his short life he acquired a cynical and hard shell to protect himself from the awful pain of watching her cry. 'Why can't we go away?' he would persistently ask her, seeing huge bruises on her face. So they would go, usually after yet another fight, either at night while Ron was in a drunken stupor, or during the day when he was at work.

It became a cat-and-mouse game. After a fight, he would worry that Rose might leave with the children, so he would take time off or suddenly pop home unexpectedly. Leaving became a very tense and dramatic event. It all fell into a pattern of drinking, fighting, Rose running, Ron pursuing with chocolates, flowers and phone-calls; then a reunion. And then it would begin all over again. Ron was mystified when I discussed it with him. 'But I love her,' he said, while trying to explain the depth of his hatred for himself. 'We have everything we need to be happy.' That was certainly true. They were a handsome couple with two lovely sons, a daughter and a beautiful house. Ron earned good money and Rose was popular in her neighbourhood. On the surface they were a successful couple, but underneath it all was a hornet's nest.

The fight that first brought her to me was the end of several weeks of bickering and tension. Rose had finally been warned by yet another set of relations that she could no longer expect to burst into their lives, exhaust them with stories of Ron's cruelty, then rush into his arms again and return home, only to come back later for more sympathy. She had joined the hundreds of families who troop through homeless family units and pop in and out of refuges, using these places as an extra dimension in the war against their husbands. Most of the tension here was to do with Rose's need for pain and Ron's need for rage. Making love had long been abandoned, and no wonder. The relationship between them had little to do with loving each other. It was actually to do with hate, fear, rage and violence.

Emotionally disabled people have to be taught love. It requires a great deal of security to be able to give yourself on trust to another human being. These two people were only able to use sex as a relief mechanism when one or other of them felt sexual tension, but that only brought more problems, as the residue of physical relief without tenderness or affection was a bitter sense of loneliness and further isolation. The problem was that Ron, because he had had at least some good parenting, was capable of a fairly healthy sex life, but Rose could only climax in pain.

At this stage Rose had not identified this need in herself. She saw the fighting and the very violent sexual sessions as manifestations of Ron's cruelty to her. It is true that Ron was by now drinking heavily. Rose would drink in bouts. The children knew that when Rose's voice became slow and precise, it was time to get out of the way. There was little they could do to shut out the sounds of the two bodies heaving and thrashing about the bedroom, or the groans and the moans which made it difficult to distinguish between agony and ecstasy. After a particularly violent sexual episode they would both be ashamed of themselves. Ron would tell Rose she was a disgusting old whore. Rose would be genuinely hurt and bewildered. Slowly Rose would need more and more pain as the ability to climax moved further and further away.

There came a time when they had been tormenting each other for days. The taunting and the jeering excited both of them and built up tension until Rose started screaming at Ron in the passage. Finally he threw her on the floor on her face in a rugby tackle, pinned her with his knees on the back of her legs, tore her clothes off, and split her anus with the first thrust. Her screams brought the children downstairs. There was blood everywhere. Ron curled up in a ball and was sick. The climax of the pair was now over, and Rose was in dreadful agony. She dragged herself to the bathroom and attempted to clean herself up. And she arrived at the Refuge the next day.

'Never again . . . I'll never go near him . . . never. This time it's finished.' I had listened to this whole story, and I felt a tremendous sympathy for a whole family so horribly trapped in their circle of violence, but I felt physically sick — so I had to go out of the office. Mike Dunne, who worked beside me for so many years, sensed what had gone on; God knows, we had seen thousands of families together. So he gave me a big warm hug, and I was able to go back and comfort her too. I knew this was not the end of her relationship with Ron. '*It's finished*' — I had heard those words so often before. Battered women who come to a refuge to sincerely get out of their violent relationships will talk about their future. They very quickly give up their pasts. However, women like Rose, who are still locked into these relationships, use the words of leaving *for ever . . . for good . . . never again . . .* like a litany. In their heads they recognise the danger and degradation of these relationships, but they are addicted to the excitement and drama that go with them.

Predictably she was on the phone to him by that evening. There was a huge bunch of flowers by the morning. She was pleased. The boys looked at me — two pairs of cynical eyes.

They were beginning to hate her now. Already they looked at all the women in the refuge with loathing and contempt. 'Slags, whores, cunts,' they would scream at the other mothers if anyone upset them. Then Ron was on the doorstep. We talked to him about their problem, about how he and Rose were on a slippery slope which could, at worst, end up with one of them dead – though it was more likely that their lives would slide in a gradual decline to where they would become hopelessly addicted to alcohol, giving them an excuse for the release of their violent needs for each other. Then, after the money ran out, Ron would find himself in prison, and Rose would be relegated to a mental hospital to be treated for drink. The children would go into care. The family might then be briefly reunited for several months of semi-stability, but they would soon degenerate again.

By this time there would be case files and conferences involving their doctor, health visitors, probation officer, social worker, hospital social worker, borough solictors. All the case workers would have a little information to contribute, mostly reflecting the to's and fro's of the various members of the family. Yet still nothing would be understood about the violent needs of these desperate people. By the time the boys were fourteen or fifteen, they would have girlfriends pregnant — and therefore they would receive accommodation and social security. Two more babies would join the rapidly growing army of the emotionally disabled. Unloved and unloving, they would inherit the mantle of violence that is passed from one generation to another — the mark of Cain.

By now I found that I was more and more drawn to the concept of these violent relationships being actually a form of addiction. Moira once explained to me why she stayed with Mike. Mike who was so dangerous that he had knifed her between the ribs and put her into an intensive-care unit; Mike, who had so nearly run her down; Mike, who had stubbed out his cigarettes on her breasts and stomach while he pinned her to the ground. But she always went back to him, and each time she conceived another child. I think it must need a lorry by now to cart round all the documents recording the history of this family.

Moira is a wanderer, and in between bouts with Mike she, like so many others, stays in various homeless family hostels or refuges. She then gets allotted a flat in a New Town, a grant to furnish it, installs her kids in school, and orders from her mail order catalogues. She is such a good hustler that before long she has £3000 to £4000 worth of goods delivered from masses of different catalogues. Then, when it's all in, she sells off the lot to neighbours and second-hand shops, and flits with the kids back to Mike, if she feels like it, or to yet another homeless family unit. When she was with us she became the life and soul of the Refuge, and all the staff loved her. But she liked to taunt Mike over the phone. She would ask him to come over and see the kids, but when he arrived she would be out, taking the kids with her.

On one occasion, when she had made yet another such arrangement which left him raging on our doorstep, I asked him why he did not just forget her. I warned him that they both had a 'till-death-us-do-part' relationship, and it looked to me highly likely that one of his onslaughts would eventually finish her off. Then the kids would go into care and he would go to jail. Although he agreed, it was hopeless talking to him. He just kept repeating that he loved her and wanted her back. 'How can you say you love someone when you torture her?' I asked. 'In the hospital after the last baby, you screwed her on the balcony and split all her stiches'. 'She wanted it as well,' he said. There was no getting through to him. Moira eventually came back and found him there, and I saw the confusion on the children's faces as they struggled to understand the violent and perverted world of their parents. Now Mike was crying and promising to take them home. This was the same Mike who went berserk and smashed their toys and beat their mother to a pulp.

'Why do you do it, Moira?' I perservered in exasperation. 'Why do you need to get killed?' If I've asked a woman that question once, I've asked a thousand times, and each time the answer is roughly the same. In this case Moira thought for a few moments, then said '*It's the moment just before he hits me*'.

It is hard to explain this need to people from non-violent backgrounds. The best way to explain it probably is to ask you to imagine a moment in your life when you are in mortal danger. Suddenly you find you are super-human. You deal with the situation perfectly. Maybe you rescue a child from in front of a car. Maybe you pull someone out of a burning house. Then after the event your knees collapse, you are shaking, and you go into a state of shock. What happened to you is that you put yourself on red alert. You perceived danger, and the message flashed from your brain to all the nerve centres of the body. Chemicals in the body alerted the system to a state of high-arousal.* You rose to the occasion. You were literally high on your own body chemicals. When the danger had passed, your chemical levels dropped dramatically, and the body suffered immediate withdrawal symptoms.

Once the danger is over, most people go back to normal, but not the violence-prone personality. This is the child that became addicted to its own body chemicals from babyhood. Probably it will one day be discovered that such children were addicted even before birth, when they were in the womb. Their entire system is constantly awash with the chemical of high arousal, as scarcely a day goes by without a violent family episode. Soon the body becomes so used to this feeling of the chemical rush that unconsciously the child looks for dangerous situations to provide it.

For Moira her high, the moment when she felt totally alive, was the point when she had so enraged Mike that he was about to hit her. She was only twenty-six, and in time her pain threshold would rise, and she would need more pain just before the blow, and she, too, like the others, might go down that dreadful road to death.

A woman named Gemma described to me how her pain threshold had become so high that she did not even feel the pain of having her finger broken. This is a transcript from one of my tapes, when she had just arrived and put her baby in my arms.

GEMMA: My finger won't go staight.
ERIN: Why?

---

*For further discussion of the chemicals involved in high-arousal and of the addiction of pain, see Chapter Six.

GEMMA: **Because he bent it right back. He didn't do it on purpose. I don't think, mind. Because I couldn't tell, you see, at the time, of course. He sort of went like that (She demonstrated his pulling the finger back. I cringed, imagining my own pain) and I couldn't tell whether he broke it or not, because I didn't go to the hospital.
ERIN: Yes, it is broken. You see, as a battered child, you've been used to quite a lot of pain.
GEMMA: Yes.
ERIN: (Seeing a horrible bruise on her thigh) I would scream blue murder if anybody kicked me like that. My God, I'd go to hospital.
GEMMA: Yes, I know. I'm used to it quite. Nothing really hurts anymore. I've been through it all, and it just doesn't hurt anymore.
ERIN: How bad did that kick hurt?
GEMMA: It didn't hardly hurt at all. I went like that, 'Aah!' and I, you know, just kept thinking there's something else, and then it just went away.

All the staff at Chiswick had noticed that many of the injuries inflicted on our women coming in would have put most people into hospital for weeks. I think I first realized this many years ago, when a CID officer's wife came in with broken ribs. Not only had he broken her ribs, but he had also made her sit on a chair and poured a kettle of boiling water over her lap. She had huge blisters between her legs. He did all this in front of her six-year-old daughter. She came to us straight from hospital. By the second day she was pushing a broom round the office. 'Can't be doing nothing,' she explained. 'You must be in agony,' I said, thinking of the blisters. 'Oh, no, I've had so many beatings all my life I don't feel nothing'. As soon as she was healed she was off back home, dragging the reluctant six-year-old with her. 'She's ever so proud of her dad . . . He won a medal for danger.' *I should co co*, I thought to myself. Of course when I thought about it later that night, it all made sense. It's like a soldier on a battlefield fighting for his life; there are countless stories on how a soldier can be horribly injured and just not notice until after the battle is over. Our families lived in a permanent state of war with their parents and their children.

We were also fascinated to watch the reactions of the mothers if they heard that a very violent man was on his way to the Refuge. Those who abhorred violence would retreat down into the safety of the basement or up to the top of the house. Those who got high on violence, on the other hand, would all congregate round the front hall and the windows. Some of the children behaved the same way: they would cluster round the front door in spite of repeated attempts to lead them away. It always saddened me to see their little faces light up at the possibility of a violent explosion and of somebody getting hurt. However, those who stayed with us for a sufficiently long time did eventually learn other patterns of behaviour.

At that time I had such a gifted play staff that the children in the Refuge probably had the best care this country could offer. Sarah Gibson was the surrogate mother figure who embraced them kindly and gave them back their childhood. Roger Blades and Michael Taylor were the first truly gentle men the children had ever met. In time I noticed, as I stood on the doorstep with yet another angry man, that some of the children who were beginning to form non-violent relationships in the Refuge would now stay away from the excited group at the doorway.

Another insight emerged from the fact that we seemed able to keep these particular families with us, in contrast to some other refuges who catered for a different type of woman. It was precisely the atmosphere of our huge, chaotic, busy house that seemed to make these families comfortable. That reminded me very much of an experience during the war. I was in Canada when relatives and friends of my mother's were returned from the concentration camps in Singapore. They were all lodged in extremely comfortable hotels, but one by one they left the hotels and moved into a nearby park. They could not, at that stage, cope with the structure and order of normal everyday life.

Once I explained my theory of 'positive' overcrowding to Anna Freud. She listened to me, and then she said it reminded her of her own work during the war, when she set up a scheme deep in the heart of peaceful countryside to cater for women and their children who were in danger of losing their lives as the bombs fell on London. They spent a lot of money to set it all up, and as the trains pulled in carrying all these families, they were made welcome and settled in. But gradually they began to return to London — to the danger, to the bombing, to the chance of getting killed. She smiled at me as she recalled this, for she *did* understand. But certainly the Department of Health and Social Security did not want to know my theory.

Dealing as I did daily with violent men, women, and children, I began to make other observations for myself. Confronted with a human being emotionally and chemically 'high' in a violent state, the one thing you must never do is to become aggressive back. That will only escalate an already violent and explosive situation. I have never, in all my ten years, been struck, though there have been two or three occasions in the Refuge when I have had to 'floor' a woman who was escalating to such a pitch of aggression that she was liable to do some damage to herself or someone else. This means pushing her gently to the floor, and holding her down until she starts to cry; usually she then cuddles into you and relaxes. Violent people are very frightened people.

I have always taught my staff not to be over wary of the big mouthy woman — it is the little quiet ones at the back that are liable to do most damage. Because the social agencies grew out of an outdated Victorian middle-class notion of philanthropy, there is no proper or practical training in this country, or elsewhere, for dealing with this problem of violence. People who are not trained to deal with violence tend to be terrified of violence, because they only see the physical manifestations of it: the swollen face, the red and purple flesh, the swelling of the neck, and the yelling and the swearing, followed possibly by physical attack. What they do not perceive is that under all that acting out is a great deal of pain. If you have been born into a violent home, you will never have had time to express sorrow or pain in any other way except through rage.

There were only very few occasions when I was seriously in danger, and they taught me a lot. The first occurred when I dropped by the Palm Court Hotel, which housed about sixty mothers and their children, and I was chatting to Anne Ashby, who was then running the place. A very flushed and breathless Dawn rushed past us, babbling that she had been home to collect some things. Now I am never terribly happy, after a mother has told you horrific stories of what went on at home, and you have seen the files to prove it, to learn that she is just popping back to collect some clothes. Somehow, if someone is out to murder you, clothes seem irrelevant, particularly as Women's Aid always had lots of spare clothes.

Anyway, Dawn proceeded to her room, and I was preparing to leave, when there came a thunderous knock on the door, and a man outside was screaming that he would 'fucking kill her'. It did not take long to establish that Dawn's husband had followed her, and was about to tear the place apart. This was an Ulster family, and not only were both parents violent, but they had also twice been bombed out of their home. The children were very disturbed, and at this stage were setting light to everything they could lay their hands on. Their only topic of conversation seemed to involve fire, and they constantly acted out the sounds of bombs falling.

For some reason best known to himself, the house's very large Alsatian, who was usually capable of removing portions of innocent passers-by was now lying quietly on the floor looking very occupied with something on the other side of the room. Fortunately, the doorway was small, with an inner porch, and I took up almost all the space, thereby effectively blocking the man out. He was so enraged that he was beside himself. He was quite a large Irishman with drink in him, so he was not liable to listen to anything reasonable. I decided to treat him as I would a badly upset Refuge child, so I threw my arms round him in a bear-hug and held him tight. He was absolutely stunned. There he was, raging and swearing, with people all round scurrying away, and here was this fat middle-aged woman enveloping him in a huge embrace. He collapsed in my arms and sobbed. All the pain and the grief ran out of him, and he became safe. His rage subsided, his body relaxed, and he calmed down.

Apparently what Dawn had done was to go home in his absence and take down all the wedding photographs, and also remove those in the album. But what had really upset him was that she had taken time to sort through his belongings, and had removed his precious insurance card. Without it, he could not get a job. I went and fetched it from Dawn, who looked a little embarrassed. She did not get the exciting smash-up she had expected. For she had already spent hours at the Palm Court boasting about his violence, describing how he would smash all the windows and kill anyone who got in his way. So I'm afraid she felt he had very much let her down. Unfortunately her urge for violence meant that she soon moved on to another relationship that offered an even more exciting level of violence.

Often violent episodes never really got out of hand because the staff were confident in their non-violent approach. Highly trained and very experienced, we would all work as a team. On one occasion Jo, who became the bane of our life because her need to fight meant that she was involved in frequent episodes in the local pubs, decided to continue her war with her current boyfriend from the safety of the Refuge. Jo had spent most of one morning recounting the grim story of how George, a Nigerian student, was promising to kill her, and indeed at that very moment was on his way over. For one about to face imminent death, Jo looked remarkably cheerful. The prospect seemed to fill her with ecstatic excitement.

Now, it is necessary for anyone working with violence to have a good understanding of how violence is expressed in different cultures. English people, on the whole, don't carry knives. West Indians do. An Irishman will respond to religion; not so a Scot. A West Indian man is more likely to attack a male member of staff because he may have little experience of men in a position of power. The West Indian mother is the supreme matriarch, so it is appropriate for a woman to go to the door, and he will not be offended. However, the reverse is true for a Nigerian, who comes from a country where it would be humiliating to be faced with a woman, their society being such a strong patriarchy.

Remembering this, I sent Mike Dunne to speak to George. He was certainly angry, and was determined to get at Jo. She had taken his wallet and car keys. I stood behind

Mike, and together we formed a barrier into the house. It did not help matters to have Jo leaning over my shoulder grinning at him. He lunged forward and threw a punch at me, but it was very half-hearted. Mike rugger-tackled him to the floor and held him while the poor man sobbed his heart out.

He had been a student here, and was terribly lonely. The eldest son of a highly successful Nigerian family, he would finish his business studies, and then return to Nigeria to care for the family all his life. Meanwhile he was cut off from the warmth and friendliness of Africa, so he was desolate. As a people, the British are far more at home with the easy-going West Indian community than with the more serious Nigerian community. So he had fallen into Jo's hands, and fortunately ended up in our arms, or he may well have got to her and injured her, and wrecked his life. He told Mike of his struggles to help her, of his need for her warmth and company, of her repeated betrayal of his trust and friendship. We explained to him that Jo behaved like this to all men.

Now was not the time to point out that over the years we had known her she was much improved. In fact, the original Jo had been a vicious animal when she first arrived, festooned with six children. When George calmed down, we let him go, and he went outside. But he asked to see her. Jo was now crouching in a very small corner of the sitting-room. All the excitement, the rush of the chemicals of high arousal had drained away, and she looked grey and shaky. 'Don't send me out there . . . he'll kill me.' Once the high has gone, the prospect of death becomes the reality it is. 'I don't think so, this time,' I said dragging her to her feet. 'Consequences, Jo. You made the mess — you clean it up.' It was a very shamefaced Jo that went down the steps to speak to George. That episode cured him of his need for Jo, but curiously enough, it also cured Jo of using us as a buffer between herself and the men against whom she warred. She recognised, I think, that we were her safe place, and that we loved her enough to risk ourselves before we would risk her.

I learned from these encounters that, as a general principle, it is better to leave a violent person no physical space in which to organise his rage. Studies on aggression and animal display have suggested that violent people require more social space in order not to become anxious and feel threatened than non-violent people. But when I read these findings I am extremely sceptical. After several years of refuge work, I noticed that whenever the Refuge was packed tight, and there was no choice of personal territory because the families had to sleep in dormitories and share all the available communal space, the aggression level would be low. As soon as our numbers dropped however, and several feet of extra space could be annexed by each woman, then the levels of aggression would rise.

It always amazed me to find that, given the antisocial behaviour and the past records for violence of many of our families, we had virtually no major incidents. In my ten years as Director, I can only recall three or four occasions when a bout of fisticuffs resulted in a black eye. Overcrowding, which began as a necessity due to lack of other refuges in the country, turned out to be of major therapeutic benefit to a community of aggressive and asocial families. So, too, I learned that those men and women most inclined to raise a wall of rage around them responded best to a gentle touch or the offer of a cigarette.

I saw a lot of verbal violence, of course. 'I'll fucking knife you, you fat cunt,' was Judy Scott's way of saying good-morning. 'I love you too,' was my stock response. Poor Judy, with such affectionate greetings, had terrified and alienated a whole shoal of well-meaning social agencies.

Then there was Jilly; who came to us from the locked wards of Holloway. She had twice burnt down her house, her children were in care, and she went from one diabolically violent relationship to another. She teamed up with Jane, whose neck was corrugated with scars from the times when she had attempted to hang herself and to slash her throat. 'It lets out the pain,' Jane would whisper. Jane came in to us after she had slashed her wrists. For her it was just time out of the nightmare that she lived in. She had finally found a man who, like her, was a middle-class reject. She told me how his rich farming father hated him so much he was forced to sleep in the barn on freezing nights. She told me how once the father broke the boy's legs with a metal rod when he was six, and his sister carried him over the fields on her back to the hospital, saying it was 'an accident'.

Anyway Jane and Jilly became drinking partners, and it was inevitable, given the pecking order of physical power in a community of this kind, that Jane would eventually need to launch a public attack on me. Again, the rooms at the Refuge were always crowded, so she had nowhere to be by herself to work up a state of rage. It is almost impossible to get ready to launch a physical attack if small children are pulling at your skirt or another woman passing by says 'Want a cup of tea, love?'

Finally, one afternoon after the pubs were closed, she came in with Jilly and seeing that most of the room was clear, because we were all sitting in a semi circle, she stood in the centre of the group, swinging her handbag and organising her attack. I decided it was best to let it happen and get it out of the way. She flung her handbag first, and then launched herself at me. But I caught her in my arms and gently pulled her to the floor, where I pinned her down for ten minutes while the rage ebbed away. All the time I talked to her as you would to a hurt child. Slowly, she began to curl into that foetal position so often seen. Then I was able to gather her in my arms, and rock her and hum to her. I was aware that this was probably the only time she had been held close in love. She was calm and happy for the next few hours, but then she departed into the night with Jilly.

She is another woman who may end up sleeping rough under the arches, and probably die from exposure. The hardest part of our work is knowing that it need not end like that. If only we could recognise that you cannot beat people better. You cannot lock them away or keep them drugged in mental hospitals forever. We must create programmes that at least give these families a *chance* to learn to live in a world which is now so highly complex. If the main part of their childhood lacked adequate training for coping in our society, they are doomed to fill the institutions which are ready and waiting to receive them.

I always remember talking to a very enlightened member of a children's home board of management. She was telling me of her frustration with a system that created more problems than it solved. We both noticed how as one child was taken into care, another rapidly replaced it in the same emotionally disabled family. It was not uncommon for some of our women to have had ten or eleven pregnancies, of which some would be miscarriages and others cot deaths. The rest of the children would be scattered like confetti across the country, in 'care'. Usually these children were abandoned in the aftermath of one violent relationship when a new partner came in and resented their presence, for the children were living reminders of the woman's past liaisons. They would then be taken in by the local social services on a voluntary basis. Then there would be a new baby to cement the new liaison, followed by further violent episodes, or else the man might abandon the woman. On her own once again, the woman would take her previous children out of care, having increased her family by one or two meanwhile, until she met another man and the whole process began again. It is a highly unsatisfactory state of affairs.

Why, I asked then as now, do we not take whole families into care? After all, if the source of the problem is the parents ignoring their children, merely concentrating on their children completely defeats the object of the exercise. But I discovered that by asking such questions, you are shaking the very foundations of a society that has never questioned its basic assumption that the privileged few should control the lives of everyone else. The class structure and social fabric of our society are so organised that any failure to comply with this assumption is met by a rigid and unyielding bureaucratic offensive. All caring agencies in this country, and in most of Western society, are based on a series of negative reactions: fail and be punished.

Overlying the basic premise that 'to punish is to improve' is the massive superstructure of the administration of misery. Millions are paid into its pocket annually to relieve the burden of conscience for the many individuals who can adapt and survive. With the old social orders decaying and crumbling, however, we can no longer afford to ignore our jails bursting at the seams, or our Welfare State being cut to ribbons. We will have to concentrate on an alternative strategy *of love and hope* for these problem families.

Chapter Three

CHILDREN OF VIOLENCE

Violence towards children brings out a passionate reaction in most adults because few of us get through childhood unhurt, either emotionally or physically. We can all remember moments of utter helplessness and impotence at the hands of an enraged adult. For the lucky ones, the angry parent soon reverts to a normal, loving self and promises the child that she or he will control their temper next time. For the others, there is no such hope, and the child is at the mercy of two entirely unpredictable human beings.

I often feel that some middle-class children have a much harder time at the hands of their parents than do working-class children, yet it is a common feeling that violence to children does not happen in 'nice' families — by which most people mean the white middle classes. I remember, in the early days of womens's aid, trying to persuade an agency worker that a woman was not only being very violent to her three children but was also neglecting them. The agency worker promised to go round to the house, and I telephoned the next day to see what had happened. She was very hesitant. 'You didn't tell me her husband was a dentist,' she said. 'It's very difficult in these cases.' I saw her point. *It is* very difficult, because middle-class people have professional resources like lawyers, whom they can use to sue anyone who dares suggest they are less than perfect.

It seems harder for a middle-class parent to ask for help. I still painfully recall going to a psychiatrist, when my daughter was little, and asking him to help me with my violent feelings towards her. I remember the shock on his face. He considered my successful husband, a national television reporter. He looked at my two well-fed, well-dressed children, and then he looked at me. 'Mrs Pizzey,' he said, sitting back in his chair, 'the problem is that you are a bad mother.' What he meant was that, firstly, I had everything anyone could want; secondly, violence, he had been trained to believe, results from bad social conditions; therefore if you could not lay claim to social deprivation, then you must be intrinsically evil or bad.

On another occasion I was in a neighbour's house. I had always suspected that it was a violent family, particularly because of the elder child's behaviour. I knew this child was being seen regularly by a child psychiatrist for educational problems. One morning I was in my bedroom, with the window open, when I heard terrible screams coming from a house in the square. The cries of a desperate child. I ran barefoot down the stairs into the street and down the pavement until I stopped outside the door of the house from which the cries were still coming. 'No, mummy! No, mummy! Don't do it . . . Don't . . . ' The screams had such ringing intensity that they must have been heard by at least a dozen of the houses round about, yet no one stirred out of a single door. The people already on the street merely turned their heads and hurried by. I banged on the front door. No answer. I banged so hard that the frame shook. The battered child in me was screaming — it was the battered child in so many people crying out for help.

Sheila finally opened the door. She was panting with rage. She was speechless. Her eyes were bulging, and her hair was sticking out in sweaty strands. She stood in silence, shaking. I pushed past her and ran upstairs. Rodney was standing in the doorway of his bedroom. He was naked, and there were red finger-marks across his chest. It was his shocked little white face that broke my heart — the dreadful acceptance by a child of six that it was his fault, he'd been naughty, and he deserved what had happened. He already knew that if you upset your parents, they beat you. He explained what had happened. His father had gone off yet again with another woman. Rodney had gone into his mother's room to phone his father, but mummy had come in and overheard him. She flew into a blinding rage, tore the telephone off the wall, and then laid into him. I cuddled him gently.

That sort of incident can happen with any parent pushed beyond endurance, but the difference here was that in Sheila's family it was a regular occurrence. The children of this family were often battered, but it was covered up by both parents. Rodney's abnormally violent and psychopathic behaviour at school was explained away as his 'giftedness'. The outpatient clinic he attended never even suspected that he was being battered.

I went downstairs to Sheila, but I felt an enormous rush of sympathy for her. 'What are you going to do?' she asked. 'Nothing,' I said. 'All you must do is to go to the clinic and see Rodney's psychiatrist and tell him the truth. I will phone him myself once you've told him, because I need to be sure you've phoned, for your own protection and for the children. Now we've been through this together, and you know I'm nearby. It will be a measure of control for you.' Poor woman. It must have been hard for her, but at least the clinic, although they had missed the signs before, had a reputation for being good and sympathetic.

But it is a mistake to think of violence as a collection of bruises and broken bones. It is not the physical attacks that do the worst of the damage; it is the slow destruction of a human soul in the hands of people already suffering from their own violent natures. Until it is accepted by everyone that verbal violence can do far more damage than even the most savage physical onslaught, we will continue to react only to stories and pictures of visibly battered children, and comfort ourselves that it only happens among the poor and the feckless.

In my experience of cases which range from one end of the social scale to the other, the truth is that the more primitive the personality, the greater the likelihood that they will lose control of their rage and batter or even kill. You will find these people in all walks of life. Among the middle classes, however, with their highly-developed methods of social control, the violence will, for the most part, be physically restrained but will acquire a mental sophistication that is far more dangerous to the survival of the other members of a family. You can destroy the physical world of other human beings by smashing up the house and beating up the inmates. The home can be mended and the bruises will fade. But in bringing up children, although you may never physically attack them, you may instead slowly decimate any sense of self they have, so that their inner world is destroyed. And then you commit the equivalent of soul murder, and the resulting adults will be the walking dead.

Middle-class violence is still a taboo subject. Because it remains largely untold and is a highly skilled vice, it goes untreated and unchecked. I see it in the eczema, in the migraines, in the epileptic fits, in the asthma. I see the violence in all the stress symptoms of childhood: in the child up the road that constantly has a red ring round his lips because he nervously sucks at them all the time; in the child that blinks furiously when you speak to her; and all the other cases taken to the doctor's surgery for him to recommend treatment for the symptoms. It would probably never cross the doctor's mind that Richard's nightmares about his mother were a result of her incestuous overtures. That Melanie's migraine was a result of the silent battle of a ten-year-old to keep her father out of the bathroom because she recognises that his feelings towards her are more sexual than paternal. Or, in the case of an eight-year-old boy attending the hospital for ulcers – his own father a doctor – that his bleeding stomach was a symptom of the family meal times when everyone round the table sat in terror of the father's moods – and continual acid remarks to his son reminding him of his failure at school, on the sportsfield, in life, as a human being.

You have a greater chance of coming to terms with your own violent childhood, which often includes sexual as well as physical attacks, if the events are actualised and visible. If you have parents that act out their damage in front of you, it is all seen, heard and experienced. The most difficult cases to treat, however, are where the violence is never all openly said, seen or heard. This is the case in the majority of middle-class homes. It will continue to be the case until enough middle-class emotionally-disabled people have the courage to get together and work to prevent it.

Just recently I became involved with a grandmother who

was extremely worried about her grandson. Her daughter, the child's mother, came to see me as a result of a hideous beating from yet another violent boyfriend. I have seldom seen a face so badly smashed up. Her little boy was three years old, but in his life he had known nothing but drugs and violence. When he was a baby he had even been taken to India on a heroin smuggling operation by his mother and a previous boyfriend. This girl had been a deb of the year, and her godfather was one of the world's richest men. Her mother was frantic with worry about her little grandson; she knew her daughter to be an alcoholic and incapable of coping with a child. She approached her local Social Services for help, and they promised to go round right away. 'Sophia fooled them,' she told me later on the phone. 'She completely fooled them.' Well, Sophia may well have fooled them, but to her own cost. A few weeks later she was found dead on the floor of her kitchen with the little boy sitting beside her watching television. The verdict was death by misadventure, and her death certificate stated that she had died of a combination of alcohol and drug abuse.

In my work I learned, to my horror, how soon children become physically and emotionally addicted to pain. I think the youngest example of this I found in a baby of three to four months old. His mother, Frieda, was well known to us at the Refuge, and was probably one of the most violent women I have ever known — at least I thought so until I met *her* mother. We despaired of Frieda's behaviour, but she was such a life-force, and such an intelligent, funny human being, that we all persevered with her. With the help of her social worker, Frieda moved out of the Refuge into a New Town. She was pregnant again at the time, and she visited the Refuge to reassure me that, in spite of all my gloomy predictions, all was well. Of course, everything looked wonderful. Frieda was always a spotlessly clean, wonderful home-maker, and a good cook. Baby Joss was all dressed in white, and looked just like his father. He lay on my lap kicking and cooing, and seemed a very contented baby. There was a sudden moist patch on my knee, where Joss had wet through his nappy. Frieda took him back and undid his terry-towelling nappy. The baby lay contentedly on her lap, looking into her face and smiling.

Frieda then began to pinch his fat little cheeks, and he smiled and gurgled. Then as she pinched she began to twist his flesh. Any other baby would have been screaming with pain, but this baby just gurgled happily. I was horrified and glanced round at Anne Ashby, who was looking aghast. 'Stop it, Frieda,' I said, 'you're hurting him.' 'I'm not,' she protested. 'See, he's laughing.' She was right. But realising our disapproval, she turned her attention to changing his nappy. Within a few minutes she was pricking his bottom with a pin. Again he laughed and gurgled. 'Stop, Frieda,' I said again. 'You're being cruel'. Frieda knew that – but mother and child were sharing a moment which excluded people who used words like love, tenderness, and affection. They were bonded in their addiction to giving and receiving pain. We could only tell her social worker of our anxiety. Several years later I heard that Joss was up for adoption. I felt sorry for the uncomprehending family who would take him in and never understand why this beautiful, healthy baby would probably grow up to be a dangerous violence-prone man. But I know why: I saw it for myself.

The observer in me often watches such interactions with fascination even while my human side is outraged and appalled. I clearly remember sitting with a young couple, both of whom were violent, as we talked about how he could alter his need to inflict pain on Jenny and she could perhaps learn to enjoy making love in preference to having a good fight. Their eighteen-month-old toddler, Anthony, on seeing that we were absorbed and ignoring him, decided to put his head on his father's knee. 'See,' said John, pleased with himself, and looking at me. 'See how much he loves me?' (Actually the child was not his, which served as another source of conflict in the family.) Jenny immediately became defensive. 'He loves me better than you. Come here, Anthony, Come here.' She stretched out her arms to him.

Anthony, who at eighteen months had already survived a series of adult fights, and attacks upon himself which would have killed most babies, looked coolly across at his mother and did not move his head. Jenny became more agitated. 'Come here, you little cunt,' she insisted. The child, gauging the situation decided to go over to his mother. When he moved over to her and sat in her lap, John felt betrayed, and began to swear at Jenny. She then raised her voice, and the situation escalated. The child sat watching, his eyes shining: he found the scene exciting. Soon he would get punched by one or other parent, then he would join in the drama. Other children watch television for excitement; but he had live drama all day and all night in his family. I intervened and put a stop to the quarrel. Yes, they admitted that was sometimes how the rows developed. Shamefaced, they could see what they were doing to the child. They acknowledged their own violence and brutal backgrounds, and they did sincerely wish to change. The last I heard, Jenny had remarried, but still kept Anthony. I pray she has changed — it can happen.

It was not only my own observations that led me to believe that pleasure and pain can be crossed in early childhood, but also observations by the staff. Nicky Hay came to see me one day and described how a three-year-old girl had come into the Refuge with a dreadfully burnt hand, encrusted in a filthy bandage. It was necessary to cut the bandage away from the hand which involved tearing away pieces of burnt skin. Nicky had expected the child to scream and struggle. But no, the child sat impassively and patiently while the doctor cut the bandage off. 'I couldn't believe it,' said Nicky. But I could. I had watched for years our children falling off walls, breaking limbs, walking into the Refuge covered in bruises, with black eyes, split lips. They did not feel pain like ordinary children.

Tony and Billy came into the Refuge with their mother. Marge lashed out at anyone and everything, particularly at her two uncontrollable boys. She had just left an extremely violent man — so extreme that he had been locked up in a hospital for the criminally insane. Although recognised as a troublemaker in his youth, he always got off any charges against him because his adopted mother was a middle-class Justice of the Peace. Nobody noticed how seriously disturbed he was until it was too late, and then he was sent to the hospital for the criminally insane.

Tony the elder boy spent his time in the Refuge fighting.

He was only really happy and content when he was punching or being punched, preferably by someone bigger. I was opening my house in Bristol at that time, and I needed to take five families with me to begin a new community. I chose Marge because I needed her administrative abilities, her energy and her humour. She could drive, and also I suspected she was not physically and emotionally addicted to violence. I believed that, given a clean break and an opportunity to achieve something in her own right, she would not go back to a violent relationship.

Tony, however, was a different matter. At five he was a bully and a thug. Living with him was a nightmare, since he smashed everything in sight. Marge, so used to years of dreadful violence from the father and then from the son, would sit at the kitchen table and throw her wooden Dr Scholl sandal at him. It would crack him on the head but he wouldn't even notice. Then Marge and I would fight about it. 'You can't beat children better,' I'd yell. 'How else can I stop him?' she'd yell back. Finally we instituted a daily pocket-money system. Pocket-money belonged to each child by right, and could only be removed for violent behaviour. It worked. We devised a long-term reward system for the children in the house, and slowly they calmed down.

Then Jimmy came into Marge's life. She could not believe that such a kind good man would ever want her, after all she had been through. The boys adored him. One day you would catch Tony leaning against Jimmy. Then another day he took his hand. They moved out together and set up home. A baby daughter was born. Marge rang up and asked if they could come to the Bristol house to see me. The boys went out into the garden to play. I was delighted as I sat in our sitting-room admiring the baby, thinking how lucky she was to be born in peace. There was a loud howl from the garden and Tony appeared, clutching his knee. It was grazed. 'Come here, son' said Jimmy. Tony flew into his new father's arms, and buried his head in his chest. Tony was crying. He could now feel pain. He had grazed his knee and it hurt and he cried. I cried, too. Those are the little miracles, the times when you know it is all worthwhile. People can change, but the younger you treat violence the faster you can effect the changing.

Amanda was two when her father Francis died. He was knifed by her mother in a moment of rage that even she could barely understand. One or other of that couple was bound to end up dead in their violent relationship, and it turned out to be Francis. Christine, the mother, was distraught. She sat beside me in the office going over and over the dreadful moment when the knife slid into his throat, when he staggered to the bed, and then fell to the floor. Amanda banged around the office, tore at her mother's skirts, sang, walked round and round in circles. 'Are you sure she didn't see what happened?' I asked. 'No. Amanda was asleep next door.'

Two or three days later, I was sitting with Christine when Amanda came banging into the office. She indicated that she wanted to draw on my large drawing-pad. I spread out my coloured pens as I always do, and she chose the red one and handed it to me. 'Draw Francis,' she said, gazing at me very intensely. I know that when a child has that sense of urgency with you, they are about to let go of something which to them is momentous. As soon as I had drawn a not very good cartoon figure of Francis, she took the pen from my hand and drew lines all round the figure, and then began stabbing the paper, over and over again, meanwhile looking at her mother. As I suspected, having encountered so many, many children who were witnesses to killings, she had been there and seen it.

I know Christine did not deliberately lie to me. She would have had no real memory of actual events in that moment of murder, because violence fuses realities. She and Francis would have been in a world of their own. This fusing of realities affected her recounting of the stabbing to the police. By the time she was talking to them she was no longer in that heightened shared reality, but was suddenly in their world. Our police and our courts should remember that when a person describes a crime he has committed, he is often not lying, but is simply speaking from a reality that is totally different from the one he was in when he committed the crime. Each different reality has its own distinct set of memories.

Christine would just not have noticed Amanda in the room at the time. But it was vital for the child to be able to tell

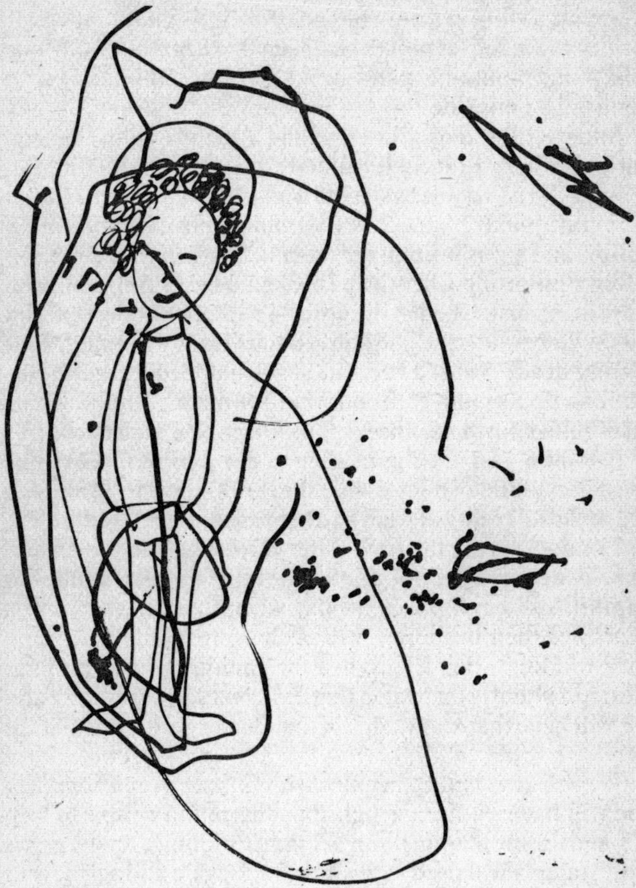

someone what had happened, to share what she had seen, and also to be angry with her mother. When the knife pierced her father's carotid artery, the blood hit the ceiling and sprayed around the walls. The last she would have seen of him was lying in a heap on the floor. It was now important for her to see him at peace. I explained to her that Daddy was asleep and would be going away. She listened intently with her head on one side.

Anne Ashby took Christine and Amanda to the funeral parlour where Francis lay quietly at rest in his coffin. Although Christine was hysterical with grief, Amanda looked at him very quietly. Anne took Polaroid photos of Francis in his coffin, and I was waiting for them both when they got back. After comforting Christine, I looked over at Amanda, who was sitting on the bed in the office. I took the photograph and sat down beside her. 'Did you see your Daddy sleeping, your Daddy dead?' I asked her. She slowly nodded her head. She put two fingers into the comfort of her mouth, and two huge tears rolled down her cheeks. She knew. She understood.

It took a year for the mother to come to trial. Christine lived at my Bristol house while she slowly came to terms with the dreadful reality of what had happened. She stayed with us in London during the trial. After three days the jury unanimously declared her not guilty. The relief was enormous, but she will still have to face the day when the children, having repressed their memories, will ask how their father died, and they will know that it was their own mother who killed him. Christine knows that when that day comes, wherever we are, we will have that knowledge of their history, and we will help her.

We will always keep in touch with Christine, and hopefully she will have learned enough about herself to be able to help Amanda come to terms with her father's killing. As she grows up, Amanda will need to work through again and again, with us and with child guidance, her memories of Francis's death. If the memories are not dealt with, they will sink into her unconscious. In later life, picking up a knife could then become a reflex action if she is fighting with a man. We hope that we have caught her young enough and can work with her thoroughly enough, so that she may recognise and understand the murder, and then use that understanding to break the pattern of violence in her own life.

The Richards family arrived at the Refuge in the middle of the night. They had travelled overnight from Yorkshire. Jody, their mother, was distraught. It took some considerable time to sort out the details of what had happened. Steve and Brian took the children off to playschool to let them talk out and draw their grief and confusion. I sat down with Jody. Jody had been living with the father of her youngest child Michael, who was seven months old. There were three other children: Julia who was two, Tyrone who was four, and Peter, aged five.

Jody had adored her own father, who seemed to have been a kind gentleman, but her mother was a monster. She hated Jody, who had been a very pretty, lively and intelligent child. Unfortunately, her father, her only protector, died when she was quite young, so she was left to the mercy of her violent bully of a mother. Jody soon decided that she would only survive if she fought back. Soon she was not only in trouble at home but also at school. The school showed little understanding, and continually punished the already abused little girl. Slowly she was transformed into a furious, intractable adolescent. Everything she did was in reaction to her mother. She deliberately dated West Indian boys, knowing how racially prejudiced her mother was. She took drugs, she drank herself silly, and soon became pregnant. Her mother fought back. All her life her mother had devoted herself to fooling the neighbours. The image of the little God-fearing woman who went out to work and scrubbed her house clean was a camouflage for an embittered, violent woman. She was one of the few human beings I found it difficult to like.

Jody was always with a new man, continually going back to her mother to scream and yell and demand attention. The first two children were born and she moved into a council flat supplied by the borough. But she could not cope with the two small children, so they were taken into care, and then returned to her, and then received back into care when she broke down again. Her restlessness made it impossible for her to stay indoors at night. She needed to be out and roaming the estate. Sometimes she would come back with men, for money and for company. Sometimes she would come back with a bottle, to drink herself into oblivion. The flat was sparse and the children had very little to wear. It was impossible for her to cope with all her own chaos.

Peter the eldest boy did his best to look after Tyrone and Julia. He learned very early to expect nothing from life and he got on with the business of seeing that they had enough to eat. He would nag and shout at his mother by the time he was three. He was used to being hit so he felt no pain.

Then Jody met Ralph. He was a giant of a man and very kind to Jody and her children. He was already living with another woman with three children, but he spent more and more time at Jody's flat. She became pregnant, and Michael arrived, but she could not bear the nights on her own when Ralph was with the 'other woman'. Soon she became obsessed with the images of Ralph somewhere else without her. She would beg and plead for him to stay. Ralph was rarely violent, but if pushed too far, he was known for his ability to explode into violent rage.

No one will ever know what it was that took him over to the other woman's house that night, and caused him to mutilate and then stab the woman to death. According to Jody, he came back to her flat covered with blood. He complained of dreadful stomach pains and told the children to wait for dinner, while he had a bath. He went into the bathroom and locked the door. Jody waited, then, hearing no sounds from the bathroom, and getting no answer to her knocks at the door, she broke it open. Ralph was lying dead in the bath. The children crowded into the room to look at him. Jody called the police, and Ralph's body was taken away. Jody was by now in an incredible state of fear. The neighbours, many of whom were Jamaican, were openly hostile to her. She picked up her children and ran to us. Now it was up to us to make sense of what happened both for her sake and for the children's.

This drawing is by Peter; he was explaining to my colleague Steve the complexity of the family relationships, as it involved four different fathers. He also showed in his drawings how he saw Ralph dead in the bathroom. He was also clearly

71

aware of the other woman's death, but he agreed with Tyrone that they were not there when she died. Peter was a very intense, moody child given to sudden outbursts of rage. Like most small children who have been robbed of the innocence of their childhood, Peter was frighteningly precocious.

Tyrone, however, was a professional charmer. He quietly got what he wanted from life by a mixture of friendly manipulation and cunning. He also was able to describe the sight of Ralph's nose under water, and he remarked on the bottles on the floor. Where as Peter showed grief and sorrow, Tyrone seemed quite cheerful, but he was the one who let me know he had a secret.

At playschool Julia spent hours stabbing at the walls and her drawing paper with a brush dipped in red paint. The play staff were all fairly new and had not worked before with any children who had witnessed murders. They were amazed at the ferocity and intensity of her attacks on the walls. Although Jody insisted that the children had not seen Ralph stabbing the other woman, Julia's behaviour was an accurate acting out of a violent event. When she raised her little hand in a stabbing motion I warned the staff, if she were left untreated, this event would go deep into her subconscious, only to reappear in a moment of crisis when she herself felt attacked. Then there was a very real possibility that she would stab someone.

It was several years before Tyrone was able to tell me that they had all watched the stabbing, as I suspected.

My immediate concern, however, was the baby, Michael. He seemed to be sleeping his little life away. At seven months he had the typical look of a neglected child. As he was unable to sit up or turn himself over, he constantly moved his head from side to side, and the friction from the sheets had made him bald. I noticed that his only form of play was to clutch his bottle with his feet which he used as hands for lack of ever being taken out of his cot. If I held him up, his little legs would dangle helplessly. I thought that if we kept him in the main sitting-room, where there were plenty of people to pick him up and cuddle him, he might be stimulated enough to come to life. It was soon apparent, however, that he did not want to join the human race. Life for him was all too painful, so he was sleeping his life away.

I talked it all over with my daughter Cleo, who was at home with a baby of the same age. I then talked to Jody who agreed that something must be done for Michael. Of course, we were in touch with the Social Services in her area, but they had nothing to offer Jody which was realistic in terms of support, so were unable to suggest any solution except to let us cope the best we could. In spite of all her problems, Jody was a woman with many excellent qualities. Because her relationship with her mother was so intense, there was really no room for anyone else. She had never trusted anyone before. Her life had been a kaleidoscope of agency workers who, one by one, gave up on her.

Her mother came by at this point, full of Hail Marys and poison. I listened to a catalogue of Jody's sins, and when the mother sat back, her eyes sparkling with malevolence, I took the wind out of her sails by completely agreeing with her. 'But,' I pointed out, 'here she is much loved. We might not like what she does, but we love her.' The old lady did not feel much like conversation after that. Swearing loudly on the heads of her babies and the graves of various departed relatives, she left the room. I then asked Jody if I could take Michael home each night and bring him back to her during the day. Not only would I have concentrated time to give to him this way, but it would also mean that Jody could have an uninterrupted night's sleep. She agreed and I took him home.

Feeding him in the peace of my own house, I noticed how fierce he was when he was sucking his bottle. I held him close to my breast with my face close to his so that he could hear me talking to him. He would suck furiously at the nipple of the bottle, and stretching out his hands he would pinch and scratch my face. I had noticed at the Refuge that he had a large area round his navel that was constantly sore and covered in half-healed scabs. Our wonderful health visitor Cilla had given us a special cream for it, but now I saw why it would not heal. As he drank from his bottle, he would tear at his skin until it bled. His pain and pleasure were already confused. I took him to the bathroom and gently lowered him into the bath, as I have with hundreds of babies before him. It was sad to watch his face completely dissolve into a pained grimace as the warm water immersed him. It was not fear; he was not afraid. He could not bear the pleasure – it hurt him. Cleo remembers from feeding and changing Michael, that he was incapable of holding food in his system. As soon as food went in one end, it came out the other. His digestive tract was as immature as a new-born child's. Michael had given up on life, so his body refused to develop and take nourishment.

Now the real work began. Cleo and the rest of the community at my house pitched in. We realised that it would take time, but in fact I always forget how wonderfully resilient children are. Given the right climate, like a drooping plant, children revive at a startling rate. My grandson at seven months was sitting up, pulling himself to his feet, and shouting garbled commands at everyone in sight. Every evening Keita and Michael would lie on the carpet together. Keita was thrilled with him and gave him all the benefit of his advice. Michael suddenly began to smile his funny, painful, crooked smile. I still had to let him pinch and scratch me when he sucked. I did not pull his hands away; I just rocked him on my rocking chair, and sang to him, and stroked his rigid little body.

Gradually he began to pinch less and less, and within a few weeks the change was dramatic. Michael decided that the world was not too bad a place at all. He became a friendly, outgoing baby. He put on weight and smiled at everyone. The day of the inquest arrived, and Anne Ashby took Jody along. It was a long, protracted affair because no one could make sense of what had happened. The coroner gave an open verdict, because they could not decide how anyone with as much alcohol in their system as Ralph could have died without vomiting.

The next hurdle was the funeral. We were very anxious about the event because there were many of Ralph's relatives who felt Jody should not attend. But Jody was determined to go. I felt that it was vital for the children to see both the coffin and the grave. I have treated so many cases of adults who were denied access to their parent's graveside by well-intentioned relatives, and these people grow up to feel forever that the parent has abandoned and betrayed them. I always advise parents to allow children to experience the reality of death.

Tina, Brian, Steve and I decided to go to the church with Jody and her children. If things grew too hectic, we would make a dignified exit. I was lucky to have always had such excellent and dedicated people working for the mothers and children. If I asked them to risk themselves, they did. This occasion was no exception. However, the funeral turned out to be fairly uneventful in terms of aggression towards Jody, and it gave us a chance to talk to the children and to explain exactly what was happening to Ralph. Tyrone, in his incredibly practical way, was fascinated by detail. Peter dealt with it all by changing moods, from racketing around noisily to withdrawing suddenly. Julia was fairly impassive, but the two moments that united the family were when Ralph's coffin was brought in and they all knew that he was in that box; and when the coffin went down out of sight into the grave, and they realised Ralph was truly gone. He had not 'gone shopping,' or run away from the children. He was dead.

Unfortunately, now that the drama was over, the Housing Department began to harass Jody about returning to her flat. Some of her social workers insisted she should return to 'normal' life, but if you are emotionally disabled, you are far too insecure to face such people who argue that you must return to what they regard as real life, and say 'No. I need support. I need a community,' because saying this would be tantamount to recognising and admitting that you are disabled. We had not yet got that far with Jody, to a point where she could feel comfortable and accept herself as a good, warm, loving woman. She still slipped back into her lifetime pattern of feeling bad about herself. So it was in one of those dark moods that she returned to her flat. We heard from her from time to time, and then we learned that all the children had been taken into care.

Jody came in to see me, and explained that she had not been able to cope on her own. I pointed out that very few women could cope on welfare with four children under six. I said that I, for one, would take to the bottle immediately. That made her laugh. I was glad that the children were at least safe for a while, because she needed time and space to herself. It was sad that her borough saw the care that we offered as such a threat to themselves that they preferred to put Jody in a position where she was forced to fail. Their solution was to put her very small children into care in Yorkshire. It must have cost the tax-payers at least four hundred pounds a week to maintain her kids in care. It would have cost only Jody's social security contribution for the whole family to stay with us.

When I went over with Jody, to see the children, it was the usual bleak children's home. The children, mostly black or half-caste, were looked after by sympathetic young girls, but the mountains of rules and standards of hygiene required left the girls little time to play with the children. I asked to see the matron, and discovered that she had been told nothing at all about Jody's children's history. She did not know anything about their traumatic experiences, or about the deaths they had witnessed. Various members of our staff subsequently visited the children, until we got a letter from the matron asking us not to come again, as we were 'disturbing' them. We weren't surprised by this — very few children's homes like or encourage visitors. I did not argue, because I knew that Jody would soon get the children out, and would still need us. So I waited.

The next time she came she had them all with her. They were delighted to be back. Tyrone went straight for Brian and tried to hustle him for money. He got tenpence and a hug, which was what he was really asking for. They had all grown taller, and the only one I was worried about that time was Peter. He still had mood swings, and could rapidly turn from a happy smiling child to a violent and sullen thug.

I was able to spend some time with Tyrone and Peter, and at one point I asked them to draw for me the story of Ralph in the bath. This session took place about eighteen months after the event. Peter, much as I expected, was still confused and angry about the event. Jeff, who was with me at this session, felt as I did: there was great danger for Peter because he could not make coherent sense of his violent past.

Tyrone was quite different. He not only drew his version of what had happened on that night, but he asked for a second piece of paper and drew what happened at the dead woman's place. They *had* been there and had seen it all; that was the secret he was now willing to share with us. It must have been an awful burden for a little three-year-old to carry. When he had finished drawing the body, he carefully drew Ralph, his mother Jody, Peter and himself. He said that Julia and Michael were left at home. He then drew some bottles rolling on the floor. 'What did your mummy do when Ralph stabbed that lady?' I asked. 'She turned her head away and ran out of the room.' Tyrone had all the events sorted out in his head. There was no confusion and no fantasy. His emotions were appropriate to the event he was remembering. I felt far more concern for Peter, who could well grow up to reach for a knife reflexively in any state of confused rage.

I begged endlessly for these children to receive child guidance. But as it takes much arranging and trudging through red tape, those children who most need child guidance are normally too peripatetic to ever stay in one place long enough to start the process. After this drawing session, Jody took the children home again. After a while they were back in care. She visited me and we talked about her feelings. The good sign was that she was on her own, with no violent men in her life. The last time I saw her, things were looking distinctly hopeful. She came back with another marvellous woman who had been at the Refuge. They brought their children, too, for Jody's kids were now out of care again, and they all looked well. Jody told me that she had met a really nice kind man who loved her and the children. He was a steady worker and she did look relaxed and happy. So far so good. Fortunately I am an optimist.

Drawing with children is an art form in itself. Talking to children is also something that adults have to be re-trained to do. Usually I take the time to get to know children before I ask them to trust me with their secrets, but sometimes I do not have much time.

In Jenny's case, I knew the mother was not going to stay long, so I had to work fast. Jenny was seven, and extremely articulate. The conversation started with me asking her about her father's violence. This is part of the transcript from my taped interview.

ERIN: I've been having a long natter with your Mum about life at home with Dad, and the fact that Dad hits her, doesn't he?'

JENNY: Yes.

ERIN: What do you do?

JENNY: I say 'Stop it'.

ERIN: Does he stop?

JENNY: He still goes on.

ERIN: Why does he hit her?

JENNY: I don't know. Only when he's drunk he hits her.

ERIN: Yes. What starts it?

JENNY: I don't know what starts it.

ERIN: Well, you do, because you're sitting there watching, aren't you?

JENNY: Yes.

ERIN: All right, give me an example.

JENNY: He's sitting down on the couch, and my Mum's sitting down, and my Dad comes over and says 'Stand up', and my Mum gets up, and then my Dad gets hold of her arm — and that's what starts it. Because he's drunk.

ERIN: Yes. He's burnt her with a cigarette, hasn't he?

JENNY: Yes.

ERIN: Did you see that happen?

JENNY: I didn't see it happen.

ERIN: How did you know he'd done that? Is it on her hand where you can see it?

JENNY: Yes. It's on my Mum's hand. My Daddy done it.

ERIN: Did you see him do it?

JENNY: Yes.

ERIN: Where were you?

JENNY: I was in Jean's room.

ERIN: Who's Jean?

JENNY: She lives down there (*in another room in the house*).

ERIN: Oh, wait a minute, yes. You share a room with your Mum and Dad.

JENNY: Yes. And the other lady lives in another room.

ERIN: So *you* all sleep in the same room. When they start fighting, and you're in bed, what do you do?

JENNY: I just go back to sleep, because I can't hear them

sometimes.

ERIN: You *do* hear them. You're pretending you don't, aren't you?

JENNY: Only sometimes. Sometimes I'm fast asleep, but when he starts shouting I wake up.

ERIN: What does he say when he shouts?

JENNY: He says 'Leave me alone'. My Mum, she knows that he'll do it again (*batter her*).

ERIN: Are you glad she's left him? Yes? Are you nodding your head or shaking it?

JENNY: Nodding it.

ERIN: You *are* glad. How do you feel about leaving him?

JENNY: It's all right.

ERIN: Really? Do you miss him at all? No? Because you know your Mum's not been well recently. She's having another baby, isn't she? And she's been in hospital. Now she's been talking to me a lot about your Dad, and she wants to try and sort it out with him — whether they can live together or not. What would you like to happen?

JENNY: I'd like to stay here.

ERIN: And not go back to him? Does he hit you?

JENNY: Sometimes.

ERIN: Hard?

JENNY: Not very hard.

ERIN: What does he hit you for?

JENNY: Once when I was sitting in bed when 'Crossroads' was on, Dad said 'Get into bed.' And I wasn't doing anything, because I was only sitting on the bed with my Mum, and then I got in and my Dad slapped me.

ERIN: On the other hand, he also gives you lots of toys and things, doesn't he? And if your Mum tells you off, he lets you off.

JENNY: Yes. He bought me a monkey, and that went missing.

ERIN: A real monkey?

JENNY: A pretending one. When you squeeze him his arms move.

ERIN: What happened? Why did he go missing?

JENNY: Because we were in this other hostel, where my friend lives, and we stayed there for a day, but then we had to come back to my Dad.

ERIN: Why? Because he found you?

JENNY: No. He never found us. In case something happened to him. And so we went back, and we left our clothes there (*at the hostel*), but when we came back in the morning there was no monkey, because this boy took it away from me.

ERIN: Do you think your Mum loves your Dad?

JENNY: I don't know.

ERIN: Honest? How many times have you left?

JENNY: Five.

ERIN: How old are you now?

JENNY: Seven. It was my birthday when we got over to Ireland, and then my Dad had to come.

ERIN: So you went to Ireland when it was your birthday? Which birthday was that?

JENNY: That was when we were over in Ireland. But my Mum had no money, so I didn't have my birthday, and I had it in care, because I didn't want to have my birthday, because my Mum didn't have any money.

ERIN: How badly have you seen your Mum hit?

JENNY: Twelve times.

ERIN: What was the worst you've ever seen?

JENNY: When he was punching my Mum.

ERIN: Yes, but where?

JENNY: In the face.

ERIN: Was there blood?

JENNY: No blood.

ERIN: Where did he hit her, then?

JENNY: On the hair.

ERIN: What stopped him?

JENNY: When we was living in this other hostel, my Dad was fighting my Mum and then I heard them shouting, and then I came up and said 'Stop it, Daddy', and he stopped.

ERIN: Your Mum said she fights back, too.

JENNY: Yes, she does fight back, too.

ERIN: What does she do?

JENNY: She tries to calm him down, to stop doing it.

ERIN: She says she throws things.

JENNY: Yes she does.
ERIN: What?
JENNY: My Dad throws things as well.
ERIN: So they both fight. They sound like children to me.
JENNY: I know.
ERIN: You sound like the grown-up. Do you think sometimes you are more grown-up? I wonder sometimes. I know you're only seven, but you know a lot about it, don't you?
JENNY: Because I'm always awake. I never go to sleep at all.
ERIN: No? You lie there all night, just pretending, eh?
JENNY: I fall asleep sometimes after the film.
ERIN: What happens when they start fighting?
JENNY: I wake up and get out of bed.
ERIN: And what do you do?
JENNY: I say 'Stop it, Daddy', and my Dad stops. But sometimes he doesn't stop and he says 'Get out of my way'.
ERIN: Then what do you do?
JENNY: I get out of his way, because he might stop if I get out of his way.
ERIN: Do you ever get frightened he might kill her?
JENNY: Yes.
ERIN: Really? How long have you been frightened he might kill her?
JENNY: Twelve days.
ERIN: Just recently then? It's got worse has it?
JENNY: It's worse.
ERIN: It's always been bad. So you've always been afraid your Mum might die. What do you see happening to you?
JENNY: You mean in my own life?
ERIN: Yes.
JENNY: Nothing.
ERIN: What happens if she dies?
JENNY: My Dad will cry, maybe.
ERIN: What happens to you if she dies?
JENNY: I'll cry.
ERIN: Where will you go?
JENNY: The two men up in the office, I'll go and tell them.
ERIN: Yes.
JENNY: Then I'll phone the police.
ERIN: Yes.

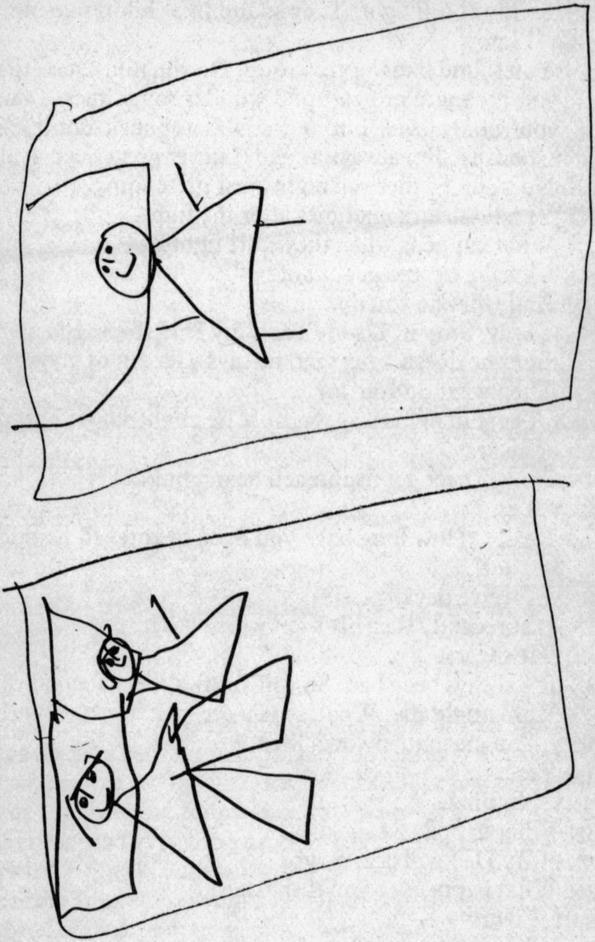

JENNY: Because I might have told them my Dad done it.
ERIN: Yes.
JENNY: And then an ambulance will come, because I would have told them that my Mum had died.
ERIN: Yes.
JENNY: And then they'll come up, won't they?
ERIN: What will they do?
JENNY: They'll get her in the ambulance because she . . . She had another little girl, you know, and she had to give her away.
ERIN: Did she? How old were you when she gave her away?
JENNY: I don't know. She just told me. We have to call her my cousin now because she gave her away. And she's a lot bigger.

After that interview, Jenny produced her drawing of family life. As you can see, it shows two beds and a very wide-awake Jenny. She knew her father had another girlfriend, so I asked a question one does not normally ask a seven-year-old child.

ERIN: How do you feel when they are making love to each other?
JENNY: All right.
ERIN: Don't you feel embarrassed? You're used to it, I suppose.
JENNY: I'm used to it.

To Jenny that is what normal life is about. She has already worked out a contingency plan for her mother's death, as the interview shows. No doubt she will go on to become tomorrow's violence-prone woman unless somewhere, somehow, someone gets her mother in a position where she is able to confront the fact that not only was she herself a battered child, but she was also raped by a bunch of youths when she was fourteen. The baby that came from that crisis in her life, whom Jenny describes as the little girl given away, was passed over to another branch of the family. We couldn't hold Jenny's mother, and she moved back to the husband. However, I know that sometimes all it takes to rescue a child is to give that child a glimpse of a possible alternative. That is why the Women's Aid playgroup staff put so much of themselves into the loving of the children.

This next interview is with five-year-old Curt, talking to me about his mother being beaten by a new boyfriend. We knew for a fact that she encouraged the children to watch her making love.

ERIN: When he hit your mother, what do you do?
CURT: I don't know.
ERIN: Do you cry?
CURT: I was in the bedroom when he done it.
ERIN: How many times does he do it?
CURT: Twelve. (*Children often use twelve as the biggest number they can imagine.*)
ERIN: What does your mum do? Does she scream?
CURT: No.
ERIN: What does she do?
CURT: She shouts.
ERIN: What does she shout? Go on, what does she shout, Curt?
CURT: What?
ERIN: What does she shout like? Show me.
CURT: A cissy.
ERIN: A cissy?
CURT: Yes.
ERIN: How does a cissy shout? Go on, tell me.
CURT: Like a girl.
ERIN: And what do girls shout?
CURT: Loud.
ERIN: Loud! What words do they say?
CURT: Languages.
ERIN: What languages?
CURT: Don't want to tell you.
ERIN: Oh yes, you do. I've heard your languages before. Go on.
CURT: No.
ERIN: Just once.
CURT: No.
ERIN: You've got your funny secret squirrel face on.
CURT: No, I haven't.

ERIN: Yes you have. I know why they're smiling, too. (*Meaning his mother and her boyfriend.*)

CURT: Why?

ERIN: Why your Daddy and Mummy used to smile at each other — same reason.

CURT: No.

ERIN: Yes.

CURT: No.

ERIN: Do you watch now? (*Watch his mother and her boyfriend making love.*)

CURT: No.

ERIN: You used to, didn't you?

CURT: No.

ERIN: Oh, oh, oh, that is a lie. Isn't it?

CURT: I do really.

ERIN: You do?

CURT: Yes.

ERIN: You still watch?

CURT: Yes.

ERIN: How do you watch now?

CURT: What?

ERIN: How do you watch now?

CURT: I don't know.

ERIN: Yes you do. Do you creep out of bed and listen? How can you see?

CURT: Because the light's on.

ERIN: Oh, I see. Yes, that's how you see. Well you've worked very hard for today . . .

Curt and his mother were with us for quite a while until, again, the borough saw her problem as a housing problem and gave her a flat. We lost them in spite of endless arguing with the Social Services over the fact that she was not ready to go. It is frightening to see how Curt already reckons it's cissy to cry if you are being battered. The 'secret squirrel' face refers to a certain look on his face which shows a mixture of mirth and sexual perversity. Seeing that expression was like looking at a deviant old man, which is what Curt will probably become.

His four-year-old brother had this to say:

ERIN: Do you want to tell me your secret?
BOBBY: Yes.
ERIN: Why do you watch?
BOBBY: Just feel like it.
ERIN: You just feel like it. How do you feel when you're watching?
BOBBY: It makes me very happy.

Here are two small boys of four and five already taking an active part in violence and sexual abuse. They were violent to each other and to other children, and their perceptions of relationships were totally distorted.

This is Eddie talking to me about his mother. He was wild, and had an obsession with blood. The sight of it excited and stimulated him.

ERIN: What does he hit her with? (*'He' here is Eddie's father.*)
EDDIE: Er.
ERIN: His fists?
EDDIE: No. Stick.
ERIN: Really?
EDDIE: Mmm.
ERIN: Does she have blood on her face sometimes?
EDDIE: No, she had blood running down her nose.
ERIN: Did she? What did you do?
EDDIE: Nothing.
ERIN: Did you cry?
EDDIE: Yes.
ERIN: How often does that happen?
EDDIE: Er. It kept coming down all the time.
ERIN: What, the blood?
EDDIE: Yes.
ERIN: Do you often see blood?
EDDIE: Yes.
ERIN: Do you like blood?
EDDIE: Yes.
ERIN: Why?
EDDIE: I don't.
ERIN: Eh?

EDDIE: I don't.
ERIN: You do.
EDDIE: I don't.
ERIN: I can see you smiling and laughing. Yes?
EDDIE: No. I don't.
ERIN: When you go to playschool you can draw pictures of it.

Even when Eddie decides it is getting unsafe to go on talking about it, he is wriggling on his chair, his face alive with glee. One has to remember that he has just described his mother's face after a beating.

This next little boy, specially asked to talk with me. When he came in he got right down to business.

ERIN: Right. What is it you want to talk about? Why are you here?
FRANK: Because Dad fights.
ERIN: Yes. With who?
FRANK: Mum.
ERIN: Yes.
FRANK: And she bites things. And he won't stop. And Mum wants him to go, and he won't go.
ERIN: Do you love him?
FRANK: Yes.
ERIN: Really?
FRANK: Yes.
ERIN: What's nice about him?
FRANK: Good.
ERIN: He's good to you, is he?
FRANK: Yes.
ERIN: What happened to you? What happened to your eye?
FRANK: Blind.
ERIN: Why?
FRANK: Because Dad picked me up and shook me, and this eye went blind.
ERIN: How do you know that?
FRANK: I'm right.
ERIN: How do you know?
FRANK: Because Dad done it, really.
ERIN: How do you know?

FRANK: I know when . . .
ERIN: Who told you?
FRANK: Dad.
ERIN: Did he?
FRANK: Yes.
ERIN: Why did he tell you?
FRANK: Because I wanted him to.
ERIN: Are you upset?
FRANK: No.
ERIN: Why?
FRANK: Because I'm all right.
ERIN: But don't you mind that he made you blind?
FRANK: Mmm.
ERIN: He didn't mean to do it, did he?
FRANK: No. I only wanted to be blind.
ERIN: Did you?
FRANK: Yes.
ERIN: Why?
FRANK: Because I like it.
ERIN: What does it feel like?
FRANK: Good. It's lovely.
ERIN: Explain it to me. I'm not blind, so I don't know what it feels like. What does it feel like?
FRANK: It feels like it's nice.
ERIN: What's better about being blind than being not blind?
FRANK: Then you can cry over everything then – when I'm not blind.
ERIN: But you can't when your blind, though. Isn't that true?
FRANK: Mmm.
ERIN: So what's good about being blind?
FRANK: About being blind is that when you can't see – and I can see a little bit.
ERIN: How much can you see? For instance can you see the tape-recorder?
FRANK: Yes. This eye. (*Frank had totally lost sight in one eye, and only partial sight remains in the other.*)
ERIN: Yes. Perfectly can you?
FRANK: Yes.
ERIN: Not that well. So you can see most things, can't you?
FRANK: Yes. That's with that eye.

ERIN: Yes.
FRANK: That eye . . .
ERIN: How long are you going to stay here, Frank?
FRANK: About . . . Mum said about Monday, Tuesday, Wednesday, Thursday, Friday.

Later on, when the tape-recorder ran out, he suddenly let go of a secret grief. 'I won't be able to drive cars,' he said. He felt so much love for his father, who really did love his son. The blinding was an act the father would regret all his life, so the little boy took it upon himself to remove as much guilt from his father as he could. 'I like it, really.' In the quiet of the office he did not have to pretend. He could allow himself to be a hurt, bewildered, blind child. Fortunately for this boy, he is at a very good special school where people truly care for him. Also, both parents, although they have a destructive addictive need for each other, separately are intelligent, and genuinely do love him. With some pluses in his life, he may just transcend their violence. I hope so.

On the 13 November 1980, I wrote an article for *New Society*, with Michael Dunne from the Refuge, on the subject of incest. I was amazed by the total silence that greeted it. I have listened over ten years to families in the Refuge pouring out their stories. I have seen the damage done to the children exposed to their parents sexual demands. I have watched adults kissing and caressing their children in a totally sexual manner, and have then realised yet again that the parents' reality shapes the reality of their children. If your father used to kiss you lasciviously on the mouth, then, unless somewhere along the line someone points out the inappropriateness of this to you, you will probably do the same to your children. I remember my first moment of shock when I saw one of our mothers lean over her nine-year-old son, who was sprawling on a sofa, and kiss him passionately on his mouth. 'Belinda', I said 'that's your son, not your lover.' She looked at me in surprise and left the room.

Father/daughter incest is a social problem that is now recognised, if not understood. Mother/son incest is still a strictly taboo subject. In fact I continually read books that state quite categorically that mother/son incest is so rare that it is virtually nonexistent. Those of us who see mother-damaged men all round us, and have suffered at their hands, would do well to raise our voices and object. Certainly it is rare for a woman to actually have sexual intercourse with her son. This, I believe, is because women do not want to risk the social stigma of getting caught in what is still a totally unacceptable act. Men seem to have an urgent sexual need to penetrate in order to achieve maximum sexual pleasure. At some point they lose control, and then they may be caught, and the matter is made public. Women get a more diffuse sexual pleasure from just touching and stroking. So many of their incestuous acts with their sons are usually very subtle and very difficult for the son to deal with or describe. A girl can say, 'This is what my father did to me,' and feel outraged at the event. A boy, however, has to say to me, 'This is what I *think* my mother did to me.'

Furthermore, mothers tend to disguise sexual acts, if they do want to penetrate their children through their role as loving nurses, giving rectal suppositories, rectal thermometers, and enemas.

Naturally, in a healthy family, the parents will kiss, cuddle, touch, and, when necessary, nurse their children. The difference, however, between the normal affection of a healthy family and the unsaid sexual acts of incestuous family is not the outward act itself but the charge behind the act which the parent feels. A kiss may be fine in one family, but in another family, when the parents act with a heavy sexual charge, and the child instinctively picks up on that charge, then the same kiss becomes an incestuous assault. One boy described how his mother had his brothers hold him down when he was as old as twelve, to push an enema tube into his rectum. He was constantly in hospital for constipation. The hospital quite unwittingly encouraged the mother to commit this gross act of indecency upon her child.

The whole subject of incest is so huge that it will be the subject of our next book, but suffice it to say that incest is endemic in our Western society. It has always been said that incest is the last taboo which, once removed, heralds the destruction of a civilisation. The Criminal Law Revision Committee suggested in its October of 1980 Working Paper on Sexual Offences that a father should no longer be prosecuted if he has sexual intercourse with his daughter, provided she is over twenty-one. If society follows this pattern of moral decline, the future for children in this country looks even bleaker than the present.

The major problem is that many of the people who organise this country and make all the major decisions, both morally and financially, do so not out of an altruistic love of mankind, but out of a deep greedy need of self-service. They got where they are by a ruthless driving ambition which is the by-product of a violent personality. Happy, contented human beings seldom seek high office. They prefer the warmth and love of good relationships to long hours spent in meetings or in offices. The people who run our society are the last people to listen to any attempts to organise changes, to improve and to protect the lives of children. Such prospects threaten their lives, their personal power over their own families, and above all, their control over the defenceless and frightened children.

Chapter Four

TILL DEATH US DO PART

'You will be the death of me.' I always thought this an ordinary, everyday expression of no significance until I began to realise how accurate a description it was of some of the relationships our families experienced. In violent families, one or other of the parents may easily die, sometimes the whole family. In middle-class households, where the violence is intellectual rather than physical, the chances are that various members may 'go mad'. I dread seeing middle-class women come in to see me who have been literally driven mad by the men they live with. It is an awful living death for them. In some cases, they would be better off really dead than end up pacing the streets muttering to themselves.

'My husband's a bank manager,' said one thin, shaken woman. 'He comes home and moves things about, so I can't find anything. Then he tells me that everything is just where it always was, and I must be going mad.' She sat waiting for me to look sceptical. I reassured her. 'I know,' I said. 'I've heard other women tell me the same story.' She looked so relieved, and her eyes were filled with tears. 'You believe me?' she said, still incredulous. 'Yes, I do,' I said, for this is a well-known sadistic pastime for the violent active partner to set about a calculated campaign to drive another member of the family mad. 'The *Fanny by Gaslight* syndrome', I call it. The terrible thing is that it works, and in most cases the perpetrator gets away with it because no one is properly trained to see into other people's inner worlds.

Many such women, having endured years of sexual, mental or physical sadism, go over the edge never to return. They haunt solicitors' offices with huge bags of files. They go everywhere looking for justice, but there is none for them to find. Eventually they end up in the back wards of our larger mental hospitals, or on the road — becoming one of the huge crowd of the dispossessed.

Talking to Sarah first concentrated my attention on the subject of *choosing* to die. She had come to us straight from hospital, with her little boy, and described the way her husband used to go completely berserk. 'He doesn't know what he's doing when he's like that,' she said. This remark reminded me very forcibly of a conversation during the early days in Women's Aid, when I was lecturing at Rhode Island in America. I was talking to Richard Gelles, a sociologist who had studied violence in the family, and made a similar remark suggesting that men were completely out of control when they battered their wives. 'No they aren't, said Richard firmly. 'They are very much in control. Otherwise you would have many more deaths.'

Now, listening to Sarah, and looking at her legs, I was still prepared to acknowledge the general truth of that comment. But this time Sarah's husband had gone *too* far: he had pushed her out of the window of their flat, to fall thirty feet to the ground, and left her lying there. She dragged herself along the ground to the nearest flat, where they called an ambulance. Both legs were broken, and one required a big operation to put a steel pin to hold the ankle together. It was that leg that we were both staring at. 'Do you think he'll kill you?' I asked. 'Yes,' she said, with a huge smile on her face, her eyes alight at the prospect. 'Yes, he will.' I knew then that she was yet another woman who would go back for more.

We talked for a long time. She said she reckoned she had a ninety per cent chance of being killed. She needed murder games to feel alive. And she probably will lose one such game, because this particular man will kill her. He is one of the men whose rage does exceed all boundaries. She knows that, and that is why she stays with him. No other man is as deadly for her. I kissed her goodbye a few days later, and subsequently I had a phone-call from her. 'They've taken my boy into care,' she said. 'Will you tell them I'm a good mother?' 'I can't, Sarah. If you can't come to terms with your own need for violence, he's safer away from you. But you don't want to give it up. I'm sorry, love.'

It was a painful conversation because, in a way, I was the last human contact in the strange lunar inner world that had dictated and directed her course through life since she had been a little girl — and her violent father's little princess. Her father the prince had kissed his daughter, thereby infecting her for the rest of her life. She had become addicted to her father and to his violence. But she could never have him to herself, because her mother had too strong a grip, so her husband now served to keep the addiction alive.

Eleanor was in the Refuge at the same time as Sarah, and I have always been particularly fond of her. She worked the 'rough trade', the bottom end of the prostitution business, where the prostitute knows she is paid to abuse or to be sexually abused. She was another one who predicted her own death with cheerful certainty. 'Cut up in little bits,' she would say, 'That's how they'll find me.' Several of her friends had already been found dismembered. She had even been asked to identify one of them who had been on ice for months because there were not enough bits to put together to allow recognition. Eleanor knew it was her friend by the tattoo on her upper arm, and she was very proud of herself for helping the coppers for a change.

Eleanor and her brother and sister had been abandoned by their mother on a doorstep in North London when she was seven. Her mother was a prostitute, and Caroline had been molested and beaten as a child. The three children were taken into care, and so passed from one mini concentration camp to another. She was on the game by the time she was fourteen. Yet she was such a lovable woman. On one occasion I had not seen her for several months, when she arrived puffing and panting through the front door. 'I've legged it from the nick,' she said. 'Oh, Eleanor, that's stupid,' I said. 'I'm not picking fucking Brussels sprouts on a prison farm in this weather,' she said. 'How would *you* feel about picking sprouts?' 'You have to pick sprouts because you did a robbery,' I explained. 'I can choose whether or not to pick sprouts because I don't commit robberies.' This piece of moralising floated straight over her head, and we grinned at each other, and I hugged her.

Everyone around her was sure she was going to kill someone sometime. She was one of those people who give off the promise of a huge and potentially catastrophic violent explosion. Certainly those over-controlled violent people can, if they ever do blow, cause incredible damage. For the most part, they internalise all their rage and look for another violent relationship to ventilate it. Eleanor did not have to choose the rough trade. She was young and attractive, and could well have chosen the Gloucester Road area, where there is a flourishing trade of sex in cars, and plenty of money to be made. Instead Eleanor insisted on concentrating on the King's Cross area where the rough trade thrives. She knew she needed pain. She was really one of the first women I met who understood her own need to reach the ultimate orgasm at the moment just before death, and then to slide into a womb-like oblivion.

Talking to her, I was reminded of the sampan girls in Hong Kong, where I lived twenty-five years ago. Although illegal, it was still a practice for rich young men to take prostitutes out to sea in those Chinese boats and then bend backwards over the sides so that their heads were submerged in the water. The goal was for the man to ejaculate and for the girl to survive the ordeal to collect a very large sum of money. In this terminal struggle, if the man was slow in ejaculating, the woman would drown. I found it very puzzling that so many of the Chinese girls who chose to do this were young, attractive, and not in need of money. It puzzled me then, but now I understand it. Like a heroin addict tenderly describing his love object, the needle, so Eleanor would describe the atrocities that were performed on her. She talked like a young girl describing a first romance. She would flush with sexual excitement at the memory of whips and chains, though she preferred to inflict pain rather than receive it.

Some women who have their pain and pleasure crossed in this way do find prostitution an acceptable way of fulfilling their needs. But the myth of the happy hooker is pernicious, as it totally denies the misery and the horror of that grim, lurid business, to say nothing of the effect prostitution has on their children. Eleanor's life will probably end up some back alley, with fancy knife-work round her vagina and breasts — the well-known trademark of a lethal mother-damaged man.

On this particular visit from Eleanor, I persuaded her she would be better off giving herself up and finishing her sentence. She said she wanted to go back to Holloway Prison where she knew everybody and felt safe, instead of having to work on the Brussels sprout farm. So I wrote a letter to Holloway explaining why I was sending her back to them, and to her delight I sent her back in style, in a taxi with a member of staff. I gather Holloway is quite unused to convicts arriving back in taxis and giving themselves up.

Brenda was not a prostitute. She came to us with a very large black eye and a small baby. She had raven-black hair and olive skin from her Jewish ancestry. Her mother and father had both been very violent to each other and to the children. Her father was confusing for her because he both spoiled her and beat her. He also molested her. I could see an old familiar pattern again. The following is an extract from a taped conversation with Brenda when I was trying to get her to look at what was happening to her. She started by telling me how her father used to take her out to the pub when she was young.

ERIN: Oh, right. And how old were you when he took you?
BRENDA: When I started going there I was thirteen.
ERIN: So he started taking you out to the darts when you were thirteen. That was what really pissed them all off (*meaning her brothers*).
BRENDA: Every Wednesday we used to go over there, and we used to play darts.
ERIN: Did he get heavy with your boyfriends? Did he not want you . . .
BRENDA: No. Because I never had boyfriends.
ERIN: You had him instead.
BRENDA: Yes. I used to go out with my Dad on the Wednesday. Every Wednesday I'd just go over.
ERIN: Didn't you know at thirteen that it was pissing your mother off?

BRENDA: No. All I used to see was the fighting and the shouting.

ERIN: Did he ever beat you up?

BRENDA: My Dad?

ERIN: Yes.

BRENDA: Yes.

ERIN: Really? And did he molest you at all, or not? He never touched you up?

BRENDA: No. I got beat up by my Dad, and then the same night I got beat up by my Mum.

ERIN: You got battered by both?

BRENDA: Yes.

ERIN: And emotionally, really. He used you like . . .

BRENDA: But the funny part about it was one day, it was Summer, you know — you sit in the garden to catch the sun. I walked in . . . The night before I was supposed to be in at eleven and I got in half-past eleven, and my Dad really hit me hard, and I had a great big black eye. And I walked into the pub to tell my Dad that . . . He was in the garden and there was a crowd of blokes sitting with him, and I was going to tell him to tell my Mum that I wasn't going to be in for dinner. I was going out for the day. And as I walked in there, Charles he was sitting with turned round and said 'That's a nice shiner. How did you get that?' And my Dad actually had the cheek to tell him 'I done that one'; and he was really proud of it.

ERIN: Yes. He brought you back here, didn't he, the other day? Your Dad.

BRENDA: Yes. My Dad came down on Saturday.

ERIN: What's he like with you now?

BRENDA: He's okay. But he's very sort of off. It's weird. I mean, it will probably sound funny but instead of like 'look at my handsome grandchild'. It's 'Look at me, I'm a grandad'. In other words, you're supposed to say to him 'You don't look like a grandad.' Not 'Look at my handsome grandson'.

ERIN: Yes. He's a narcissus, isn't he?

BRENDA: Yes. He's very ego . . . you know.

ERIN: Yes.

BRENDA: That's why he used to get a kick out of these pregnant women knocking on the door.
ERIN: Yes. And then he laughed when he hurt them.
BRENDA: Yes.
ERIN: He must have hated women you know.
BRENDA: He gets a kick out of them.
ERIN: What happened in his family? Do you know?
BRENDA: He's got lots of brothers and sisters, and he's the black sheep of the family now. Because of how he treated my Mum.
ERIN: Was his family violent, though?
BRENDA: His Mum and Dad, no.
ERIN: Where did he learn all that violence?
BRENDA: He used to fight a lot. He was always in trouble at school. And he used to go round with a gang. He used to like do nasty things to people just for the kick of it, you know, like they'd knock someone's walking-stick and laugh.
ERIN: Yes, and laugh. Yes.
BRENDA: It's . . . you know it's evil the things he used to do. He'd just sit and tell you about it all, and think it's funny. His sister is very violent, though.
ERIN: There must have been some violence, though, in the family if . . . Because you don't get born like that. You learn it.
BRENDA: From the other children?
ERIN: Yes.
BRENDA: He still fights with his favourite sister.
ERIN: Really! Physically?
BRENDA: To this day.
ERIN: What about your brothers? Do you fight with them still?
BRENDA: I don't fight with my brothers now. Because of the fact that when I do see them it's such a long time in between that it's nice to see them.
ERIN: Yes. Were you the favourite once? Were there any favourites?
BRENDA: Well. In the family, my big brother Stan. He's my favourite because he was the first-born, and when he was born he had to have . . . He's got a scar from there

to there (*all around the abdomen*). He had to have all his insides unblocked. He was supposed to die, and he was christened because he was supposed to die. They worried about him so much. They really loved him. And then I came ten months later, so I was an accident and then my little brother, came. And my Mum was sterilised at the age of nineteen, so she couldn't have any more. Nick, the little one, was loved because he was the last child that she'd ever have.

ERIN: She was nineteen when she was sterilised. So how old when she started having babies? Fifteen?

BRENDA: Yes. They were forced to get married.

ERIN: Why? Because she was pregnant?

BRENDA: My Mum's dad went after my Dad.

ERIN: Went after him?

BRENDA: Yes.

ERIN: Made him marry her?

BRENDA: Because she was pregnant.

ERIN: Yes.

BRENDA: With me . . . She had my brother. But when she got married she was pregnant with me.

ERIN: Yes. So they were forced to marry, and then she had you, and in a way she could blame you for that as well. Was she ever good to you?

BRENDA: Sometimes we'd get on. But I couldn't sit in the same room. I mean if I sat down in the same room as my Mum, she'd find something to start on me about like 'Go and do the washing-up'.

ERIN: She'd pick on you.

BRENDA: She's got to pick on something, my Mum. We could not sit in the same room. You know, you wouldn't see us together. I mean I've had fights with her and . . .

ERIN: Well, she beat you a lot as a child, didn't she?

BRENDA: One day the police were called about her being stupid. One night my Mum was doing the washing — you know the tongs that you move by . . . All I did was walk through the back door, and she said, 'Get off the grass, I've just cut it', or something stupid. And I walked off the grass, and as I went into the kitchen she had the tongs in her hand, and she hit me with them. So I ran out into the back garden. I just thought 'Right, that's it', and I just ran out . . . and it really hurt, it got me right on the shoulder, and she ran after me. To stop her from getting me, I held her hand. But she went on her knees and her arm twisted back. My brothers came running out and they started to hit me for hitting my Mum. My Mum told them that I attacked her, and really all I was doing was trying to stop her from hitting me again.

ERIN: Yes, I know.

BRENDA: And so my brothers beat me up for hitting my Mum.

ERIN: Terrible jealousies in that family, there, really?

BRENDA: Yes. They're both living there now.

ERIN: They live with her now? (*The brothers*.) Haven't left her?

BRENDA: Yes.

ERIN: How old are they?

BRENDA: One's twenty-one and one's nineteen.

ERIN: And they're probably violent.

BRENDA: Nick's not. He's very quiet. He's very deceiving.

ERIN: Yes. But you never know. You see . . .

BRENDA: Because when . . . He's a bastard. He really is a imbecile.

ERIN: Yes?

BRENDA: But he's very quiet. He's nice. Really nice. Do anything for anybody.

ERIN: What's he doing about your mother? What do you think he'll do?

BRENDA: He'll kill her.

ERIN: Yes. If I asked you what chance you thought you had of dying, what chance would you give yourself of living or dying in the next few years?

BRENDA: Dying?

ERIN: Dying. What chance are you going to give? Ellen (*also in the Refuge*) told me she'd give herself eighty per cent chance of being killed.

BRENDA: I'd say ninety.

ERIN: Why do you want to die? Do you know?

BRENDA: No. Not that I want to die, but I just think I will.

ERIN: Behind it is a need. While your slagging a man down, you don't really know him very well, but at any moment he could take out a knife.

BRENDA: Yes.

ERIN: How do you think it will happen?

BRENDA: Yes, that's how I'm looking at it. I know someone's going to kill me.

ERIN: How are they going to kill you?

BRENDA: I don't know actually. As . . .

ERIN: Have you thought? Have you got any imagination of how it would happen?

BRENDA: Yes. I think I'm going to . . . I think what's going to happen is like – all the times I used to come home when I'd hopped off school. So I'd go home and say like 'The dinner was really horrible today, Mum', or something like that. Just the sense of guilt knowing that I hadn't been to school. I'd say something about school – what happened. And yet they've known that I hadn't been to school; and they'd turn round and say 'Well, you haven't been to school. Why are you lying?' You know. But I had this sense of guilt. But I know that one day I'm going to say something. I'm going to tell a lie to somebody. They're going to find out and it's going to be telling the wrong person the wrong lie. And they're going to get me for it.

ERIN: How are they going to kill you?

BRENDA: Well. I just know that I'm going to tell a lie to somebody and . . .

ERIN: Yes. I can see that, but what I'm saying is: how? With a knife, or strangling, or hitting, or what?

BRENDA: Knife.

ERIN: A knife.

BRENDA: I've got a feeling, an axe.

ERIN: An axeman. Right. So where will he actually axe you? Your head off, or what? Which way will you die?

BRENDA: I don't know. I've always had a feeling of an axeman, the last three years. I've had this fear that someone's going to break in with an axe.

ERIN: Axe?

BRENDA: And hack me.
ERIN: And where?
BRENDA: Well across there (*pointing to her neck*).
ERIN: Across your neck?
BRENDA: Yes.
ERIN: Yes. It's interesting, because people who think they're going to die have usually worked out how it's going to happen.
BRENDA: Because when I was living with Harry (*her violent boyfriend and Ned's father*) the house was not a very safe house; the back doors were faulty. And the week we moved in there, was the week that five girls had been murdered; and where the Brixton Road is, it was all in there, and that was at the back of my garden; and I was really frightened. And Harry said he was going to the pub and you know sort of . . . And I used to literally take my blankets down to the front door and sleep next to the front door. And every bit of noise I heard . . . I used to stand on the doorstep sometimes, just stand on the doorstep, and yet that's more dangerous than actually being behind the door.
ERIN: Now, that's something you've picked up about yourself. How to explain it is very simple. When you were born, there are two parts of your brain, if you like. There's pain and there's pleasure. Now if you're loved and cuddled you learn that love — a pleasure comes from being loved and cuddled. You feel pleasure from being loved and cuddled. If you're battered, the only time you feel real pleasure is when you're in pain. I don't expect you to understand, but it's true. Now, I've talked to thousands of women about this. What's happening to you is . . . when you were standing on that step, with the possibility of an axeman somewhere around you, your adrenalin must have been so high that you were probably higher than you could ever be on heroin. Because of partly fear . . .
BRENDA: So what you're more or less saying is that I actually stood on the doorstep and I was saying 'Do it. Get it over and done with.'
ERIN: Yes, probably. And you're looking — and, I mean, I

know Ellen's going down dark alleys.

BRENDA: Yes. But I wouldn't. I mean even in the daytime I would walk down Chiswick High Road . . .

ERIN: Yes. But you look at it differently. She actually goes out on the streets and will fight. You are quite different. The axeman will be somebody — as you say, you will get drunk; you'll pick him out. He'll know that that's what you want, and then you'll end up dead. Or he'll end up dead.

BRENDA: It's a really stupid thing to have, is the fear of an axeman. I mean why an axeman? And why couldn't I pick a knife maniac? But an axeman — why an axe?

ERIN: Well, I think that's what we're going to work on. Shall we try and work that out? I'll finish today because we've both worked very hard. We've got down to what it is, and now I've got to start right back at the beginning, and we'll have to work out why an axe, and why do you have to die. Why is that the end that you see?

BRENDA: Because I know my mouth will get me into trouble.

ERIN: Yes. That's right.

BRENDA: It won't be me or what I do; it's my mouth and what I say.

ERIN: Yes. Well, do you know what you actually say when you start slagging down?

BRENDA: No. I mean, when I'm lying, it just comes so natural — I even convince myself.

ERIN: Oh, I know. That's why I believe you. I mean, I know you believe yourself so you're not lying in your eyes.

BRENDA: I mean, I can say 'Yes, I was there at school', and I've really convinced myself that I was at school.

ERIN: No. But the other things, too, love, is this is what happens. There's another side of you that doesn't want to admit what you do. You bunk off school, you come home, and you set it up. You know your parents know you weren't at school. So you tell a lie which is 'We had a good dinner'. They have the right then to beat you. For you being battered is pleasure — in a way, if you think about it. Because that's all you've ever known as love. At least when they were beating you, you were feeling something.

BRENDA: Because they were touching me.
ERIN: They were touching you, and so were the men touching you, and you start to slag, and the trouble is that you get your black eye, like you did the other day, one way or another, because you get driven to it. You're all right for a little while, then suddenly that need comes again, and that's when you go looking for it. And that's the work we've got to do.
BRENDA: Well, Harry once told me that I . . . Like the night that he bust them couple of ribs and he literally smashed the whole flat up; the television went; everything went. And he still swears to this day I begged for it.
ERIN: You probably did.
BRENDA: He said I really begged for it. He said no way would he ever have done it, and he hit me right in the face, and hit my head against the wall.
ERIN: You know what's interesting about that, though. We were talking about this another time — this is another whole discussion, this whole thing of pain and pleasure. And many women can't climax normally, because it's when they're in pain, when they're actually being battered, that is a climax for them; and that's why they keep going back to look for pain. For quite a lot of women, it's the moment before the man loses control. That's the moment — the exciting element for them. Women whose pleasure and pain haven't been confused can have ordinary sexual climaxes. But the trouble with that game, where it's pain and pleasure confused, is that pain has to get worse, and worse, and worse for the pleasure to increase and increase and increase. And that's where you end up with the axeman. For that's the ultimate. It's almost like the ultimate orgasm, isn't it? Frightening, but it's true.
BRENDA: And yet I still would like to be loved.
ERIN: You see, there's two sides of Brenda. There's the side that . . . and her head knows all this and knows that she wants love and comfort. But there's the other side, which is the side we have to work on. I have to work on it with you — which in fact's dragging you off the other

way, to a certain death.

BRENDA: But there's no two ways it can go, though. I mean, it's not knowing how to give love. I don't know how to receive it.

ERIN: No. Right. Oh, it's very frightening for someone, being loved . . .

BRENDA: I mean, someone could say that they loved me, and I wouldn't know.

ERIN: Because you wouldn't know what they meant.

Since that conversation, Brenda has left the Refuge. I heard from her only once subsequently. She sounded happy, and said that she and Ned were no longer living with Harry, but now with a man who apparently was not violent. In all honesty I cannot say how happy she became in that relationship, or how long it lasted, for Brenda did not keep in touch afterwards. I worry that her addiction to pain and her need to die are so strong and deepseated that she may well find her axeman one day.

Brenda was able to understand much of what I said. It was with her that I fully realised the damage often done to children by the grandmother laying claim to a favourite grandchild. Brenda had been brought up by her grandmother, who had virtually seduced her away from her mother. The grandmother (on her father's side) then used the little girl against her daughter-in-law. When the grandmother grew bored with the game (usually when the girl is around six or seven) she was sent back to the family. By that time the child was already at war with her mother, who hated her. The mother saw her daughter as a betrayer. From then on the little girl was at her mercy.

Brenda's ability to start fights in the local pubs was legendary. On one occasion a very violent woman received a batch of stolen watches and shared them with Brenda. They agreed to sell the watches for six pounds each in the pub that night. Brenda got into the pub before this woman, and sold all her watches for four pounds each. By the time the woman arrived, there were almost no takers, and she was forced to drop her price. In the ensuing fight, Brenda got very badly beaten. When she presented her woebegone face to me I refused to discuss her plans to prosecute the other woman. 'You needed a fix, a dose of pain. You set it up, and you got it. No one else would risk upsetting a lady as violent as that one, but you did. Learn from it,' I said. She took the point.

I think it might be interesting here to look at a drawing done by Ellen, referred to in my talk with Brenda as the woman who walked down dark alleys at night. When she came in she was 'high' with the excitement of getting away from Max, her very dangerous husband. There was something about Ellen that did not fit into my checklist of ingredients that make up a profile of a woman who is so addicted to violence that it will be a long-term project to help her change herself. Like Brenda she was taken hostage by her grandmother. Again, her grandmother used her in a war against her own daughter, Ellen's mother. None of this came up in conversation, because she was locked into complaining about her husband, who was indeed a very violent, explosive bully. It was when she had completed the following drawing that I was able to grasp the origin of the problem.

Firstly we discussed the figure of her kneeling at her grandmother's grave. She even remembered her grandmother's moment of death, and her feelings of being isolated from her mother and father, and fenced off from their happy and loving relationship with each other. The grandmother had always lived with the family and spoiled Ellen. Ellen realised very soon that there was a family war on, and she was to be on her grandmother's side. Soon her mother shut her out. Ellen learned to provoke her mother and to rebel against her parents, egged on by her grandmother. The poor child was in a no-win situation. Finally her grandmother died, but the pattern of provoking, for a violent reaction from her mother, was set and continued.

Ellen had since found an even more exciting person to provoke: her husband Max. After their marriage, Ellen continued down the path that could have lead to her own destruction. She did have a bonus though: her parents were essentially good ones, in that they did love and care for her even if they could not cope with her. They were not aware of the relationship between Ellen and the grandmother. They saw Ellen as the problem, not the grandmother.

107

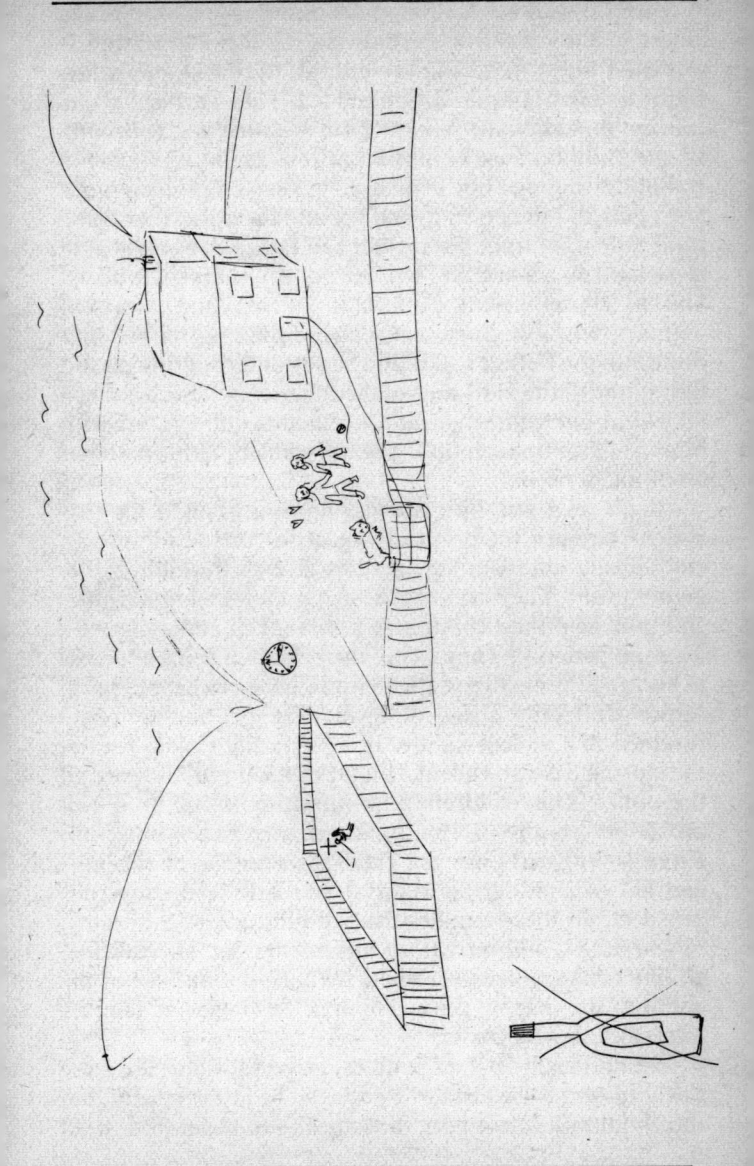

After we worked our way through that, we looked at the object in the corner of the drawing. 'It looks like a bottle to me,' I said. 'Yes,' she agreed. 'You provoke him when you're drunk,' I inquired. She nodded. Then I explained our concept of addiction* to her. 'I can see what you're driving at' she said, 'because I knew every time that he was going to end up hitting me, but I still used to keep on pushing him.' She really did understand, and because there had been some good parenting from her mother and father, she was able to work hard on herself. As I write this down, she is still with us. She has left her violent relationship with Max and has settled with her two boys. She is not at all the same person who first came into the Refuge and would be out all night drinking and fighting with the hard-nuts of the community. She has met a very kind and gentle man, and is contemplating a future with him. She has transcended. She has come to terms with her own violent needs.

Ellen's goal was life. Brenda, however, taught me that violent families set death as a goal for their children. In emotionally able families, parents give their children life-giving goals. They are realistic about their children's gifts, and they help their children to achieve their ambitions with love and patience. They talk of their children being a success in life, and the children experience a feeling of a happy, warm future stretching ahead of them. The position is totally reversed in a violent family. In a physically violent family, the language is also violent. 'I'll fucking kill you,' is heard all the time. The children grow up with death as a real possibility, as the parents fight and smash each other up. From a very early age the child has a feeling of urgency, and has to consider his survival as a risky and dangerous prospect. In these families many deaths occur: cot-deaths, miscarriages, still-births, accidents, murder and suicide. Unlike in happy families, where the goals internalised by the children are happy goals, children from violent families internalise deadly goals.

In emotionally-violent families, however, which are more likely to be middle-class, the goals can be just as deadly, but the children will not hear the language of violence; instead

*See Chapter Six.

they will be given totally unrealistic goals to achieve. Then the screaming and the mockery that meets the failure to achieve will last with them all their lives. The guilt will line their internal world, so they may never be able to express any of their real gifts. They will literally believe they are nothing – No thing – and they will form relationships expressing that same message. They often finally commit suicide. Occasionally a child from such a family will turn and kill its parents, bringing out a rush of newspaper articles simply because it is a middle-class child from a privileged background. No one will look behind the murderous event. The child will be locked away, and the middle-class fortress will close its gates, secure in the knowledge that it is only 'those people out there' who suffer the problem of violence.

The trouble is that it is the middle-class emotionally disabled, not able to ask for help because of their position in society, who often become social workers and probation officers, and join agencies involved in the care of human beings. Unfortunately, as they have done nothing about their own damage, they are a menace to the very people they are paid to help. Working from their own damage, they create havoc in social-work teams and elsewhere, as they collude with and manipulate the clients. There is no better training in my opinion than life-experience, but experience is useless if it is seen only as 'bad experience'. It must be put to work and turned into wisdom.

There are many excellent people working in this field of family violence who would relate to and understand Brenda, but unfortunately, due to lack of understanding, there are also too many emotionally disabled people let loose with the label of 'agency workers'. Of course, they were the ones who did not see Brenda's bruises as a child, or did not recognise that her repeated running away was not just a naughty act. In their own childhoods, they shared the emotionally or physically violent reality, and grew to accept violence as normal. If you grow up seeing bruises, you do not find bruising abnormal. If you are molested, you will not find other people molesting children as abnormal.

A young girl of fourteen complained to me that her father was insisting on bathing and drying her. She had run away to us because she wanted this to stop. He claimed that he was only performing his rights as a father. The social worker who followed hot on the heels of the girl tried to argue with us that it was perfectly normal for a father to behave this way. We gently pointed out that he was speaking from his own damaged and molested childhood.

There is a dangerous assumption commonly held by those who have never known real violence. It is expressed by people saying, 'But surely if someone is born into a violent family, they will learn from that experience and spend the rest of their lives avoiding violence like the plague?' I wish this was true. The fact is, if you are born into a violent family, the chances are that you will become emotionally, physically, and chemically addicted to violence.

Stephen, a boy of eleven, came to us with his mother. She was a very beautiful, childlike woman who drifted from one violent man to another, dragging Stephen with her. Poor Stephen was totally confused by her attitude towards him. One moment, when she was manless, he was the most important thing in her life, 'the man of the family,' her protector, her friend, and also the 'lover'. Then, just as suddenly, he would be pitchforked into yet another of her violent relationships, and be expected to stand between her and her new man. Stephen was hopelessly addicted to his mother. I could rarely lure him away from her side. He stole for her, and brought her jewellery, clothes, sweets, anything to keep her. 'Stephen's so wonderful to his mother,' unsuspecting visitors would say. I knew it was not like that at all.

One day Stephen came running in to me, obviously very pleased with himself. He held out his hand and showed me a drawing he had just done that made him so proud. It depicted a skeleton pointing its bony finger to an arched doorway labelled 'The Door to Hell'. The skeleton, marked 'Dead Wife' grinned horribly as she showed the way to the door over which hung the sign 'Wives Only'. This is the terrifying attitude to women with which Stephen will grow as he makes his future relationships. The light in his eyes was unmistakable. Unless he receives extensive treatment it is likely that this boy may well grown up to torture other women. He has been storing away his violence and his pain, and, given a certain type of woman, he may well act out all his confused rage on her.

This brings me to the well-documented case of Eunice and Gerald. During the ten years I have spent listening to people in pain, I have often had occasions when they related to me events such as occurred between these two human beings. Most of the time they are left in a fantasy world, largely ignored by doctors and psychiatrists, until as for Peter Sutcliffe, the fantasy becomes a reality and they begin to act it all out. As long as the mutilator and the mutilated meet in the dark sea of the criminal underworld, a body in a black plastic bag attracts little attention.

Our society's schizophrenic attitude to violence was well illustrated during the Yorkshire Ripper trial. The whole country expressed outrage at what he had done. He was called a monster, a beast, inhuman, but there seemed absolutely no attempt to understand why he did what he did. Who should really be standing in the dock with him? In my time I have warned agencies of other potential rippers, and got precious little response. Who failed to spot the troubled child? Soon after the trial, the opera *Lulu* was staged in London, and people flocked to buy expensive tickets to watch a prostitute die by sexual misadventure. A month later the film *Pandora's Box* was shown on television. As the main character feels the knife sliding into her, she smiles ecstatically at the camera over the shoulder of her murderer. How can we condemn a murderer when we finance opera and film which celebrate identical events?

Eunice came into the Refuge asking to see me. She was a big woman; handsome is probably how one would describe her. She carried herself well, and if you did not know her, you would never suspect she was anything other than a successful business woman. As we talked around the problem she had come to discuss, I realised that she was yet another woman in the grip of such a serious addiction to pain that she could eventually die from it. Her confusion was enormous, and even her recital of events could raise her emotional and chemical levels to a point where she slipped into that reality shared only by herself and by the man,

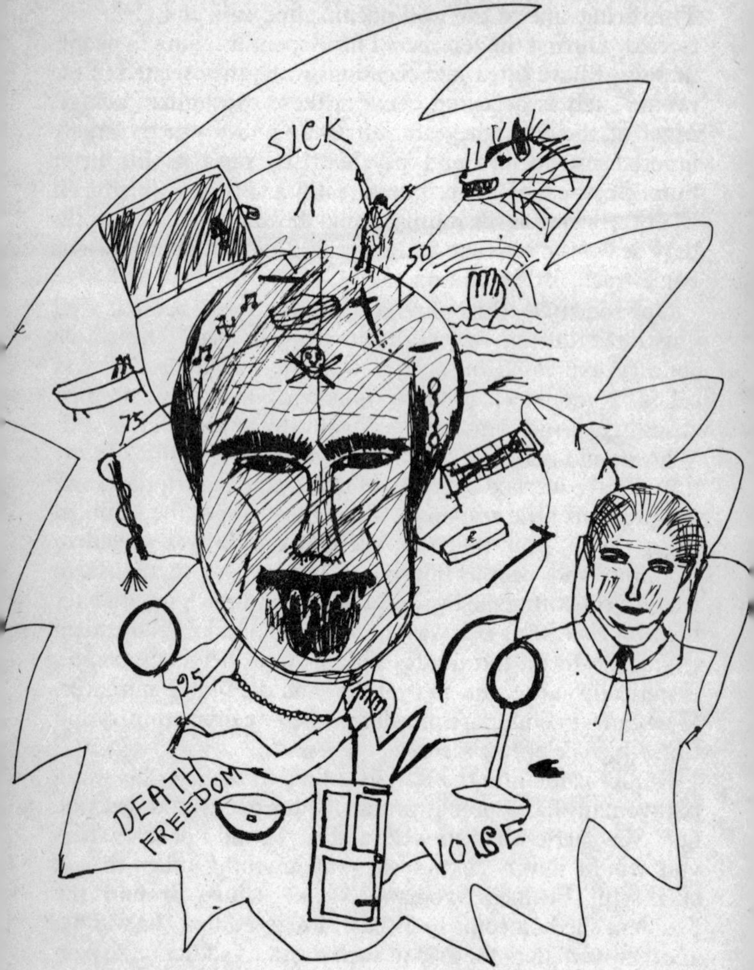

SICK
50
75
25
DEATH
FREEDOM
VOICE

Gerald, who mutilated her.

Most of this work I shared with my colleague Tina Wood. The first thing we had to do was to gain entry into that reality, which meant interviewing Gerald, once I had Eunice's trust. I asked her to draw 'the Beast', as she called him. To draw him she sat in a chair outside the office. When she had finished, she lay slumped over the drawing pad; and I reminded myself that people in love recall their sexual pleasure with love, but people who know only pain must recall their sexual pleasure with pain. I comforted her, and we began our first session. The following is the first recorded interview with Eunice:

ERIN: (*looking over the drawing*) Yep! It's very good, actually. Look, everything you've told me.

EUNICE: Normally, this is what's taking a hell of a lot out of me. It's taking me apart – the fact that I've had to. I've even let anybody know what I feel about it. You know – that drawing.

ERIN: That's right, I knew that would do it. Now I'm going to put you back together again. Yes? Fine. Well, there you have – what made me cry, or makes me want to cry, we speak about, is not him, but that's your father, isn't it? (*pointing to the face on the right of the drawing*).

EUNICE: No.

ERIN: No? Isn't it?

EUNICE: No.

ERIN: Who is it?

EUNICE: That's the other him (*Gerald*).

ERIN: Funny.

EUNICE: That's the small image I see of the person that was the one that I thought was him.

ERIN: It *was* him?

EUNICE: That took me in, and you can see I've linked it up with the person that he was. Because that part of him was such a small part of it.

ERIN: Isn't it extraordinary, but you also told me, at the same time that your father had a beautiful voice and sang.

EUNICE: Oh, yes.

ERIN: To me, that's the microphone, and then you've written

the word 'voice'.
EUNICE: Perhaps I thought it without realising that's so.
ERIN: It's your subconscious.
EUNICE: Yes.
ERIN: Because you've been looking for your father through men. Every relationship, you're looking for someone, because you loved him.
EUNICE: I like the person he was.
ERIN: He's lovely?
EUNICE: That he was happy and genuine, straightforward, and he gave a lot of pleasure to people, by entertaining, and he was an intelligent man and he had a . . .
ERIN: And yet what he (*Gerald*) should have been, was like him — instead you've got this very very sick man. Now, explain — I don't understand that. (*Pointing to the rectangular shape in the upper corner of the drawing.*)
EUNICE: That's that room. (*In the house where Eunice lived with her mutilating partner.*)
ERIN: Explain this now. Just go through the room again for me.
EUNICE: That's what should have been the, umm, like you've got a big living-room, right. This is a massive house, and you come along the passage and then there's the room off to the left hand, and that room was the breakfast room, where there was a hatchway.
ERIN: That's right.
EUNICE: The hatchway was about, maybe the size of this book, or maybe that, like that. Umm, on the left-hand side of the room there's some french windows — french doors. Wood at the bottom and the glass halfway down. Well, what he done with a week or two, or a week. I can't remember the question to that extent — we moved in. He went round and he nailed . . .
ERIN: Did you choose this house together?
EUNICE: Yes.
ERIN: You didn't know what he was going to use that room for?
EUNICE: Oh no. No, I got no idea. I had to go out and buy furniture, thinking we'd got plenty of bedrooms —

putting furniture upstairs, planned it as a home you know. Oh, yes, I looked on it, you know, as a home. And after two weeks he went out the back and he got some wooden planks and nailed the French doors from outside with six inch nails, and he said that was because, umm, in case, you look, when we're out and things, with people being able to burgle and that — it makes the place more secure. And I'd got no reason not to think that.

He had some heavy curtains put up at the French window, er, thick velvet ones, and it wasn't till some weeks later, that . . . what he used to do. He used to get a piece of hardboard — because — through the archway was the kitchen part with the big steel cabinets, and he'd either get a cabinet and move that along so the hatchway was blocked. Or, he'd get a piece of hardboard and shove that. So in that room there was only the lamp and that was an orange lamp. There was no main light.

ERIN: With an orange bulb?

EUNICE: Yes. He wouldn't have no main light on. And using that as a bedroom. But of course, later on I realised that, that wasn't just a bedroom. That was a room which made an isolated chamber. And when I was in there and he'd got a wireless, and he used to put the wireless through from the kitchen. He'd got a hole where the wire came through, and he would bring it into the bedroom, so that he could turn it up. One of them old box wirelesses — turn the volume up. And for me, when it was getting bad or, when at that time . . . the place was the place where quite a lot of things happened.

ERIN: Most of them really.

EUNICE: Most of them — but also in the living-room.

ERIN: This is when you've been tied up?

EUNICE: Yes.

ERIN: And that, umm — what are the marks?

EUNICE: They're the ones that I was smothered in after the cutting, or with marks from sticks, or whips and that.

ERIN: When you see him like this — remember you called him the Beast. (*Pointing to the large face in the centre of the drawing.*)

EUNICE: Yes. Well, there were times when he used to get so het up that he — it was like he couldn't destroy me enough. He'd get hold of me and he'd rip me down with his nails. And the first year when I was with him, he'd got all rotten teeth, absolutely terrible teeth; they were all jagged. And he fright to death about going to the dentist, but that wasn't it. They looked really horrible. And when he used to go into this thing and he used to bite me and try to gnaw at my head, and he'd growl like a dog, and he'd get his teeth like this and he'd drag them all down like that. That was long before he started doing the cutting, and I used to have ridges down my back like that with his jagged teeth, and they used to go bad, you know. And that's when I think about whether he's a dog. This bit here is the amount of punching I took which always began . . .

ERIN: He'd say 'It's eight o'clock.'

EUNICE: He'd say 'It's time, it's time,' or some remark like that, and then he'd sort of come across and he'd sort of — we could sometimes be, say, in the living-room. The telly could be on, and, er, he'd put the record-player on and the telly at the same time, and he'd say 'It's time.' And he'd just come over to me and he'd start taking my dress off, or my skirts, and my jumpers and everything off, and he'd just literally fold them; he'd fold everything. This is at certain times when he folded them up, and I never used to look to see where he was putting my things or anything, you know.

ERIN: You used to shut your eyes once it was time.

EUNICE: Oh, yes.

ERIN: Then, you just never opened your eyes?

EUNICE: I only ever opened my eyes when I was forced to stand at the wall, or to get down on the couch, or to make any movement. Then I'd got to open my eyes to do that. But the minute I was down, or whatever how I was doing, I didn't open my eyes at all.

ERIN: Who is this then? (*Pointing to the drawing.*)

EUNICE: That's me there the same, er, that, er, upstairs later on there was — I brought the single bed down as well, because I had single furniture with me. And there's one room at the back that looked out onto open space at the balcony part, where he put that single bed in there, and he made up some reason about he was going to have the plumber in and he was going to let the rooms out, which never did occur, you know. It never happened. But there were times, especially — sometimes it used to be on a Saturday — a Saturday morning, and he would take me upstairs. Only very rarely, so this is why I don't remember a lot about it. Sometimes he would say it's time to go in the bathroom, you know, which is that. And whenever that happened, umm, he used to take me in there and he used to get me down in a kneeling position, and he'd hold my hair, and, as I say, he's an expert, this is what he kept digging into me. He's an expert in how to do a hell of a lot of pain without, you know — not that it don't show, but he can do — you know. And then he would start slapping my face backwards and forwards like that, anything up to fifty or sixty times, which seems bloody impossible, but it can happen.

ERIN: He's got all night.

EUNICE: No. He did this in the morning, and he used to run the taps. What he used to do — what he used to do. He used to turn the taps on in the bath, and the taps on in the sink, so that the slapping wouldn't be heard. And then sometimes he used to chop down on my face like that, so he chopped on it like that. Sometimes after that, and after he'd perhaps tired himself out and everything, then I used to go back downstairs, because I'm sad about that bedroom and that, and I knew that I'd got to go out, but I'd have to be ready to be out by 4.30 that day, no matter what. So, what I used to do — I used to go to the fridge and I used to get ice and I used to get the towel, get the ice and put it in it, and have it on my face. But my face used to come up. Funny thing is, it never bruised, but it used to bloat up like a balloon and inside of my mouth was swollen. But he'd got a way of doing it, so it didn't bruise – but it did. It come out like that, and the ice was the only thing that would make the swelling go down. But unless – the terrific pain you can get was forcing the swelling down, and the pounding, it's like having a terrific burning on your tooth like that, all the time.

ERIN: Did he ever try putting you in the bath?

EUNICE: No, No. The funny thing, he never did, and in fact he – that's another strange thing. He never used that bath in that house. Never once did he use our own bath. He used to go to a public bath. And when he used to come back, he used to undo his – that's where he used to go Saturday mornings after he'd either beaten me up in bed and done the slapping and everything else. Then he'd just go out. He'd say 'I'll see you later. I'll be back for lunch at whatever time'. He always went out that Saturday morning, always. I never knew, only for the fact he went to the baths. And when he came back, he used to walk in and he used to pull his jumper up like that and he'd have one of the corporation bath towels wrapped round his waist, and he used to laugh and he used to say 'That's done them one. I might have had my bath, but I got a new towel as well.'

ERIN: He obviously hates society, doesn't he?

EUNICE: I think he hates everything going. And when the police raided the house, they found over, I don't know whether it's forty or forty-odd towels, different towels, what he collected every Saturday morning.

ERIN: If something about the Ripper came on the telly, what would happen to him?

EUNICE: He would get very excited and very agitated, and, I know, once when I was with him and there was some write-up, some bloke decided to do a write-up about the Ripper and he never bought newspapers, but he'd heard about this because he used to get papers from work, off the blokes he worked with. But he heard about they're going to do a three-day series on the Ripper, and when, er – the only time I've known him to go out and spend his own money to get a paper, and he'd have it open like that, and he'd be reading and reading, and whenever that happened, I was bloody shaking. I was getting sick, because I knew, knew that when he'd read anything like that it excited him. It would excite him to such an extent, he couldn't wait to get going. He couldn't wait to get hold of me and just sling me around.

ERIN: What about violent films?

EUNICE: Umm, I don't know. Anything to do with Germans.

ERIN: War films?

EUNICE: Yes, and things like that, you know, tortures. I couldn't watch them. In fact even now, even now today, I hate anything to do with violence, you know. I don't like it. But, umm, he used to . . . I forget what I was talking about, now.

ERIN: You were telling me about — we got as far as, he got back from the corporation bath Saturday morning and got a towel round him.

EUNICE: That's right, yes. And then, say, about 4.30. This is winter-time, because summertime we go out for the day. That's one thing I used to think, that thank God it was a sunny day. Because if it's a sunny day, we'd go right over the market. We'd go off round the East End. This is how I know the East End so well. I know every Pub and every place and every walk, and sometimes he used to walk me around for hours. You know, I'd be in terrific pain from Friday night, my back, my legs and everything. And he'd walk and walk and walk, and we'd go in the pubs and that. But say it's like a winter day, and I hadn't been out for the day. By 5 o'clock I knew I'd got to be ready — no matter what. My face would have to be okay, or whatever I could do with it. I always used to dress everything covered up, and he used to look and say, 'nobody would know, would they? ' And so I used to have to mentally make myself . . .

ERIN: I want you to talk to an Irish lady who was in yesterday evening, because she told me about a man, nothing like as bad as yours, but she's just been in hospital because he put beer bottles up inside her. He ripped her vagina, her bladder and everything else. But he did this sort of thing to you didn't he?

EUNICE: Yes, I had bottles inside me. But the thing that he used to mostly, was the whip handle. And that was a solid handle; it was that length.

ERIN: Didn't it tear you up?

EUNICE: Yes, that's right. He caused me terrific pain. He used to make me bleed.

ERIN: This is the thing, yes? (*Pointing to the whip in the drawing.*)

EUNICE: And he used to put it in, and then he used to wrap it, put it round and round and round, like that inside, to cause as much pain. And another thing, he used to get me in a position with my wrist and tie me down, so that I was in a squat position down, so that he could ram it up more, and he'd order me to come. He'd say 'You've got to come. I'm giving you two minutes to come. You're going to have an orgasm. You've got to.' And he would literally, you know, satisfy himself that you were doing it.

ERIN: What, he'd have to wank off?

EUNICE: No, he'd be telling me, he'd be ordering me, I'd got to come.

ERIN: So you'd come and then you were safe.

EUNICE: Well, I don't know whether I come, or whether I didn't, as long as he thought in himself that I was coming, and he'd sometimes, you can imagine how he then understand a woman, he'd demand about fourteen or fifteen times, I think. You got to come, you got to come, and all the time there he was nearly taking me apart with the bloody thing.

ERIN: But in fact, there's a very, very close line between pain and pleasure, and the trouble is he could actually make you come that way, isn't it?

EUNICE: I can't think about whether I came or not. All I know is that he'd be doing me inside, and between everything else you know it's . . .

ERIN: That's you drowning, isn't it? 'Help!' Is it? (*Pointing to the drawing of water.*)

EUNICE: It could be. There are times when I feel like it.

ERIN: Look at that. It's your coffin with your name on it, and the only freedom you feel is when you die.

EUNICE: Yes, I suppose I felt that way, yes.

ERIN: What worries me, is that he is going to draw you back to him, and draw you back, and draw you back.

EUNICE: No way, no way, will I ever go near him. I might want to kill him. I might want to . . .

ERIN: Yes. You're also obsessed by him. That is the trouble.

EUNICE: I don't think I've ever been free from the time when he came into my life, because the things that he put into me, the things that he, that he brainwashed and talked to me, and the — I can't, I couldn't even put into words.

ERIN: I want to ask you a question that's worrying me. We'll talk about pain another time. What I am worried about is this. He's lost you, he's trained you, you are specially trained by him now. So you could satisfy him, right? You've gone. He's back by Euston Station. Who's he going to find next? (*Eunice and Gerald met outside Euston Station*)

EUNICE: I don't know. This is the reason I put my life on the line. I knew, I knew, that when a man's like this, he won't change. He can't alter. There was times when he used to get very agitated as well, because — when he used to want me to wear a blonde wig. He got this wig, he got this wig; I don't know where the hell he got it from. But, as I say, he used to have several wigs, when he done certain things, and first of all I had to put this blonde wig on. Then he used to go really, really mad.

ERIN: What colour was his Mum's hair, do you know?

EUNICE: I don't know.

ERIN: Never saw a picture of her?

EUNICE: No.

ERIN: You knew little about his private life, did you?

EUNICE: He would never talk to me about it.

ERIN: Give me an example. I mean, as a kid, everybody gets smacked, right? Or in trouble. I mean, you came, as you say, from a home where you're all right, but you must have been smacked occasionally . . .

EUNICE: Yes, I suppose so, but our Mum, if she said something, we knew if we were playing her up, how far we'd go, and then, you know — and knew that she meant it if she said it.

ERIN: So, until you met your first husband and he went bad — he was all right in the beginning. Just describe the worst smack you ever had in your happy life.

EUNICE: I can't remember.

ERIN: Mine was when I was caught stealing as a kid. My mum got the ironing cord and let me have it. I mean, I remember that, that I'd been caught stealing. You must be able to think of one like that. You can't be perfect.

EUNICE: No, I don't think it's a matter of perfect. I think, you see, Mum had got so many of us, and I suppose when we were playing her up she got tired and everything else. We were all in the bedroom, you know, because then you had about three or four kids in a bedroom in them days. And she used to shout upstairs, you know, and of course if we were still banging pillows around, swinging on to one thing or another, all of a sudden we'd hear her running upstairs, you know, and then we would dive under the covers — but I can't really remember anybody really hurting me at all.

ERIN: So she was powerful enough to control you with her voice.

EUNICE: Yes, just with her talking, her authority.

ERIN: How many of you were there?

EUNICE: Pardon?

ERIN: How many of you were there?

EUNICE: There were seven of us, besides my Mum and Dad.

ERIN: And all those seven are happy except you?

EUNICE: Yes. Yes.

ERIN: Poor you. You've had a hell of a time.

EUNICE: These numbers round here (*Pointing to the numbers on the drawing*) are the amount of, um, he'd actually talk it over with me, and discuss about how many strokes I was going to get, and one of the things that used to bring a lot of dreading. About say my husband said, 'You're going to get twenty-five, right' of the whip, and he'd say, 'two of them, two out of them strokes are going to be really hard, the rest are going to be medium', and you'd never know. I'd never know. I'd never know when that really hard two were going to come. And when they come, they'd come down with all the bloody force he could put in them.

ERIN: I would imagine that he would actually save the two for when he was trying to force you to come.

EUNICE: No, no. He'd just do the whipping — was a completely separate thing.

ERIN: Completely? Nothing to do with coming?

EUNICE: Oh, no, no. He'd just do that. He'd do that because he wanted to. He'd tie me down on the bed and then . . .

ERIN: It wouldn't actually make him come. What were the things that made him come? The blood?

EUNICE: I never had to be involved in whatever he were coming, because it wasn't like that. The things he was doing or whatever the hell he was doing to me was the things that made him come. He'd come and come all in me hair, or up me face, you know.

ERIN: But he wouldn't let you touch him?

EUNICE: No. I can't ever remember, no. Not sort of rub him up.

ERIN: No, or suck him off?

EUNICE: No. He'd do it himself, or put it in me. Or he'd get my . . . when he went on to the blood thing like, he'd get my blood and he'd put it all over his own private parts.

ERIN: Incredible, isn't it?

EUNICE: Yes. It was damn terrifying, especially when I realised he'd gone blood crazy.

ERIN: And this all came out in court?

EUNICE: I don't know what came out in court, Erin. I wasn't there.

ERIN: Well we do know that several judges thought he was so dangerous, he had to be kept on remand for eight months.

EUNICE: That's right. Two judges remanded him.

ERIN: And one judge decided to let him go.

Eunice was quite right to feel outraged with the law, because again she was confused about what the law can do in a situation like this. I had to explain to her that courts are not there to treat people. The good judge had to decide whether a crime had been committed. Having listened to the case brought by the police, and having considered that Eunice was free to leave Gerald's house at any moment, he decided that, as Gerald had been in remand already for eight months, he would wash his hands of the matter. This immediately put Eunice in an awful situation. While Gerald was locked up, she could control her addiction to a certain extent, but when he was out and available, the urge to go back was overpowering, and she was terrified of it. When she was emotionally and chemically calm, she could see all the dangers that lay in that relationship. She could admit that Gerald was merely an expression of her own needs. Remove Gerald and she would continue to roam in a desperate search for the same sort of relationship. She put herself in danger in such episodes, as well as endangering anyone she met because she was aware of her volcanic rage, which felt as if it could erupt and destroy the whole planet. Indeed, when she was upset, her power could be felt throughout the room. Yet there was such a gentle, lovable person trapped in that nightmare. Other people who had dealings with her all commented on how much they liked her. She had many talents, and as we worked together, she was able to draw her feelings. Often when they were too painful, she would draw a set piece, like a picture of some houses; then on the back of the paper would be drawn the broken-hearted child — the real drawing.

I knew she was working her way back to Gerald. I also knew it was important we let her go with our love. If we had insisted she stay away from him, we would have created a barrier between her and ourselves. She had unfinished business with Gerald, and we recognised that.

Eunice had never really intended to leave Gerald. She had begun to tell her next-door neighbour of the happenings in the house, and to show her the marks. Now, in my experience, it is an essential part of a relationship of this kind that the participants feel compelled to share what is happening to them with a third party. I believe Peter Sutcliffe would have told someone else about his exploits,

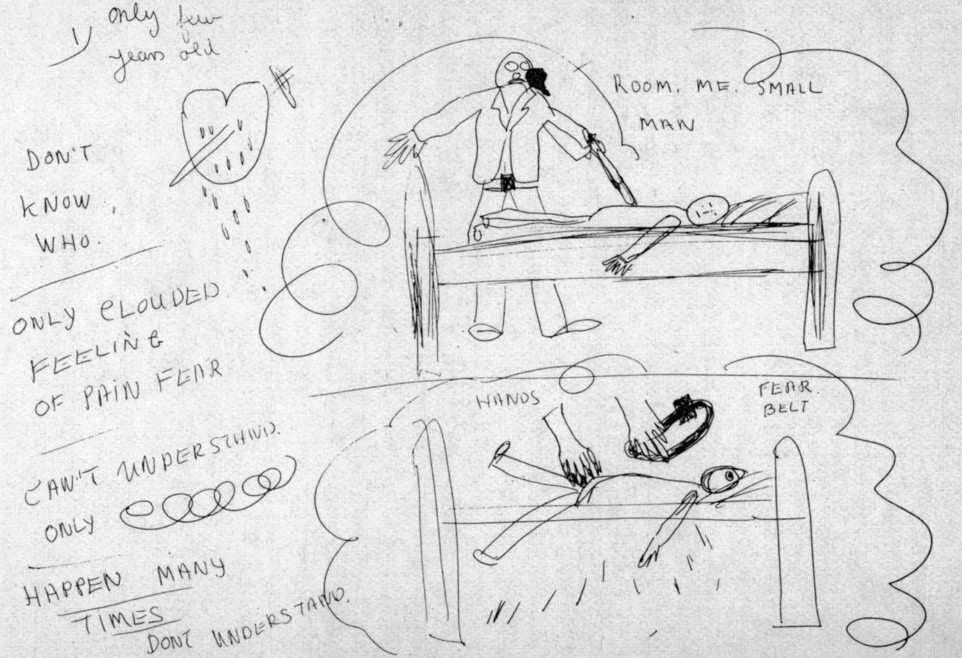
I only few years old
DON'T KNOW, WHO.
ONLY CLOUDED FEELING OF PAIN FEAR
CAN'T UNDERSTAND.
ONLY
HAPPEN MANY TIMES
DONT UNDERSTAND.
ROOM. ME. SMALL MAN
HANDS
FEAR. BELT

AFTER
UNKOWN FEAR.

DON'T WHANT TO THINK
ABOUT IT. I ONLY KNOW THAT THE HOUSE
I FELT FEAR AND DREAD, NEVER KNOW.

because between intense bursts of activity, the addicted parties can only keep themselves 'high' by recounting the events to someone else. Eunice had no one to talk to during the day, because Gerald was at work, so the next-door neighbour became her confidante. After several months of listening, the neighbour became so upset that she got in touch with a local refuge which, on being told of a woman kept in such a state of fear that she was unable to leave a man who might well kill her, quite understandably swept into Eunice's rescue. Eunice could recount the moment when her able-side knew she must go with these good women who were flinging her possessions into a suitcase, but her disabled-side was furiously trying to put the clothes back into the cupboard. Finally, the women bundled her into the car and took her away.

As soon as she told her story to a sympathetic woman, she was taken to see a psychiatrist. He heard her out and said that in his opinion a man like Gerald should be in Broadmoor for life, so he called in the police. Eunice was asked to give evidence for a police prosecution against Gerald.

Her evidence filled fifty pages. Gerald was arrested and the bloodstained implements were found in the house, just as Eunice had described. Gerald spent eight months in jail, and the psychiatrist there said he was not insane.

During the time Gerald was locked away, Eunice was seen by various members of the medical profession, all of whom tended to feel there was little they could do for her. When the matter came to court, the police were feeling more than a little embarrassed. What they had mounted as a huge prosecution against Gerald had turned into a nightmare, for it was obvious from the evidence before them that this was not a case of an innocent victim of aggression. This was a case of two people in the grip of a hopelessly complicated addiction to each other, and the matter had no business in a court of law. It should have been properly referred to experts working in the field of human behaviour.

Thus Gerald suffered eight months in jail, where he had no chance of anyone helping him. He was finally allowed to go free, carrying the stigma of being labelled a bloodthirsty monster, when he really was a frightened man in the hold of something he really did not understand. People prefer to think of child-molesters and sexually disturbed people as monsters; that way they can suspend human feeling and compassion, and righteously hate them. I have never truly met a monster, only vulnerable, confused, grief-stricken people expressing their pain in rage and despair.

Eunice came to us, as she had to so many other agencies beforehand, for help. 'Keep him away from me,' is what she said, but what she meant was 'Keep me away from him.' We did so for a while, and I began work with her that was to spread over seven months. It was hard work because Eunice was a highly intelligent woman, and had built a solid wall around herself. Gradually she learned that we could be trusted, and she began to paint and to draw her feelings. I bought her an excellent set of paints and lots of pads. Every week I worked through the material with her. She began to put the story of her childhood into some sort of realistic perspective, rather than maintaining her original statement that it had all been perfect.

Every time I sit with someone who says 'It was all perfect', I groan inwardly. It is a sure sign of an emotionally disabled adult defending the hurt child in himself. There is no such thing as a perfect childhood. Emotionally able people are secure enough to acknowledge the bits that were not too good, but they agree that, on balance, their upbringing had more pluses than minuses. People like Eunice either totally deny their past, thereby sitting on huge piles of conflicting emotion; or they go the other way, and a sympathetic glance is enough to set them off with a veritable diarrhoea of stories which shock and horrify the listener. These latter are often the people who love the story, and have no intention of creating a happy ending for themselves. They very much see themselves as Hamlet or Ophelia, and the rest of the world as a huge stage. Most helpers of mankind are not trained to realise that in such cases they become merely part of the cast of characters. Agency workers often think they represent the directors in the plays of their clients' lives; actually, they are walk-ons, used as props by the main characters.

This is what happened to Eunice. An awful lot of good people got fed up with helping her, because they were

(see page 130)

working on the generally-accepted view that 'If a man treats you like that, surely you must want to get away, and stay away.' We at least were able to say, 'We know why you need to go back to him, but we have got to find out why you need him at all.' Eunice's second drawing was a complete history of her family life. Her father is drawn in the parlour, which he kept locked until Sunday afternoons. She remembers the room as a treasure-house stuffed full of all the pretty things that he loved, and his gramophone. He had a beautiful voice and he used to sing for her. The poverty of the rest of the house was reflected in the drawing.

Gradually Eunice was able to describe her bitter, angry mother, who saw her husband as weak and ineffectual. They had many children, far too many to cope with on so little money. There was also a grandmother dying of stomach cancer in an upstairs bedroom. In those days she would have died in agony. Somewhere there was a lodger, an un-remembered man. What was coming clear at this point was that someone, when Eunice was under the age of three, must have molested her sexually. Certainly she was battered by her mother. She could never gain her mother's love, even though all her life she strived for it. I suspect Eunice was a gifted child, and those children are always difficult to rear, because although intellectually way beyond their years, emotionally they take far longer to mature than normal children, and the risk of damaging them is much greater.

Her first happy memory was her first day at school. It was probably her first experience of sanity, and her first recognition that there was a good world outside the nightmare at home. She remembered sitting in the dark on the top stairs of her house, crying for hours. Her drawings began to give hints. Stairs appeared, a little figure, a door with a cord tying the door-handle to the banisters. 'What was that?' I asked. 'That's the room my grandmother was in,' she remembered. How much screaming and moaning must have gone on behind that door. Her memories of her father included times when he would take her to the pub in the evening, and she would sit in the audience and listen to him sing. How much did her mother's anger against her reflect her relationship with her father? Her mother was never able to acknowledge his singing. He made all the clothes for the family himself. He told Eunice about *his* mother, an ardent Salvation Army follower; one day Eunice opened the door of a cupboard in her parents' bedroom and found a picture of her grandmother's face inside. There were constant visits to the hospital with a sick sister who demanded all the mother's time. The memories were mostly grim.

When we got close to the central question of who it was who sexually abused her and beat her as a child, she would close up, and I would see the anxiety surrounding that question cause her face and neck to flush. You could see the emotional reaction trigger off a chemical charge, and she would become restless and shift about in her chair.

I know that at some point in her life she must be allowed to come to terms with that deeply felt pain and hurt. Sitting before me was yet another betrayed child, crippled by events before the age of five. However, I also knew that the Refuge did not have the facilities to offer a safe place for her to let go of all those years of damage. It would be dangerous for us and disastrous for her to open her up without being in a position to put her back together again. At this point I realised that she had a problem with hypertension, and I was able to refer her to a very gifted specialist, who took her into hospital and put her on sleep therapy. Not only did it cure her hypertension, but it also gave us a chance to be with her when she was relaxed and unflustered by the trivia of everyday life.

Tina and I visited her every day, and let her talk about her first marriage, which was a disaster; about her beloved only son, who died in a motor accident; about her childhood, about her mother who never loved her, about the crying, the fear, the empty blackness. Before she went into hospital she drew her rage for me; it was frightening. I hoped that the time in hospital would give us time to get closer to the truth, but the hospital was not the right place. She had already been in most of the mental hospitals, and she had seen psychiatrists. By now most women in Eunice's position would be dead, either from the hours of beating, or from the pills she took to keep her calm. But Eunice had the most amazing stamina.

She also recognised the moments in the torture sessions

with Gerald when she was near to death, and would draw back from it. 'All of a sudden there was a sound that came from in me, and yet where the hell it came from . . . I suppose you'd call it basic primitive,' she said.

ERIN: Yes.
EUNICE: The thing that, you know, I felt so much: I was like a bloody animal, that was, you know . . .
ERIN: Roaring?
EUNICE: Yes. And I made this noise, terrific noise, and at any time I did say at this particular time if I'd have been able to, I would have done something . . . but it only lasted five minutes.
ERIN: Done what?
EUNICE: I just wanted to finish with it.
ERIN: Why is that? . . . Do you ever hear that noise again? Have you ever heard it again?
EUNICE: No, it's the only one time when it . . . and the funny thing was . . .
ERIN: Did you feel you were very near death then? Or were you very much alive?

Gerald stopped the mutilation when he heard her roar. He turned his head and walked away. In that moment he could have taken her life. But he gave it back to her. In these relationships the balance goes back and forth — death is on the side-lines waiting.

While Eunice was in hospital, Tina and I agreed that we would visit Gerald, so wrote and asked if we could see him. He wrote back and said he would be pleased to see us, and said he hoped Eunice was well. On the appointed day we drove to his house: a beautifully kept terraced house in a middle-class suburban area. We knocked on the door and were ushered into the narrow hall, and Gerald showed us into his warm, comfortable kitchen. Before me stood a powerfully built man, immaculately dressed, and very nervous. He made us a cup of coffee each and we got on with the talking. He seemed completely isolated in his house, and expressed a very real affection for Eunice. The most amazing thing about talking to both Eunice and Gerald was that the bits of their personalities which did function normally really enjoyed each other's company immensely. She would describe the times they would laugh and joke. He would make a cup of tea for her, or she would cook a special dinner for him. I felt that here were two really nice people with plenty of good potential.

He was a good worker and respected among his colleagues. Looking round the room, I could see he was able to create a very warm and organised environment round him. He was a great reader and knowledgeable to talk to. Both Tina and I liked him very much. He was very concerned about Eunice, and we both pointed out the dangers of her returning to him. He might either kill her by accident, or her heart might give out. He agreed, but complained that after a hard day's work she used to demand that he beat her for hours, and that used to exhaust him, because he had to put in a hard day's work the next day. He made it sound such a normal complaint that Tina and I had to look at each other to restore our own sense of reality.

He, like Eunice, both wanted and did not want this relationship. He described how Eunice would fall on the floor in a totally passive state during these sessions, and she would seem to be in a world of her own. Actually, they were both in a world of their own. Gerald himself, Eunice eventually told me, had come from a very violent family, in which he was savagely battered. Apart from the violence in the family, his task as a child during the war years was to loot the bombed-out houses in his area. He would tell Eunice about the broken and maimed bodies strewn around the rooms he visited, the raw lumps of flesh that were once human beings. He had been given very little chance to find love or happiness in his early years.

We finished our coffee and left. We both felt that we had a clear picture of why Gerald needed his relationship with Eunice, but no clear picture of what more could be done. Certainly, Gerald was not unusual in our case histories of women coming to the Refuge telling us about this kind of abusive sexual practice. What was different was that her description of their practices together could not be dismissed as merely 'fantasy'. There was solid police evidence to prove it. I telephoned various people for advice, but the net result of hours of talking was that no one really wanted to take her on. 'These are difficult cases,' they would say. We were faced with the prospect of Eunice coming out of hospital and going back to him, which she did.

Eunice phoned me to describe how she had met him and spent the day with him. 'How did you feel when you saw him?' I asked. 'Before I went in, I felt like I'd got twenty butterflies in my stomach.' 'You must have been very frightened,' I said. 'I was coming out in such a heat I felt I'd got a temperature.' There it was again — that accurate description of an addiction. You hear it said by an alcoholic as he reaches for his bottle. You hear it said by a heroin addict reaching for his needle. The buzz, the click, and then the intense warmth.

So they were together again. After a few weeks Eunice came back to see me. It was all happening again. 'I want to leave him,' she said. 'I really do want to leave him.' 'All right,' I said. 'This time I'll arrange for you to leave England, and you won't know where you're going till you come to say goodbye to me.' I made the arrangements, and when she came along she brought with her a roll of drawings. 'Don't open them until I've gone,' she said. 'I won't,' I promised, and kissed her goodbye, before sending her off to a refuge abroad. 'If you filter back to him from there, you will have to acknowledge your need for his violence, won't you?' I said. She smiled and left. I unrolled the drawings, and saw we were one step closer to the pain. She could now at least draw what happened in her childhood. But it would take time for her to draw who did it. As I write, she has returned to this country, and is in touch with me. She is in yet another hospital and I only hope they can help her. Gerald will be waiting for her, unless he meets another woman like her, and unless he kills or gets killed. Only then will the matter rest.

One day, Jeff and I will have a place that will specialise in caring for the Geralds and Eunices of this world — hopefully, finding them before they are adults.

Chapter Five

WHICH WAY NOW?

On 6 October 1977, having lost the appeal to the House of Lords, I was taken back to Acton Magistrates' Court for sentencing, and was found guilty of allowing overcrowding in the refuge. I was given a twelve-month conditional discharge: the condition being, of course, that I in future refused further mothers and children entry when we had reached our limit of thirty-six bodies. Again, I stood on the steps of Acton Court and looked out at the crowd of mothers and their children.

One was Liza, and she should have had a baby in her arms. But the baby was dead, the victim of an uncomprehending maternity hospital. The hospital had insisted that, because of our 'overcrowded' conditions, Liza should be taken to a homeless family hostel and installed in a room of her own with her three disturbed children, rather than be left in a community that knew her and loved her. But we knew that Liza would not cope on her own, and the baby died — a cot-death.

There, too, was Gwen, whose arms were also empty. She orignally came to us with thirty-two charges for theft, burglary, and illegal scrap-dealing. She was a big, healthy girl, yet her baby boy was stillborn. 'What happened?' I asked her when she came home from the hospital. She shrugged. 'Don't know. Just dead.' Gwen herself had been discovered, at the age of six weeks, hanging in a wardrobe, suspended by her neck by her father's tie. Coming from a violent childhood, she knew only how to recreate violence in later relationships.

'I think you'd rather have a good fight than make love with your Arthur,' I said to her in exasperation — after yet another fracas with him had sent her catapulting through our doors again, trailing her brood of children. 'Least you don't have to give in to the buggers,' she said, snorting with laughter. You *have* to know how to laugh in this business.

Again looking round the crowd, I realised just how many pointless adult deaths there had been. One was Mr Simmonds, who killed himself in his car by filling it with carbon-monoxide, at the bottom of our garden. The young policeman who came to inform Mrs Simmonds took at least five minutes to get to the point. 'Thank God for that,' said Emma with much feeling when the PC finally mustered the courage to tell her. I had to help the policeman to a chair; he had not expected the bereaved to be just as violent as the deceased.

Also absent was Mrs X, now in another country after having been rehoused from the Refuge. Her very violent husband had been discharged from the mental hospital for a weekend visit, and knowing he was suicidal the psychiatrist had insisted that only contact with his family would save his life. When he arrived he was still heavily drugged from the hospital. The next day, it was alleged, he went to the local shop and bought some paraffin, climbed into the bathtub and poured it over himself, then set himself alight. 'Go in peace,' I said to Mrs X when she came to say goodbye to me.

There on the courthouse steps I wondered if official interference would always make it such a struggle for us to give these people a second chance.

Within just a few hours of coming back to the Refuge, I had broken the condition of my discharge. A very tired woman arrived with her children, who had travelled from the other side of England. We took her in. Sue asked me: 'What happens if you go to jail? Shall I write to the Queen?'

'Write to anyone you like,' I said in despair. 'It won't make any difference.'

So on 10 February 1978, a letter for Sue arrived from Buckingham Palace:

> I acknowledge your letter of 19th January on 23rd January and I am now writing to say that the letter has

been laid before The Queen. Her Majesty has told me to thank you for your letter of 19th January about Chiswick Women's Aid. She is most concerned about the plight of battered women and pleased that since 1972, when Mrs Erin Pizzey founded the first refuge at Chiswick, much has been done to help alleviate the problem.

It is most unfortunate that there should still be disagreement between Chiswick Women's Aid and the London Borough of Hounslow but this is not a situation in which Her Majesty can personally intervene. She has been assured, however, that there is no question of residents at 369, High Road, Chiswick, being evicted.

That letter signified the end of the struggle. Various central and local government departments were called together with the Social Services. They co-operated with Hounslow, and I was called to the offices of the Greater London Council, where my colleague Steve and I heard George Tremlett, deputy head of the Conservative Party, outline a course of action that included the allocation of a quarter of a million pounds towards the building of a refuge.

I looked at Lord Goodman and David Astor. 'Does that mean no one will ever be turned away?' I asked. They confirmed that this would be enshrined in any interdepartmental discussions that would occur in the future. Peace at last!

Steve and I went straight back to the Refuge and called a house-meeting. We asked the mothers present to vote on whether they wanted to accept the money, and the conditions that went with it – one being that a Board of Management would be established, composed of people from outside the Refuge; another being that policy decisions would be made in future by a business manager, specially appointed, instead of by the community as a whole – or whether they preferred to continue operating in our present more haphazard way.

There was no argument, really, and the mothers voted to accept the Government proposal — which we did.

Our guiding principle had always been that we would never turn anyone away. In the early days, this practice was vital, and sometimes we used to have over a hundred mothers and children living in the nine rooms and in sheds in the back garden. Indeed, on one occasion Anne and I rehoused in a squat thirty-eight mothers and children during the early hours of one morning, only to have a similar number arrive at the Refuge by the evening of the same day. This overcrowding had brought upon us a continuous barrage of criticism and legal prosecutions in the past. But now the Government concessions showed that public attitudes had changed.

The social agencies had become far more aware of the needs of *battered* women and their children, and these women were being given the help and support they needed to get away from their violent home situations. However, the more difficult problem of women from *violence-prone* relationships was still being overlooked or misunderstood, as new refuges opened and these families poured through the doors. Many of the genuinely caring people in charge of these refuges were so horrified by the violent attitudes of such women, that they quickly created selection procedures to protect other innocently battered wives from the chaos created by *violence-prone* families. Other refuges, unable to make that distinction, disintegrated into anarchy, and were forced to close down. But some had social workers who proved able to cope with, say, four or five *violence-prone* families at a time, and they did, and still do, excellent work.

However, it seems a lot of the refuges chose to exist merely to justify the political beliefs of the people who ran them. They encouraged violence-prone women to continue to see themselves as victims of male oppression, and of capitalism. Occasionally I have winced to see a dreadfully violent and destructive woman, who had left us because she refused to recognise the truth about herself, later emerge on a public platform with her refuge workers to vividly describe her 'brute' of a husband — when both she and I knew she was just as violent as he was.

After the vote to accept the GLC offer — with peace finally established between ourselves and the Borough of Hounslow, and the future of Chiswick assured — I could now think about giving up my full-time participation at the Refuge. 'Chiswick Family Rescue' was then formed, with

David Astor as Chairman, to take charge of the buildings and staff at Chiswick High Road. Anne Ashby became the new Director. For two years I continued to act as consultant for Chiswick Family Rescue; and under its umbrella Jeff and I wrote up some of our findings. (Now Jeff and I have withdrawn from Chiswick Family Rescue, and we continue our work and our research in our own original charity, Women's Aid).

Soon after, I was asked by the new Board of Management to design my ideal refuge. This I did with the help of Gil Chambers, who had originally produced some drawings for me while we were working on the future ideals of shared living for single-parent families. Porter-Wright, our architects, who worked with him, then produced a clients' brief which outlined the needs of violence-prone families, and they came up with the design which is reproduced in Appendix C at the back of this book. This groundplan for a purpose-built centre was my solution for containing these highly anti-social families within the same locale without disrupting the everyday lives of their neighbours. My plan was immediately attacked in the prestigious *Architect's Journal*, which – like so many other bodies – did not understand that I was not designing a refuge just for battered wives, but an inward-looking sanctuary for people outcast from society. Certainly, I feel there are many refuge groups and social agencies who will find both the brief and the groundplan of interest.

Unfortunately, there were insufficient funds to construct this building, and anyway Anne Ashby the new Director of Chiswick Family Rescue, quite rightly had her own views on how to run her own project. Anne and I have worked together for so long and have survived so many battles through our unswerving support for each other, that we will always share a deep and abiding friendship even though our paths have taken different directions. Jeff and I have retained our direct interest in Women's Aid Ltd, whose aim as a charity is to train and teach people how to identify and treat families that are addicted to violence.

Part of my own experience arises from work I have shared in and observed in my travels all over the world. As an example, once in a training programme in Anchorage, Alaska I was lecturing on 'The Uses of Inappropriate Behaviour in Violent Situations' when a social worker related an incident that occurred when she was called out to deal with a domestic crisis, and was met at the door by an enraged man holding a double-barrel shotgun. As he stood there, huge and sweating with anger, she asked him 'Have you got a typewriter?' in an ordinary, everyday voice. He looked completely amazed. 'No,' he said. 'Why do you ask?' 'I want to type my resignation,' she said smiling. He burst out laughing. That was an excellent example of defusing anger, letting someone off the hook. She survived the situation because of her training.

It must always be remembered that, since violent people have had to survive all their lives in a world that they perceive as hostile towards them, they are constantly on the alert, and therefore finely tuned to every flicker of emotion in other people, and can immediately pick up fear or tension. To work effectively with these families, it is essential for workers in this field to be trained to come to terms with their *own* aggression and their *own* internal fears, so that they can handle a confrontation without danger to themselves or to the person they are trying to help. Thus I often tell students to consider a violent person before them as being an unexploded bomb. And though rigorous training is given to anyone whose job it is to defuse live bombs; we make almost no attempt to train people adequately on how to defuse an explosive human being.

Fortunately, my own turbulent and violent background gave me a sound training for survival in this very dangerous field. What other people may have learned in books, *I* knew by heart. No amount of book-learning will teach you how to manoeuvre yourself out of danger when confronted with a man literally frothing at the mouth with rage. What you need to know is that a gentle touch of the hand will calm him. And using words will be useless, because at a certain point of rage, when the chemicals and emotions are flowing, he cannot even hear words.

When I first began taking in women, we all assumed that the address of the Refuge should be kept secret, to protect us against their violent menfolk. So, for the first few weeks I did not allow the newspapers to reveal our whereabouts. But as most of the women coming in to us soon told their men anyway, I decided it was safer to meet these men in a spirit of sympathy. For this way we would not be seen as the 'enemy', and therefore we would not make the community vulnerable to physical attack. This policy involved a commitment to tell a man the truth, even if sometimes we had to tell him that his wife and children were indeed in the Refuge, but refused to see him. I gradually discovered that, provided I told them the truth and did not betray their trust, I could talk constructively to even the most violent of men.

At this point I realised I must have a project for the men, too. This was brought home to me by an interview on the front doorstep with a man who had regularly beaten his wife and sexually molested all his daughters, who were subsequently taken into care. He went to jail for these offences, but on release his wife took him back; whereupon they lived in a caravan and she gave birth again. One day he was left to babysit his eighteen-month-old daughter, and hit her in a fit of rage when she cried. She died as a result of cracking her head against a wall, and he put her little body in a suitcase and left it at a local golf-course. Again he was imprisoned, but on his release again returned to his wife. At the time I met him, she had come to us for shelter, complaining that he was yet again sexually interfering with their two new children and also with the wife's sisters. So I knew his history by heart, and indeed he looked a dreadful villain, with one lone tooth sticking out of the middle of his bottom gum.

Speaking with him on the doorstep, we reached the bit about him killing the baby. 'I didn't mean to kill her,' he said. This I came to believe, for he went on to explain how he had carefully packed the child's favourite toys around her before disposing of the body. Looking at him then, I knew there was potential for good in him — as there is in any human being. From then on I actively encouraged a policy of working with the men, too, even if there was no chance of a reconciliation with the women concerned. Later on, I did secure a 'men's house' from the Greater London Council — and it was fully booked up even before it opened. However, we soon had to shut it, because the Department of Health and Social security withdrew our grant. But just the fact that it existed proved the need for a therapeutic community to handle men who otherwise would find themselves in prison. For there you can cage their bodies, but if you ignore their inner worlds there is no possibility of changing them for the better.

As far as the security of the Refuge was concerned, I also came to realise that violent men are far more intimidated by a large group of women than if faced by a similar group of men. So while the community contained twenty-five or more women we were safe. By the time we moved into a bigger house I had sufficient experience to realise that we should let our address be made public. Violence-prone women had no trouble finding us; most of them knew every agency going. But it was the genuine battered wives — so trapped by their net-curtain respectability that they could never tell anyone they were being beaten — who needed to know where to find us.

And each time I dealt with an angry man, I learned a little more about the techniques of violence. For instance, I recognised the fact that the more violent a man is, the less likely he is to leave his own territory. Therefore, provided I moved the woman from his local area to another refuge I did not expect any problems from him, except perhaps the odd broken window. It was Junior who presented one of the very few serious physical threats in all my ten years' experience.

Junior confronted me on the doorstep. He was African and I was a woman. We did not have any male house-staff at this point, just one man who worked in the playgroup — and I would not risk him, as he was untrained for this sort of confrontation. Junior was very angry: he was shaking with rage, and had worked himself up to such a pitch that there was white froth at the corners of his mouth. He demanded to see his wife. 'She is here but she doesn't want to see you,' I replied. I should have touched him then, to let his rage ebb away. Contained in his body, it had no way of leaving him except through some violent and explosive act. As he walked away down the steps and began pacing up and down, he seemed in the grip of something he could not control. So I warned the rest of the house — including a German film crew in the basement, who were making a documentary. Junior's wife went up to the attic of the house with her two children and barricaded herself in. I observed which of the other children found the situation exciting and were trying to get near the front door, and which were frightened and crying and looking for their mothers. I registered which of the staff were paralysed with fear, rushing ineffectively around, and which were able to function coolly, following my instructions to gather all the children into the basement.

There was a sudden crash and the sound of breaking glass, as Junior came through the basement window and tore up the stairs onto the first landing. Anne Ashby stood barring the stairs with a small posse of women. I took up my position in front of the door to the basement, to stop him getting back down to the children and frightening them. I had a plastic orange-squash bottle in my hand. I heard sounds of fighting from the upstairs landing, then the sound of running feet. Suddenly Junior turned the corner and charged towards me. I faced him very calmly and he screeched to a halt. We looked at each other — and both acknowledged that there would be no contest between us. He turned away.

Unfortunately, the police had been called, and as Junior left by the front door, he ran straight into them. There was a dreadful fight — it took six policemen to get him into the van. Finally they managed to close the door of the Black Maria on him, and drove off. I have discussed this problem of involving themselves with domestic violence with the police, both here and in other countries. They suffer from the usual misunderstanding of two different family dynamics. On the one hand they will find themselves called out by a woman who has genuinely decided that she can no longer tolerate her husband's violence. It takes a great deal of courage for such a woman to summon the police, because she is usually deeply ashamed of the circumstances she is in, but here the police are more than willing to help. On the other hand, however, their more usual experience is to be called out to one of those notoriously violent families in their area, and be asked to intervene in a fight that could result in the policeman getting badly hurt, and the warring couple falling back into each other's arms.

Little Mo described to me a characteristic situation when she came into the Refuge with her two-year-old son, a broken nose, and many bruises. She had been having a fight with her lunatically violent boyfriend, the terror of his patch and of the local police station, but it was getting out of hand, so she screamed for her neighbour to call the police. 'I really thought I was a goner that time,' she said with some relish. On hearing the address, the police turned up in full force and set about Mo's boyfriend, who did his best to kill them all. Then Mo pitched into the police to stop them harming her loved one. In the ensuing mêlée Mo received a broken nose. So she had taken refuge with us to nurse her bruises, to set about suing the police, and to mend a broken heart because the boyfriend had now ditched her for another woman.

The police in any country in the world are more likely to get hurt (or where carrying guns is legal, even killed) when intervening in family quarrels than in any of their other policing duties. It is tantamount to suicide for a man to enter a violent man's territory when he is in a fit of rage. It would be far wiser to send two female social workers in first — one to pacify the man, the other to see to the woman and children. Then the woman should be asked if she wishes to be taken to a refuge. Then it becomes her own responsibility, with advice from the legal services at the shelters, to decide what action she should take.

Anyway, after this drama with Junior, it was time to see how it had affected the Refuge. I could instantly see the community was divided into two camps: those staff and mothers who were shaking and upset, and their children crying; and those who seemed excited and 'high'. The latter talked animatedly about the event, gesticulating and capping each other's stories; meanwhile their children were bombing around the house, fighting and wrecking the place. But not all crying mothers had crying children; some were clearly excited. And the same was true of the 'high' mothers — some of their children were crying and shaking. As I went home that night I knew there would be trouble, not necessarily in the Refuge — there was a house rule against fighting — but more likely because those mothers so 'high' they couldn't contain themselves would be looking for a fight somewhere else, to release their aggression in order to calm down.

Sure enough, at the next morning's house-meeting, I had to deal with a group of women who had gone to the local Palais and started brawling with some of the men there. They had very virtuously kept the fighting outside the Refuge, and were now loudly insisting that it was all the men's fault, anyway. But when the whole community examined the dynamics of the event, these women were forced to admit that they had gone out deliberately to pick a fight, and that the men involved were merely unknowing victims of an event that had occurred earlier in the day. When I pointed out that this was just the sort of behaviour they complained of in their own men, some of them at least had the grace to look embarrassed.

In the early days after we moved from Belmont Terrace (a packed community in just four rooms) to Chiswick High Road, I already had ideas of how a community containing so many emotionally disabled and disruptive people could best be managed. I realised that a large majority of these mothers had come from institutional backgrounds, as well as violent families, and because of this their internal life was chaotic. After all, I myself had spent many years in a boarding school, and vacations in a holiday home. Improperly parented, and brought up largely in servants' quarters in the Far East, I remembered my own early struggles even to begin to understand the highly complex rules of socially acceptable behaviour. Institutions may create external order, but without that emotional and chemical bonding between parents and children which is necessary to create a learning situation as soon as the external rules are removed, the emotionally disabled person is bereft. It is like removing crutches from crippled patients before training them to walk. Their own internal world has no social structures for such emotionally disabled people to fall back on; no internal clock to help get them up in the morning; no internal message to go to the lavatory regularly; to eat at spaced intervals; to sleep regularly, not only when they are exhausted. For them all is confusion — and finally they will find their way back to institutions for safe-keeping. This structureless behaviour is also very evident in people from the background of violent families, which are by nature chaotic.

Most institutions have been designed by the emotionally able for the emotionally disabled on the 'But surely . . .' principle. 'But surely if you *train* people to get up, after a while they will get up automatically?' No they won't — if all you do is train them to become addicted to the sound of a bell, like Pavlov's dogs. Unless they develop an internal response to the need to get up in the morning, they will sleep on. If you need the sound of a bell to elicit the response of hunger three times a day, once that sound is absent, you will have no internal messages telling you that you are hungry and need food in regular amounts. The result of this is usually stomach disorders.

All this I knew and observed among a middle-class elite that inhabited the rigid world of public schools. Where there was no confirming love and reassuring family life, there was also no internalised structure that enabled a child to cope once on his or her own. Thus, among twenty-year-olds living in the smartest areas of London, endowed by their parents with the best education and social advantages the country had to offer, there still grew up men and women just as dirty, just as violent, just as deviant, and just as promiscuous as any of those in our Refuge. The difference was that they were protected by money, and if things got too rough, they would be sent abroad — Rhodesia and South Africa being very popular lands of exile in my time.

It was with a great deal of enthusiasm that I approached the problem of how to create a thriving community which would enable people to grow and change out of the negative conditioning of their emotionally deprived backgrounds.

Many of the women arriving first seemed to expect me to be running an institution which would perform certain functions they could perfectly well perform for themselves. I realised I would have to make it clear to everyone that Anne and I were *not* social workers, and did not intend to act as nannies to them. Rather we saw ourselves as 'enablers' — and that our role was to enable them to cope with themselves.*

This was no problem with the 'battered wives' leaving

violent relationships never to return. For these relationships arose from the accidental choice of one violent man; the women concerned did not have a whole lifetime of emotional damage behind them. They still had plenty of their own resources; and could co-operate with us and utilise the help we were able to give them. But violence-prone women only had a lifetime of survival techniques to fall back on, which meant that they had survived mostly at the expense of other people. The first lesson they learned from me was that I was not prepared to be manipulated in the same way.

It was extremely difficult for such women and their families to live in a community where the people they wanted to see as 'staff' refused to be drawn into playing a role that would enable them to be manipulated or organised against. In thinking about the day-to-day running of the Refuge, firstly I decided that there should never be an 'office'. For me, an office meant a place for the staff to hide, and territory for the families to invest with a sense of alienation, which would then allow them to behave one way in the office (with the staff) and another way in the community (their equals). This is precisely how most of them had operated in their social agency offices, with their social workers or probation officers — on their best behaviour there but always reverting to their real behaviour once outside the office door. In fact we did have a little side room called 'the office', but this contained only old clothes and junk. I had as much of a problem de-officing this room for staff who wanted office status, as for the mothers seeking 'social worker' type of control over their lives so that they could relinquish responsibility for their own lives. At times, after being away on lecturing tours, I would return to the Refuge and have to physically remove tables and chairs from this room. On one occasion I turned it into a

---

*I used to joke with the mothers that while the rich had nannies, the poor had social workers trained to act as nannies — and that was not our way. (This curious situation arises because when the upper middle-class designed the social services, they modelled social-workers after their own nannies). What *we* could do for ourselves we would teach *them* to do for themselves. Above all, we were there because we *wanted* to be there. Ours was not a nine-to-five job; it was a deep commitment, and we expected a reciprocal commitment from the women and children in our care.

bedroom, so there would be no chance of staff making a territory out of it for themselves, or the more hesitant mothers becoming afraid to approach a door that seemed to be a symbol of authority.

The only telephones were in the sitting-room, and no staff were allowed to answer them. All information that came into the community belonged to the people who lived there, and it was their job to see that messages and phone-calls were relayed to those concerned. All post for the Refuge, addressed either to myself or to the house, except for mothers' private letters, was opened publicly in the sitting-room each morning, and was read out before the morning house-meeting. This included all bills, bank statements, donations, and anything else that came in. During those early years the post was of intense interest, as much of it involved major incidents in our fight for the 'open door' principle. And letters came in from all over the world asking for information — from groups as far away as Japan who wished to open refuges. The benefit of the house-meeting was that they constituted a safe coming-together of a group of people who, for better or for worse, were learning to co-operate with each other in order to survive the cramped and potentially hazardous conditions of a very overcrowded house. For in this situation antisocial and unruly families found themselves living with other families who behaved in exactly the same way. Normally, an antisocial family living in a street of quiet, peace-loving people will ride roughshod over their neighbours and terrorise them into accepting their behaviour for fear of reprisals. In our Refuge this type of intimidation did not work. There were no divisions between the Refuge workers and the families who lived there. The violent women were therefore unable to police the path to an office, and so all information about events in the Refuge would come to my ears immediately. Anyone attempting to bully or coerce other members of the community found themselves publicly answerable in a house-meeting, and often the bullies began to realise there were ways of achieving their goals other than terrorising someone else.

In these house-meetings a lot of the time was spent explaining simple concepts of love and caring in relationships to people who had no language other than the language of violence. I found poetry the best medium for teaching, because of its immediacy. I would read some poetry and then encourage mothers to write down their own feelings. Sometimes the mothers would write with such passion and clarity that we would all sit spellbound as they read out their own words. On other days we would spend the afternoon singing, and all the pain and hurt would then leak out, since people could express themselves with song in a way that they could never risk with words.

I will always remember the afternoon when an American girl dropped by with a guitar. Whether it was the sweetness of her playing or a particular chord, I shall never know, but the music had an amazing affect on Jewel. Jewel was African, and only about four feet high. She had come to us two years before this event, having walked out on her husband and five children. On checking her background I learned that she was the despair of the local mental hospital and social services. She had a hard-working husband, and all her children did the best they could with a mother who seemed unable to share any part of anyone else's reality. Most of the time she behaved like a naughty, spoiled child, but it was interesting to see how the rest of the community protected her and loved her. Her contribution to the house-meetings was a series of interruptions that were so bizarre we would always go into fits of laughter. On one occasion I was delivering a dire warning about the perils of bringing stolen goods into the Refuge. I was particularly admonishing several mothers who had been born and bred to shop-lift, and who were now training their own children in the fine art of stealing. I told them firmly I was not prepared to accept the well-worn excuse that they were only stealing for survival, since most of their haul consisted of nail-varnish and dresses for the local dance-hall. Furthermore, I was going to shop them myself to the police station. '333,' I intoned pompously – this being the number of the local-beat policeman, 'will be called in.' Jewel could contain herself no longer. 'What about 222?' she enquired ingenuously, and everyone erupted with laughter. She had done it again.

It was always a dreadful struggle to get Jewel to pay her

rent on a Monday morning. We were not an institution, and it was vital that when the mothers cashed their welfare cheques they should pay their rent to us on a Monday morning. For many of our mothers it was a culture shock to be expected to actually part with money for anything as pointless as rent. Most of these families were up to their necks in hire-purchase debts and rent arrears. They had always relied on repeated evictions eventually as a means of clearing rent arrears and avoiding pursuit by catalogue companies. But in the Refuge there were no evictions for arrears, only the house-meeting, where those who chose not to pay their rent had to face those who did. The consequences for non-payment were decided by the community and not by the staff, and this group pressure meant virtually no non-payment, except in the case of Jewel, who would not recognise group pressure if she saw it.

After several house discussions it was decided that if she refused to pay her rent, she should be carried to the front door and left outside every Monday morning, before the house-meeting began. I was chosen to carry her, as I was by far the largest member of the community, and there was no other way of removing her. On the first occasion, I scooped her up and carried her out to the front doorstep and left her there. We all felt confident that because Jewel so loved house-meetings, particularly the Monday morning ones when the whole of the weekend was under discussion, she would not take long to reconsider. It did not work. She just bounced back into the sitting-room unrepentant. However, for all her lovable side, there was an untouchable part of Jewel I could never reach.

On this particular day we were singing old cockney songs. Many of the community at that time came from the East End of London, and it was a pleasure to hear the original words of many songs that are passing from our musical heritage. As I listened to the words, I became aware that these songs were the oral history of the emotionally disabled, who passed them down from generation to generation. For instance, 'My old man said follow the van and don't dilly dally on the way' is a Victorian song about a family doing a moonlight flit before the bailiffs arrived.

After a while, the American girl started playing 'We Shall Overcome', and as that was particularly appropriate to our current struggle to survive we all joined in. Jewel was listening intently, and suddenly from this tiny, wrinkled, little black figure came this huge melodious voice. It filled the room and we all fell silent. The words were those of an African lament, and Jewel sang with her eyes closed and tears running down her cheeks. Her voice rose and fell with a rhythm that seemed to be an eternal prayer for black Africans in exile from their homeland. She was truly in exile, for now there was no one to go back to; her tribe had been disbanded. There was no going home.

When she stopped, we all began singing softly again. From that day on she decided not to live any more: she took to her bed and refused to eat. Everyone tried everything. Eventually, because we could not nurse her efficiently, we took her back to the mental hospital where they knew her and also loved her as we did. We all missed her dreadfully, though from time to time we would hear news of her. (She is still in a mental hospital). One of the advantages of the world I work in is that, just as there is a *Who's Who* of the emotionally enabled, listing their clubs, like the Athenaeum and Boodle's, there are also clubs for the emotionally disabled: homeless family hostels, mental hospitals, borstals, hospitals for the criminally insane, like Broadmoor and Rampton. This is why in my own entry in *Who's Who* I list my club as Women's Aid.

Often the community would contain several women who always reacted to events by exploding with rage. Many of the women would also regularly batter their children. As I explained earlier, in the Refuge there was no territorial space for anyone to organise their rage. I grew up in places like Hong Kong and India, where I saw families living ten to a room. I knew many of the children of these families, and was aware of the high level of sensitivity that these families displayed towards each other so that they could survive in those living conditions. There was similarly no privacy in the Refuge in which to beat children, and this acted as a controlling factor for violent mothers. If you have been brought up by the rule of the boot and the fist, then all conflict between yourself and anyone else, including your children, is resolved by the impact of pain.

If a violent person hits a non-violent person, the latter will react by feeling pain, and will very quickly give in and obey. In our problem families, however, where the constant level of pain is very high, the mother would have to really lay into her children to get them even to pay attention. Usually, it was possible, with a lot of group pressure, to get a mother to give up beating her children, but then we were left with the problem of children who used their mother's violent behaviour as a means of achieving satisfaction.

I had often heard stories and read accounts of battered children clinging to the parent who battered them. Various analytical discussions grew out of these reports, but I could see that — as with many of the women and their violent men — these children were often not particularly fond of their mothers. Indeed, they often expressed a great deal of hostility and dislike. But they were addicted to their mother's violence, and would return time and time again to receive a blow or a kick which would then produce a feeling of calm and satisfaction. Once we had established a relationship with a mother where she herself no longer looked for violence, it was then the job of the staff to effect a change in the relationship between the mother and her children.

The dormitory conditions provided a living experience of co-operation between families. I would oversee the mix of families to make sure that the 'heavy mob' did not organise themselves into one room and then dominate and terrorise the other members of the community. By ensuring a mix of those who were good physical copers with those who could not physically manage themselves and their children, we achieved a good atmosphere of people helping themselves and each other. The absence of rules imposed from outside meant that everyone had to pull their weight to keep the house in some sort of working order. For the community voted its own rules.

I had only two rules. The first was: no violence in the house. But if this rule was broken, I had no sanction, because the only sanction lay in the hands of the women. They were the only ones who were able to vote for a mother to be asked to leave. If they did vote this, it had to be unanimous, and it was also their responsibility to find a place for her to go. In my time voting out very rarely happened, but certainly it did occur. The house could also vote out a member of staff. I remember once wanting to get rid of a member of the play-group, but the house disagreed, so the staff member stayed.

My second rule was: no men in the house, other than male staff and professional visitors. This rule was introduced by the mothers themselves in 1973. Before then we had struggled with the idea of allowing men friends in to visit, because so many women were there for a year or more. But jealousies would break out, and women would go home and tell their husbands we were a 'knocking shop', which was totally untrue. Apart from anything else, there was no room to tie a shoelace, let alone make love. By this time I was well aware that some of the women were attempting to use the Refuge as an extra weapon in the war against their partners. And enticing a man inside in order to further excite the community was also intolerable.

On one 5 November, Guy Fawkes night, we organised a spectacular event for the children in the back garden. At the house-meeting it was voted that boyfriends could attend so that they too could 'share the joy of the children at the sight of exploding rockets and help them wave the sparklers in their little hands'. (They really thought I'd swallow that story.) All day the mothers worked in the kitchen to prepare food, and we all contributed to wine, beer and juice. The party went off without a hitch — but also without any sign of the boy-friends. As I was leaving at about 9 o'clock, I found the sitting-room full of men, all obviously waiting for the real party to begin.

Now I am well aware that most social institutions are designed to suppress any deviant behaviour. That is why they are singularly unable to change the behaviour and responses of the people who fill their beds. It would have been perfectly easy to have asked the men to leave; to tell them what they already knew, which is that they had missed the firework party. But I realised that this particular group of mothers had deliberately organised with their boyfriends a party that would take place after the children were in bed. So

I left thinking to myself that the next day's house-meeting would be hectic. It was.

Patsy, who usually manipulated from the wings and looked as though butter would not melt in her mouth, had gone for Gloria, who was the house bully, and had removed handfuls of Gloria's hair. The party itself never got off the ground, because the men, on witnessing these two women fighting, all fled. I was asked to climb to the top of the house and see the damage for myself. Sure enough, Gloria lay in bed feeling very sorry for herself, bald as a coot at the front of her head, and with handfuls of hair lying in a saucer beside her bed for my inspection. The ensuing house-meeting was one of the most constructive ever. It was a result of this incident that the house voted to keep all men out, except for male staff and business visitors. Alcohol was also voted out, though occasionally it was voted back. They usually voted it out again soon because we had too many heavy drinkers among the violence-prone families. And there was no point in 'breaking rules' for the thrill of it. If the community was self-determining, even the most determinedly deviant woman had to co-operate with the group or attract the group's displeasure.

We also had to tackle the problem of women who acted out their violence and released their feelings through rage; and those who released their feelings through attracting pain. An example of this behaviour occurred in the relationship between Jenny Moland and Patti. Jenny M was a vital, intelligent, energetic woman. She had a voice like a fog-horn, and a terrific sense of humour. The problem was that she totally refused to accept that she was violent. House-meeting after house-meeting there would be complaints that she had terrorised some poor soul with threats. 'If you don't fucking get your dinner eaten, I'll plaster you to the ceiling,' was her way of saying 'There's a love, eat your dinner quickly,' when she was on kitchen duty. It was impossible to get through to her about this. She had no idea of her aggressive behaviour — in her reality she did not actually hit anyone, therefore she was not violent. The fact that she was totally intimidating meant nothing to her. In her own background everyone behaved that way, and only those who actually lashed out were considered violent.

However, she met her match in Patti. Patti was a whinger. Women who keep themselves high on their own adrenalin are a bloody nuisance in that they tend to jack themselves up with deviant acts like shop-lifting and a lot of noisy behaviour. Yet I find them far easier to work with, because they externalise all their problems. It is the Pattis of this world, who turn all their rage and violence inwards, who prove far more difficult to treat. Patti never raised her voice but, where there was a violent scene, there you would find Patti. In house-meetings she would be seen virtuously wagging her finger at others and telling everyone about her good mothering, her immaculate children, and how life had ill-treated her when all she did was be a good and faithful wife.

Patti was the sort of woman everyone wanted to hit occasionally. If you did not have to live with Patti, I suppose you could be fooled by her, but for those of us who had to endure her, and other women like her, day by day, she was a terrible trial. If the whole community was going to have a football match, Patti would not join in. If we all decided to have a party, Patti would stay upstairs. If we were singing, she would sit there looking mournful. If the play-staff were organising an expedition for the children, she would refuse to let hers go. She talked about herself incessantly. In a house-meeting, it would take only a few minutes before Patti drew the discussion round to herself. If she was reprimanded, she would shake. If shaking did not get her anywhere, she'd cry. If crying did not get her anywhere, she would leave the room, only to burst in again demanding attention. But she met her match in Jenny.

People tended to avoid Jenny Moland when she had had a few drinks. She was usually quite amicable, but experience with violent families teaches you to treat with caution, anyone who has a hair-trigger temper and a few drinks inside them, unless you are looking for trouble. Patti was looking for trouble. So she stood in front of Jenny Moland, wagging her finger at her, and holding forth on her own virtuous avoidance of alcohol. Jenny, maddened beyond endurance by the monologue and the finger-wagging, leaned forward and bit off the top of it. Patti was taken off to hospital and duly bandaged, and I was confronted with a severely shaken and overhung Jenny in the Refuge the next morning. She expected me to be angry, but I only wanted her to acknowledge that even she would have to agree that biting off the top of someone's finger was the act of a violent person.

I explained that they were both equally violent people, it was just that they expressed their violence differently. Jenny was sufficiently shaken by her own behaviour to be able to begin to admit that she was violent. That event changed her whole perspective of herself. 'What happened to the top of the finger?' I enquired. 'Don't know,' said Jenny, green with her hangover. 'You probably swallowed it,' I said. Jenny heaved and bolted past me for the lavatory. After this she used her energy positively. She became an active member of the building team that repaired the various properties. She also was known affectionately as 'Jaws' by everyone. Eventually, she moved out into her own flat and is happily remarried. On the other hand, we never got through to Patti. She left us vowing her innocence. Her kind of violent behaviour is very commonly practised by both men and women.

People who are addicted to their own adrenalin from early childhood choose outgoing methods of externalising their damage. As soon as they are irritated by some event they go into a rage and then seek a climax in explosion. But there are other people addicted to their cortisone — the chemical in the body which should balance the adrenalin. When the cortisone level shoots up in response to an event, then the cortisone personality will *im*plode. In other words they internalise their damage. Watching women in a housemeeting you can clearly see those that yell and scream if they are very angry, and then sit back satisfied, having got it off their chests. There are those, too, who cry and shake with silent fury. But they do not get any relief, and they will be the ones to suffer migraines, asthma, hay-fever, eczema, so-called epileptic fits, and any of the other stress diseases. The adrenalin users will pay a different price for their aggressive rage, because they tend to suffer from hypertension and heart diseases. Children exhibit the same symptoms, too, depending on their way of expressing rage.

All these people trooping through my door came with bottles full of pills to treat the symptoms of violence. In my experience of dealing with these families, I must have seen several hundreds of women and children diagnosed as epileptic. I would always have them taken to hospital for an EEG. They were not epileptic; the pills to control their fits were unnecessary. They threw fits because of an inability to express emotions. Once they were able to ventilate their rage the fits disappeared. Certainly I accept there are medical conditions that require medical treatment for all the above diseases, but stress diseases are too often dismissed by the medical profession as purely physical, when in fact they are symptoms of internal emotional and chemical upheaval. Pills are merely bandages over gaping wounds. Fifty years ago, Freud said that all emotions will be found in the chemicals of the brain. Now in the 1980s, with the discovery of the enkephalins, which are the body's own pain inhibitors, and of the opioid-peptides, which are the body's own opium, it looks as though he was right.*

Probably, in the future, it will be found that a child is affected by the mother's emotions and chemical reaction to those emotions from the moment of conception. For myself, and particularly through my discussions and work with Jeff, I began to formulate a theory that maternal bonding, which is a necessary biological link between a mother and baby to ensure its survival, is also a chemical bonding. However, where the child's natural development has been disturbed by the parents' own violent and incestuous needs, the bonding turns to addiction.

I came to this rather odd conclusion because I had watched so many thousands of men and women totally unable to leave what was in fact a truly dreadful and painful relationship. On one level I could understand it in emotional terms: I could understand the intensity of a violent relationship, the passion and the excitement. But I also knew the degradation, the physical abuse, the self-loathing that the people in those violent relationships expressed about themselves. I also spent many years visiting refuges in Europe, in New Zealand, and

*See Chapter Six.

all over America. It is the same everywhere. I remember speaking to an audience in the American Mid-West. I had just finished talking about the 'high' of a violent relationship, when I noticed a woman six rows in front of me. Her eyes were full of tears. '*You* know what I am talking about,' I said to her. She nodded. 'I'm married,' she said, 'for a second time, to a man who loves me, who is so kind to me.' 'But you miss the high,' I said. She nodded. It wasn't the man she missed, it was the addiction. I thought about that for a long time.

Women came in, pregnant with babies that did not move, afraid that the babies were dead. They weren't dead; but the babies seemed aware of the danger to themselves, so they stayed still. In violence-prone families these babies are born to women who have no mothering skills at all. They are very rarely breast-fed, and if they are handled at all, they are treated roughly. If a baby cries in an emotionally able family, the cry will usually arouse in the breast of the parent pity and compassion and an urge to comfort and protect. In an emotionally disabled family, the cry of a baby arouses rage and resentment and the urge to destroy. This is why you get such horrific injuries inflicted on young children. The cry of a loved baby in distress is also quite different from the cry of an already neglected baby in a violent family. It is interesting to see even ordinary non-violent people react in a hostile fashion to the disturbed cry of a baby who expects pain from contact with adults.

I began explaining to such women that their need for violence was no different from a drug addict's for his needle, or an alcoholic's need for his bottle. Hopefully, a happy, loved baby would eventually grow up to express emotional and sexual pleasure in making love with another human being. However, where a baby knew only pain and betrayal, that child would grow up to find its sexual and emotional goal in various deviant and painful outlets. I used to draw a little diagram like the one opposite.

Then I would ask a man or woman, or a teenager, where applicable, to tell me where they found themselves on that chart. Women usually identified themselves in pain, and their men in rage. We would discuss how deadly that com-

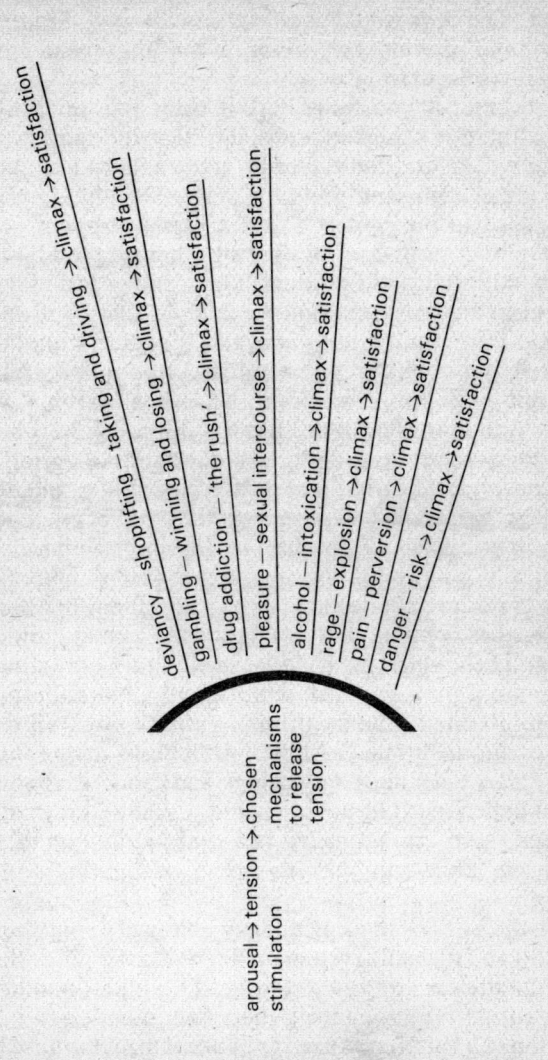

deviancy — shoplifting — taking and driving →climax →satisfaction
gambling — winning and losing →climax →satisfaction
drug addiction — 'the rush' →climax →satisfaction
pleasure — sexual intercourse →climax →satisfaction
alcohol — intoxication →climax →satisfaction
rage — explosion →climax →satisfaction
pain — perversion →climax →satisfaction
danger — risk →climax →satisfaction

arousal →tension →chosen
stimulation   mechanisms
              to release
              tension

bination was because the escalation could lead to death. Teenage girls would tend to choose shop-lifting because of the excitement. In fact they would describe the thrill as a climax. The boys would usually choose danger, for instance taking and driving away cars, when they would often ejaculate while driving away.

Of course, if you translate this chart into middle-class terms, there is a higher probability that the same type of people would find more socially acceptable and rewarding methods of achieving the same goals. Shop-lifting can be transposed to the climactic thrill of asset-stripping, which effectively destroys and steals away other people's jobs and livelihoods. A violent policeman or member of the armed forces can legitimise his violence in a way that a wife-beater cannot. Taking and driving away cars is a crime, while killing yourself and others on a racing-track is acceptable. Asking for pain is seen as masochism, while boxing is a popular sport. And how many women can confirm the overt hatred and violence they have endured at the hands of doctors and surgeons, particularly some gynaecologists. In talking to middle-class people I merely adjust the terms of reference.

If you accept, as we do, that you are both emotionally and chemically bonded to your parenting, then it becomes so much easier to understand your own addiction. In a healthy family, that bonding plays its part while a child grows and learns. Then, when the child is ready to turn outwards, the bonds are slowly loosened, while the parents readjust their lives to use their time for themselves and enjoy their future with each other. The child meanwhile seeks to recreate the good, warm, loving relationships and home environment that it experienced in its own home. Usually, this child will succeed. An emotionally and chemically synthesised maturing adult will seek the same relationship with its partner.

On the whole, the emotionally able will avoid the discomfort and turmoil of the emotionally disabled. If by chance they do attempt to form a relationship with an emotionally disabled person, they will then find themselves in the position of a battered woman or battered man. Confused and bewildered, they continually misunderstand the messages they get from their partners. It is very rare that they can actually do very much to change their partner. If their partner will not seek help, their best bet is to get out before children are born and they become the unwitting parents of another generation of damage.

Children born into violent homes will usually express the violence and betrayal of their childhood according to how it personally affects them, their position in the family, and their genetic inheritance. Instead of flowing with the warmth and the love of a happy family, they have had to survive against the violent and often incestuous onslaughts of their parents. Violent and incestuous families do not let each other go. The parents take little pleasure in each other's company, and use one or all of the children in the highly complex emotional theatre and battleground of the family. Betrayal is the key word in these families. Betrayed parents in turn betray their children. They rob them of their childhoods. They exploit them physically. They exploit them emotionally. They keep them on edge in a jealous rage for attention. Then when the children do finally break away, the rest of their lives are spent in reaction against their parents.

Should a girl from a non-violent home marry a boy from such a family, the chances are that no amount of reassurance will ever convince him that she will be faithful to him. That primary betrayal of a faithless or promiscuous mother will make him morbidly jealous for life. His only hope is that he can find someone who can help him not only to come to terms emotionally with the damage, but also to be able to identify the moment when an event can trigger a chemical reaction in him that sets off the emotion of jealousy, and then to relate it to the past, not the present. Sometimes it can be a smell, a perfume, an inflection in a voice, which can stimulate the feelings of betrayal, and bring the rage flooding back into the present. He then behaves in such a way that it is out of proportion with the current event.

Unfortunately, so far, very little work has been done in this field in Britain, where there is noticeable resistance to any attempt to understand why human beings behave as they do. In other countries where I lecture, I find a great deal of interest and research going on.

ONE PERSON

Where the children leave violent families in an attempt to create a happy and loving relationship that they were unable to find in their own circle, they are largely doomed to disaster. Because they have not been able to emotionally and chemically synthesise their personalities, they tend to look for a partner who will fulfil their bad and damaged needs. This drawing done by Eunice when she went back to Gerald (Chapter Four) perfectly describes what happens. They have a symbiotic relationship where they perfectly meet each other's worst needs. The adrenalin personality finds the cortisone. The exploder meets the imploder. The sadist finds the masochist.

Only the ignorant ignore the fact that there are many men who ask for pain and instead insist it is totally a woman's condition. It is time to say that more boys are physically battered than girls, and then tend to become batterers in their adult life, whereas girls tend to be emotionally violated, internalising pain and suffering. On the surface, it often looks as though the dominant partner holds the power. Actually, in my experience this is very rarely true. Usually the adrenalin personality has the drive, the creativity and the energy which seems to be a by-product of violence and chaos. Indeed if you study the lives of world-famous leaders and artists and musicians, a high proportion of them were violent people.

The cortisone personality, on the other hand, is usually structured and seeks to impose that structure on its partner and to feed off their adrenalin. You will often see a couple where only one of them is gifted and creative. Certainly it is true of famous couples in history that people will say 'Why on earth is he/she with that awful woman/man?' The answer is that the chaotic adrenalin personality is looking for structure because they were given none in childhood. The cortisone personality is trying to feed off the adrenalin of their partner, because they adopted structure as a method of survival in childhood. Either way it leads to various levels of disaster.

Jeff and I attempted to get a dialogue going concerning violence-prone families through the pages of *New Society*, but we had almost no positive response. The description of adrenalin personalities was rewritten by a biochemist who, fortunately knew and approved of our work. This article appears as Appendix B. We were roundly attacked by various women's groups who insisted that all women were victims, and we were also plagued by male journalists who again argued that they had always known that women both liked being beaten and deserved it. The problem is that when you publicly discuss a social problem, the people you tend to hear from are those who suffer from it. For example the violent women will furiously deny their violence under the guise of victim, and the violent men will defend their need to beat and torture women under the banner of 'They like it'. Either way, those people to whom the world of the emotionally disabled is completely foreign go along their own path occasionally muttering 'But surely not' when they read about a mother battering her child, or they put a donation in the post to the NSPCC or – less likely – to us. What we say is uncomfortable for people to hear.

The time has now come, however, for everyone to take notice. For the last thirty years there have been no wars to clear off our violent men. There have been no shipments of children from children's homes to Canada or Australia since 1949. The social order is rapidly breaking down. Our jails are full to bursting. Our mental hospitals can no longer cope. The cost of taking children into care is prohibitive, and now it is officially accepted that institutional care for children has bred several generations of sociopaths. The violence that has for so long been contained behind the family front doors has now finally erupted onto the streets.

The western world is now paying the price for the dream of our Industrial Revolution that would free man from the enslavement of the soil. A hundred years have been spent in fulfilling that dream. All man's ingenuity and gifts have been poured into machines and into the fields of the sciences. We have all benefited immeasureably from improvements in housing, hygiene, medicine, and standards of health. But in the race for advanced technology we have lost sight of our essentially spiritual natures. Hopefully as we create a new micro-chip technology that will free us from the enslavement of machines, we will be able to devote the next decade to exploring and understanding our own inner world. All human beings need to love and be loved. Every child has the right to its childhood, and we are all responsible, both within our own family life and as regards other less fortunate families, to see that those rights of children are protected.

The eighties will be a time when the Western world must address itself to the question of the future of the family. We must publicly declare the role of parenting as the most valuable contribution a human being can perform on this earth. To split an atom is but a minor miracle compared to the birth of a child. To walk on the moon is a feat of technology that cannot hold a candle to the miracle of conception. Both Jeff and I look forward to the next two decades with a great deal of hope. We believe that as a result of all the excellent work being done here in Britain, and all over the world, new findings will make it possible to treat emotionally disabled people with love and understanding. We hope that the old primitive institutions will be seen as obsolete, and that in their place there will be established warm, accepting community care for those who need sanctuary and refuge to heal their inner worlds.

Chapter Six

IS IT ALL IN THE CHEMICALS?

For centuries scientists and philosophers have predicted that some day we would understand all emotions and thoughts in terms of the chemicals of the brain. We already quote chemicals to describe feelings in everyday speech. When two people feel an attraction for each other, we say, 'There's a certain chemistry between them.' When a relationship breaks up, we say, 'It will take some time to get him/her out of my system.' On a purely physical level, when the brain works in a thought or an emotion or a pattern of behaviour, there is not only a series of electrical impulses, but also a wave of chemicals among the brain cells and throughout the body.

Recent work in America shows that when a person feels pleasure, a rush of warm happiness, they experience a chemical called the 'opioid-peptide', the body's own opium. Everyone needs to feel this happiness, but we do not feel it automatically in response to circumstances; we are trained by our early childhoods in which situations we feel pleasure and in which situations we feel pain. In a healthy, warm, loving family where a baby feels safe and secure, the child produces its own opium and feels pleasure and happiness in response to warm, loving situations — when it is held in its parents' arms, when it is nurtured, kissed, and cuddled.

An emotionally disabled, violent* family is not a safe place for a baby; the baby is in a state of almost constant alarm and danger, for at any time it may see its parents screaming at or hitting each other, and at any time the baby itself may be screamed at or hit. The baby is often neglected: left untouched and unfed. In such families a baby cannot learn to feel happiness in peace and safety and love, because there is no such thing as safe loving in that situation. Any moment of affection can suddenly switch to a scene of anger and violence. The baby is born into living on the knife-edge, where danger stands a step behind any kind word or gesture. It is our understanding that in this state of perpetual high-arousal a baby learns to attach its feelings of pleasure or satisfaction to the only situation regularly available — situations of danger and pain. The experience of pleasure and pain become emotionally and chemically crossed, so that as the baby grows, it feels uncomfortable in what we would all commonly agree are pleasant circumstances, and it feels its satisfaction, the opioid state, that warm rush of the opioid-peptide, in what we would all call pain.

The crossing of pleasure and pain can be seen very clearly in Chapter Three in the case of Frieda's baby Joss. Having been raised in an atmosphere in which he was always exposed to physical and emotional danger, Joss felt extreme satisfaction in the receiving of sharp pain. When Frieda pricked him with a nappy-pin, Joss gurgled and cooed. We believe that this chemical pattern quickly develops into an actual addiction, so that in its addictive need to renew its opioid state, a baby grows to create situations of pain to feel its satisfaction. In Chapter Three, you saw how baby Michael in the peace of Erin's home, simply could not stand the absence of pain. To find his own womb-like satisfaction, he clawed at his stomach until it bled. On the other hand, when Michael was put into the pleasant situation of a warm bath, the warm water seemed to hurt him, as acid would hurt a healthy baby who had not become addicted to pain and violence.

In the extreme cases of this addiction, we believe a baby can become autistic. In the past, the cause of autism has been regarded as a mystery. It seems possible to us, however, that

---

*It is important to restate that violence can be emotional as well as physical, and that violence occurs in all economic classes of society, although middle-class violence tends to be emotional for the most part. The workings of middle-class violence are so sophisticated that the subject deserves a book all to itself. Indeed, middle-class emotional violence, like incest, will be the subject of one of our books in the future. For the purposes of this present book, it must be understood that we see emotional violence and emotional (non-physical) incest as just as, if not more, soul-destroying as physical abuse. All that we have to say about the emotional and chemical addiction to pain certainly relates directly to emotional violence, too.

a certain form of autism is simply a state in which an infant has become so addicted to pain, and so unable to tolerate pleasure, that it shuts off from the rest of the world and lives in the warm, womb-like world of self-inflicted pain. In its pain, it feels the glow of the opioid state and has found its own kind of happiness.

It is not surprising that babies can become addicted to violence so young, for we believe that in years to come, medical research will prove that addiction begins while the baby is in its mother's womb. When the baby is in the womb, the placenta separates the mother's and the baby's bloodstreams, for each has its own heartbeat. Still the placenta does allow chemicals to flow freely between the two bloodstreams. Because of this, chemicals in the blood are shared between mother and child. Medical science has already proved that if the mother injects herself with heroin while pregnant, her baby may be born a heroin addict. We believe that, likewise, a mother who is chemically addicted to violence will share these chemicals with her unborn child, and the baby will be born with the same addiction to violence and pain.

Being in the womb is the absolute opioid state for a baby. We asked ourselves why a strong and healthy baby in the womb does not injure its mother with its kicks. The answer would be that the baby is heavily opiated. In this opioid state, a baby feels total contentment, as if all its wishes have already been fulfilled. There is no motivation to move or to act or to change its state, because change would only mean a step away from contentment.

In the womb, the baby experiences not only this opioid state, but also, as its brain and nervous system develop, it learns which chemicals are associated with this happiness. In a healthy non-violent family, a pregnant woman is given VIP treatment. The people around her try as far as possible to make her life calm and restful. If she is relaxed, the chemicals of quiet happiness flow through her, and through her baby. By the time the baby is born, it already knows peace.

In violent families, on the other hand, great scenes of drama and anger often surround a pregnancy. The baby is often unwanted, and its conception is not celebrated with love but punished or attended by screams and fights. Many women coming into the Refuge describe how they were beaten during their pregnancies. To the baby in the womb, then, the chemicals of high-arousal and danger experienced by the pregnant mother rush into the baby's newly-forming bloodstream and brain-cells. The chemicals of high-arousal impose themselves on the baby's opioid sleep, and pain has already become intertwined with its happiness, and satisfaction.

Babies resulting from this sort of pregnancy are often born extremely tense and anxious, addicted to a state of high arousal. In some cases, even life in the womb becomes simply too painful. The baby then opts out of life, and slips into the ultimate opioid state where no movement or effort is necessary, the deepest of sleeps — death. Among the violent families that we treat, there is an extraordinarily high incidence of miscarriages, stillbirths, and cot-deaths — all are ways in which a baby chooses the peace of death over the pain of life.

The emotionally disabled families that we treat are, then, truly prone to violence. In fact, they are deeply addicted to violence. As mentioned before, this does not include the genuine battered wife who accidentally finds herself in a violent relationship, and who, with proper support, can get out and form happy loving relationships elsewhere. But our truly violence-prone women have themselves inevitably come from violent families.

Everyone learns what happiness is in their childhood, and then seeks to recreate a similar happiness in later life, and in future relationships. Warm loving families produce children who can be happy in gentleness and affection, and who will go on to recreate that warmth in families of their own. In emotionally disabled families, children are reared in danger, even from the moment of conception, and have learned no satisfaction other than the high arousal of violent situations. Chemically they are addicted to situations of pain in order to feel the warm satisfaction of the opioid state.

In a violent relationship, a man and a woman find the violent sort of satisfaction that they learned in childhood. When there is a violent explosion between the two, somewhere behind the dramatic climax, behind the rage and the screams, the partners have stirred their own chemicals to such an extent that the opioid state has been reached, and that quiet peace inside every person has been found.

We were once talking to a man, himself the victim of a battered childhood, who had attempted to strangle his wife. Tension between the pair had been mounting for weeks. Finally, when he felt pushed beyond endurance, he jumped on her and began to strangle her until she started to pass out. He then stood up, walked away, and went to bed. 'You know, it's funny,' he explained to us, 'I slept like a baby that night. Best night of sleep I had in weeks.' 'That's because it was the best orgasm you experienced,' Erin told him. 'You're right,' he said. And she was right. We all learn to climax differently. In his rage, he found release. That moment of anger brought him deep peace: the opioid state he had experienced in childhood.

We then had to ask ourselves why his wife had needed to get herself strangled. Why did she need to push him beyond his boiling point, so that he would explode and give her pain? It is far too easy and flippant an answer to say that women stay in battering relationships 'because they like it', or 'because they want it', or 'because they deserve it'.

A violence-prone woman can tell you in all honesty that she really does want to get away, and does not want any more violent relationships. Yet she then often goes straight back to her violent partner, or to an equally violent man. At the time though, she is not lying. On one level, an intellectual level, she means what she says: she desperately wants to get out. But on another level, the chemical level, she is powerfully addicted to the amount of violence in their relationship, and cannot help but go back to it. Having been reared on violence, she will only feel *alive* and satisfied in a situation of great danger, so she often deliberately provokes a man to the point where he will hit her. Then in her pain she returns to her quiet and peaceful inner-womb of the opioid state.

The grave danger in these relationships is that since pleasure is found through pain, the ultimate orgasm is death. To die would be to return to the ultimate opioid sleep of the womb. There is a great deal of well-documented evidence describing how a person on the verge of drowning or freezing to death suddenly feels a great surge of physical warmth and a deep feeling of well-being and bliss. This is the opioid state. When imbalanced in the body, the happiness chemical becomes the chemical of death.

For violence-prone people, this end of happiness or satisfaction is sought through the means learned in childhood — pain and danger. We have seen many 'till death us do part' relationships, where it is obvious that one or other of the partners *must* die if the relationship is to reach its climax. If you ask a person from a non-violent family how they see themselves dying, they will probably describe some death-bed scene where the aged, having lived a full life, passes away quietly in his sleep. In violent families, however, children grow up with death as a constant companion. They are reared on the language of death – 'One of these days, I'll fucking kill you,' – and, with violence all round, death becomes a very real and ever-present possibility. Therefore if you ask a violence-prone person how they see themselves dying, they will usually confess that indeed they fantasise about death often, and that they expect to die young in some gruesome and violent way.

Seeking that final opioid state, violence-prone people often steer their ways definitely towards their imagined violent deaths. Eunice sees herself finally found hacked to bits in Epping Forest. As described in Chapter Four, she has chosen for herself a man who regularly and ritualistically slashes and mutilates her. Caroline, also in Chapter Four, imagines she will be found dismembered in a black plastic bag. In pursuit of this end, she has become a prostitute working the rough trade, and indeed, bits of her two best friends have already been found in black bags. Brenda describes in Chapter Four how, when there was an axeman loose in her neighbourhood, she waited nightly for him at the front door, imagining precisely where his axe would fall on her waiting neck.

Bobby was four years old when he came to us. He had been beaten by both parents since birth, and his mother continued to beat him in the Refuge. We worked hard with his mother, and soon helped her to stop beating Bobby. Once she had stopped, however, we suddenly noticed horrible burns all over Bobby's hands. We asked him how he got them. 'I burn myself with Mummy's fag when she isn't looking,' he said, smiling. He was already so addicted to pain, that when his mother stopped hitting him, he needed to inflict pain on himself to maintain his opioid state of satisfaction.

As you read in Chapter Four, before going back to her husband (who had already pushed her out of a 30-foot window), Sarah predicted that there was a ninety per cent chance that her husband would kill her. 'But why do you need to go back?' Erin asked her. 'Because we love each other,' she answered. In the world where she had been a child, in a horribly violent family, love was hopelessly intertwined with pain. For her, the ultimate expression of love seemed to be a violent and painful death.

In working with a woman like Sarah we are trying to reverse a chemical process that has been going on since conception. We attempt to uncross pleasure and pain so that happiness may be felt in situations of love and pleasure, and so that pain is no longer the ultimate happy state leading to death. The first step in this treatment is to separate love from pain. When a woman explains that she is going back to a battering husband 'because he loves me', we firmly remind her that people do not hurt the people they truly love. She only *thinks* he loves her, because that is the only sort of love she has ever received. 'It's not love. It's addiction', we tell her. 'Every time you see him, think of him as a hypodermic needle, about to inject you with the pain you're addicted to.'

Along with this uncrossing of *pleasure* and *pain*, the most important part of treatment is to show the violence-prone person genuine, unselfish pleasurable love. Most of our women have never known real loving, for in their childhood the idea of love became horribly crossed with violence. You can only change a person by loving them. Women's Aid has always been designed as a community in which genuine love engulfs the mothers and children.

Through this love, a great deal of change took place in Ellen, as described in Chapter Four. When she first came to us, Ellen was as frantic as a wild animal. She described to Jeff how she would walk down alley-ways alone at night with a knife in her pocket, hoping to meet up with the man who was, at the time, killing and dismembering people. She was waiting to die. Fortunately, she was gifted with great intelligence, and through the love and work of the community, she is now a calm and good mother, and is happy in a steady relationship with a gentle and loving man. It is the joy of helping a woman like Ellen that lets us continue our work. Ellen was able to break her own addiction.

In coming to understand the addiction that emotionally disabled people feel to violence, and to each other, we arrived at a very important emotional and chemical distinction. Why is it, we asked ourselves, that some people (both men and women) derive pleasure through inflicting pain, and other people (both men and women) derive pleasure through receiving pain? Why do some people need to explode in rage, while others need to provoke their partners to make them explode with rage? What holds together the relationship between aggressor and victim? We found what we believe to be the answer to these questions in two different chemicals that the body produces in response to situations of danger: adrenalin and cortisone.

Adrenalin* is basically the body's own activating chemical. In times of emergency, adrenalin gives a person strength beyond their usual powers, creating drive and energy. In dangerous situations, adrenalin activates the fight-or-flight mechanism, energising a person either to run effectively or to fight with great strength and aggression. Whereas adrenalin makes a person active, cortisone, on the other hand, renders a person passive. In the body cortisone inhibits energy, preventing blood vessels from opening wide, thereby limiting how much energising blood can flow. In a cortisone response to danger, a person neither flees nor fights; they adopt the animal strategy of camouflage, or 'playing possum' – playing dead.

Coming from a violent childhood, a person addicted to pain learns to achieve satisfaction either through the adrenalin-role of giving pain, or through the cortisone-role of

---

*We use the word 'adrenalin' in our layman's terms, to include both adrenalin and nor-adrenalin.

We look forward to future research in this field to discover the precise chemical workings that lie behind human behaviour.

receiving pain. Both roles are equally violent, for the cortisone-personality and the adrenalin-personality are the two opposite sides of the one coin of violence.

Although in a violent relationship it is often true that the man assumes the adrenalin role of aggressor while the women acts as the cortisone-type victim, this is by no means always the case. We all know of many couples where the apparently meek man is tongue-lashed into submission by the domineering wife. It is interesting to note that the cortisone role is often a much more powerful position. We notice, particularly where the violence-prone woman provokes her partner to violence, that the explosive partner is very straightforward; if pushed too far, he will erupt. The chronic victim, however, holds the control, for she knows how to manipulate her man, how to press the right buttons, so that he will explode.

Naturally, everyone has some of both chemicals in them, and it is impossible to say that a person is strictly an 'adrenalin personality' or strictly a 'cortisone personality'. We often rely on one chemical in one situation and on the other in other circumstances, and with respect to other relationships. In an office, for example, the boss may take the adrenalin role by bullying the sales director. Turning from the cortisone submissive role to the adrenalin aggressive role, the sales director bullies the public relations director and so on down the rungs of the office ladder of power.

Neither of us is a biochemist. It seems likely that chemical occurrences in the body are actually a series of reactions far more intricate than this broad distinction could adequately describe. Still, our layman's distinction between adrenalin personalities and cortisone personalities seems valid and extremely important. In the future we hope to see research carried out in the fields of biochemistry, pharmacology and neurophysics to work out the specific chemical mechanisms of these emotional and behavioural interactions.

The emotionally able can switch in a balanced way from one chemical to the other, as the situation necessitates. The emotionally disabled, however, are locked for the most part into one role or the other. Although the parts they play will differ to some degree from situation to situation, it is still possible to look from an overview and see which side of the giving and receiving of pain they usually stand on, especially in the context of a given relationship.

What makes a violent relationship so difficult to break is that there is usually a perfect lock-and-key fit between one partner's addiction to adrenalin and the other partner's addiction to cortisone. In the case of Eunice and Gerald (as described in Chapter Four), Gerald can only climax in the acting out of rage, while Eunice can only climax while receiving pain.

In their sessions of mutilation, Gerald's adrenalin level is pushed up to a satisfying level by watching Eunice be passive and helpless as she is being slashed. Eunice, on the other hand, needs Gerald's high level of rage for her to reach a satisfying level of cortisone. Their different paths of adrenalin and cortisone are means to the same end — the satisfaction of the opioid state. Gerald, from his childhood, learned to achieve 'happiness' or satisfaction – to stimulate his own opium – by pumping adrenalin through his system in aggressive behaviour. Eunice learned through her horribly molested childhood to find 'happiness' by having cortisone rushed through her body in the submissive receiving of pain. Both their addictions feed into each other in a deadly vicious circle.

In the healthy person, a balance exists between the levels of adrenalin and cortisone. Among the emotionally disabled, there is no balance, only addiction. Although there is no such thing as balance *within* emotionally disabled people, they can find an external balance with a partner who has the addiction opposite to their own. In Eunice's drawings of what it was like to see Gerald again (see page 162), she drew them together as sharing a common bloodstream. She labelled the drawing 'One Person'. She was right, because between the two of them, their addiction forms one system in equilibrium. The problem here is that when a relationship is formed out of mutual addiction, its ultimate goal is death – since that is the aim of the addiction to violence.

For a person to be whole, they must have balance in themselves. However, this balance can grow only out of a loving family in which a child has the freedom and encouragement to develop a strong independent central sense of self. It is this independence that allows a person to be a choosing self, choosing its chemicals and its reactions to situations. Without this central sense of self, a person does not choose to act, but only *reacts* as a helpless slave to his or her chemistry. A person then lives on an unthinking animal level instead of on a consciously choosing human level.

The problem with emotionally violent families is that children are never given the time, nor the peace, nor the love, nor the support necessary to develop a sense of self to thus gain their independence. Instead, growing up in fear and danger, the children develop a shell of behaviours learned as survival techniques. They 'make themselves up', while the real person inside the shell shrinks and shrivels. They become unconscious puppets to the chemicals in their own brain, and since they cannot choose, they become prone to addiction.

In the emotionally disabled person's addiction to violence, whether he learns the role of adrenalin-aggressor or cortisone-victim, he is first addicted to the family. In the intensity and passion of family violence, every member of the family acts as each other's hypodermics, keeping each other high on their chemicals of violence. That is why a violent family holds on to its members so tightly, and often excludes the outside world — because the members are addicted to each other.

When the children do go on to form relationships of their own, the relationships they form are not real relationships between choosing people. Instead, they are merely the replacement of one mechanism for satisfying an addiction, with another. In this new relationship, the emotionally disabled merely recreate their past into the future.

We believe that this fundamental addiction to reaching the opioid-state through pain lies behind other addictions that have in the past been regarded as entirely separate syndromes. We see addictions such as drug abuse, alcoholism, and compulsive gambling all as branches of the same tree. Those branches are merely different mechanisms to trigger off either the adrenalin or cortisone necessary for the emotionally disabled to reach the opioid state, and they all arise from the original bonding to pain in early childhood. The addiction to pain is therefore the addiction behind the addictions.

Rupert, who comes from a middle-class family, and had been diagnosed as a heroin addict, was talking to us about his mother and about his use of drugs. His mother is a loud, hysterical, aggressive, adrenalin-high woman, and Rupert was strongly addicted to the pain that her hysterical fits inflicted upon him. He did not use drugs when he was anywhere near his mother; he did not have to. She was a satisfying enough drug in herself. In her absence, Rupert would shoot up with heroin. He described to us the feeling of shooting up: 'First there's this really fast rush, and then I feel this great happy warmth coming all over me.'

That is his perspective of the experience. The heroin brings him into the same opioid state as his mother's hysterics. Interestingly enough, Rupert's girlfriend described his use of heroin from her perspective. She said that when Rupert is high, he behaves like a stubborn and naughty little boy. Exactly. In the arms of his drug, his mother's substitute, he becomes the little boy who knows how to provoke an explosive mother.

Without a strong central sense of self, Rupert and other emotionally disabled people spend their lives in reaction to their past, not in independent and positive action for their future. For a sense of self to develop, another chemical is called into play. Work from America shows this chemical to be the anti-opioid. Whereas the opioid-peptide creates such a strong sense of contentment in inertia that there is no motivation for effort or movement, the anti-opioid is an activating chemical which is triggered off in states of necessary pain.

The early part of a baby's life consists of a series of painful events which are absolutely necessary if the child is ever to separate from the parents and to lead an independent life of its own. First the baby must leave the womb and take its first lungful of air. Next the baby experiences the pain of hunger. The baby is then forced to further leave the opioid state of comfortable sleep as teething pains set in. These vital pains force the baby to chew in an attempt to ease the pain. The baby then faces the separation pain of being weaned from the mother's breast or from the bottle, and has to learn to manage with more solid foods.

All of these pains rouse the baby from complacent opioid stages and force it to learn more new techniques through which to live. Therefore the anti-opioid state, triggered off by healthy pain, is a learning state, and is vital in the development of an independent self. The Buddhists say that one learns only through pain. Indeed, they are correct. But this is true only in a healthy family environment, where the parents love and support the child enough for the pain to be made positive, as the parents try their best to ease the child's pain.

In the emotionally disabled family, however, the babies are already so addicted to emotional and physical pain that these necessary growing-pains do not rouse them from a healthy opioid state and make them learn and become independent. These pains do not trigger off the anti-opioid chemical; they serve only to reinforce the addiction to the opioid state derived through pain. Without enough of this vital anti-opioid to balance with the opioid-peptide, the emotionally disabled person remains prone to addictions, and lives without an independent sense of self.

We all know of people who learn from painful experiences, and others who are doomed to repeat their mistakes again and again. The chances are that the person who *learns* came from a healthy family, and has a strong enough choosing sense of self to endure the anti-opioid state aroused by the painful experience, and can go on to learn. What emotionally able people like this have achieved is the ability to synthesise and to integrate most parts of their personalities, as well as their chemicals, so that their strong *self* chooses their behaviour. Our less fortunate friend, however, who always seems to be in the same trouble, is addicted to the opioid state that pain brings him, and does not have the anti-opioid facility to sit back and change his behaviour.

The ideas of addiction to the opioid state found in pain, and of the addiction to adrenalin or cortisone as means to attaining the opioid state, have wide and powerful implications in many fields of social service. In the realm of medicine, many diseases can be seen as expressions of adrenalin and cortisone addiction.

The adrenalin-aggressive personality is prone to diseases that result from the body's operating in an adrenalin-high state of constant arousal. Such personalities often suffer from heart conditions, high blood-pressure, and hyperactivity. The stomach is in such a state of perpetual activation that the stomach acids begin to eat away at the stomach walls, and peptic ulcers often result. In short, adrenalin-related symptoms and diseases occur when the body has been so overworked that bits of the body wear out and can no longer stand the strain.

Cortisone-related symptoms and diseases work in just the opposite way. Instead of resulting in over-activation of the body, cortisone-related diseases immobilise the body, making it less able to operate. We believe that cortisone-related diseases include migraines, epilepsy, narcolepsy eczema, allergies, anemia, rheumatoid arthritis, anorexia, obesity, fainting spells, hysterical paralysis, and cancer. Medical research has already proved that when cortisone appears in excessive amounts in the body, tumours are quick to form. We believe that excessive cortisone also keeps a body from maturing. You can see this in bodies that apparently refuse to grow, or remain androgynous and will not sprout fully into womanhood or manhood. If a person is chemically addicted to a childlike, dependent, inactive, opioid state, how can his or her body develop and function fully?

Think how many people we all know who display these cortisone symptoms. It is likely that these people will be the sort who turn all their anger and pain inwards in typical cortisone-personality fashion. Our more aggressive friends, however, who explode in anger when faced with any difficult situation, tend to be the adrenalin-type, prone to adrenalin-related diseases.

Diabetes appears to be a very interesting case. Although it seems to occur mostly among adrenalin-personalities, the nature of diabetes would seem to be cortisone-related, for the disease immobilises the body by rendering it unable to metabolise energy-giving sugar. Through personal observation, we believe diabetes to be a carry-over from a submissive response to an aggressively incestuous parent. Although the child may grow to become an overtly aggressive adrenalin-type, part of that person remains forever responding with cortisone to the parent's adrenalin overtures.

Genetic inheritance is often cited by doctors as the cause for diabetes, as it is for heart diseases, migraines, epilepsy, allergies, and even cancer. We believe however, that these adrenalin and cortisone-related diseases are not directly inherited. It makes sense to acknowledge that there can be a genetic predisposition or susceptibility to any of these diseases. Whether or not a person grows to actually display a disease then depends upon how he learns, in his childhood, to deal with pain and anger; whether or not he is addicted to the opioid-peptide — the addiction behind the addictions, the disease behind the diseases.*

Our understanding of these medical conditions comes from personal observation through ten years of work with emotionally disabled families. We are extremely anxious for medical research to continue in its study of the causes of all these diseases. We hope that some day patients suffering from these adrenalin- and cortisone-related conditions will be seen not as people showing purely physical symptoms, but will be understood and treated on all levels in terms of the chemical and emotional addictions resulting from their childhoods.

Some doctors are coming to realise that giving valium to hyperactive and adrenalin-type people only tends to make these people behave even more aggressively violent. If you give them stimulants, on the other hand, they seem quite calm. This paradox is explained when we recognise that chemically, pleasure and pain, peace and tense anxiety have all been crossed in these addicted people. Calming them down only makes them anxious. Pumping up their adrenalin levels, however, allows them to return to the opioid state.

Emotionally disabled people do not need only pills, which throw their moods one way or the other; they need treatment

*It seems likely that all these diseases, both adrenalin-related and cortisone-related, can arise from purely organic, physical causes. We believe, however, that in some cases they result from an excess of cortisone or adrenalin which is caused by the addiction to pain through childhood conditioning.

to help them come to terms with their own addiction to their way of finding the opioid state. The difficulty in treatment is that an addicted person can be either so high and cut off in their opioid state, or so threatened if they are not in an opioid state, that they simply cannot hear or take in what one is saying to them. We hope to see pharmaceutical companies working to find a whole new spectrum of drugs that could be used to aid the internal work with the emotionally disabled. These drugs would need to temporarily allow a state of chemical equilibrium in the body, so that the person is neither high nor anxious. In this period of drug-induced balance, intensive treatment can then be practicable, so that the person can learn to control his or her own chemicals.

Many, many emotionally disabled, violence-prone people coming to us suffer from a whole slew of adrenalin-related or cortisone-related symptoms. We look forward to a time when their medical conditions will not be seen by doctors as purely physical problems separate from their emotional disability; and when we will be able to work together with the medical profession to understand and treat the emotionally disabled so that they can be helped to overcome their fundamental addiction to finding happiness through pain — the addiction that lies behind the emotional and physical symptoms.

This idea of addiction relates even to work with the elderly. Think of the people you know who, once they reach a certain age, are no longer able to learn or incorporate any new ideas or information. Basically, they are stuck in a 'time-warp', because to them the anti-opioid state is not an exciting period of learning, but merely a time of great anxiousness and unrest. Addicted to their opioid-peptides, they suffer a deficiency of the anti-opioid, and remain forever in a time when life was comfortable. What is senility if not an attempt to return to a state of child-like dependency, the opioid state?

Some old people lose their hair, their teeth, their ability to live in the present, to feed themselves, to keep themselves from soiling themselves. Other old people retain all their capabilities right up to their deaths. Those who 'escape' into senility really return to the opioid state that they were always addicted to. We believe that if a person is able to integrate and synthesise their chemicals, and to choose their behaviour, instead of remaining addicted to chemicals, then unless some purely physical condition impairs the brain's functioning, a person is usually able to remain fully capable through to the end of their life.

Understanding the chemical addiction behind violence and emotional disability also has great implications as to the nature of psychology. All of the fields that deal with human emotions — including psychology, psychiatry, social work, and sociology — have historically been passed off by academics and by scientists as the 'soft sciences'. Now, in light of the addiction to the brain's chemicals, the study of the mind can take its proper place among the very real sciences. We hope to see research programmes initiated which will measure the blood-levels of cortisone, adrenalin, the anti-opioid, and the opioid-peptide itself, in emotionally disabled people before, during, and after treatment. We believe that such programmes would prove that when a person learns to break their pattern of violence, they also change their body chemistry and go from a state of chemical addiction to a state of equilibrium in which they can consciously choose their behaviour.

This understanding has a bearing on political behaviour. The world is in grave danger now, for many nations suffer severe anxiety as their economic situations worsen, unemployment increases, and life becomes harder and harder. When a people are in such a vulnerable state of anxiety, it is very easy for a charismatic leader to sweep in and lull a nation into a 'group opioid state'. Charisma itself is the power to elicit a chemical response in the minds of a group of people. This power can be used for good, or exploited for ill. Mahatma Ghandi had the power to pull his people into peaceful action, thank God. But let us be wary, so that, in fleeing from our insecurity, we are not drawn collectively into the opioid state of group aggression, and thus find ourselves basking in the security offered by another Hitler.

Finally, properly understanding the chemicals of addiction must change the way we treat and deal with our society's emotionally disabled. When will we learn that prison and legal punishment are ineffective for those addicted to violence? Punishment then only reinforces the addiction to violence, because, at its roots, the addiction to violence is an addiction to pain. People from violent families cannot be punished better; they can only be loved better. Through being loved, the emotionally disabled can learn to synthesise their personalities. Instead of punishing our emotionally disabled, we must train workers to establish and run loving and caring communities designed to break the pattern of violence by teaching love instead.

For those who would like to make donations for our work, these would be most gratefully received, and should be sent to *Women's Aid Ltd c/o National Westminster Bank, Redfield Bristol Branch*, 112a Church Road, Redfield, Bristol: charity no. 266924, account no. 02157829. If anyone wishes to write to us, please send letters to the community at 114 Whitehall Road, Easton, Bristol.

APPENDIX A

Introduction to the 1976-77 Report from Chiswick Women's Aid

In 1971 Chiswick Women's Aid was originally conceived as a safe refuge for women and children on the run from violent relationships. It was at this point that the phrase 'battered wives' was coined. However, in the course of the last five and a half years one of the conclusions we have come to is that a more apt description of the families involved would be 'violence prone'. That is to say, that the members of these families have a tendency to be attracted to violent relationships or are themselves violent. We see the term 'battered wives' as too simplistic. We do not claim that this description fits all our families or indeed all women who find themselves in a violent relationship. But what we do claim is the majority of families who come to Chiswick are in such a state of confusion and despair, having fallen through the net of all caring social agencies, that to be offered accommodation in homeless family units, bed and breakfast or temporary hostel accommodation is an unrealistic solution. What they need is for society to understand that the chaos, anarchy and drama of the violent relationships which they have lived through has created within them a special urge to continually relive the excitement of what they have left behind. The dramas in their relationships seem endless and in these conflagrations chaos reigns. Children in such a situation feel the ebb and flow of fear and excitement. Soon they grow from terrified unwilling spectators to active manipulators in the family war. These are the violence-prone adults of tomorrow. These families have failed to build the structures necessary to provide the community with law-abiding citizens. Instead we have a percentage of the population whose drive stems from fear, flight and rage which appear to produce puzzling symptoms of addiction.

In everyday life the emotions of fear, rage and flight cause the adrenalin to flow through the body preparing it urgently for action. Most human beings rarely need this sort of protection. Our families have lived at this level of excitement for many, many years and when deprived of excitement tend to re-create hazardous situations which bring back the thrill of the moment of 'adrenalin high'. Racing drivers, mountaineers, test pilots, occasions of war — are acceptable high-adrenalin pursuits and it is our job to get our families to be aware of their addiction and the catastrophies they create for themselves and their children. It is also our job to realise that these families have largely been abandoned by the caring agencies who have tried valiantly over the years to find solutions to their problems. What we offer is to accept the damage and lack of inner structure that causes them to fail again and again and to try and re-integrate their disordered personalities to where they can leave our care having learned satisfactory methods of making relationships and standards of child care and home-making that enables them to exist happily within the community. Of course, often we fail but we have achieved sufficient success to hopefully attract funds to continue our work. One major hurdle is to get the Government to accept that these families urgently need help of a special nature and using techniques that we have developed over the years that we have been running based on some 5,000 women and children who have passed through our hands.

Erin Pizzey and the staff of Chiswick Women's Aid

Graph showing numbers of families in residence during May 76 to April 77, and their borough of origin.

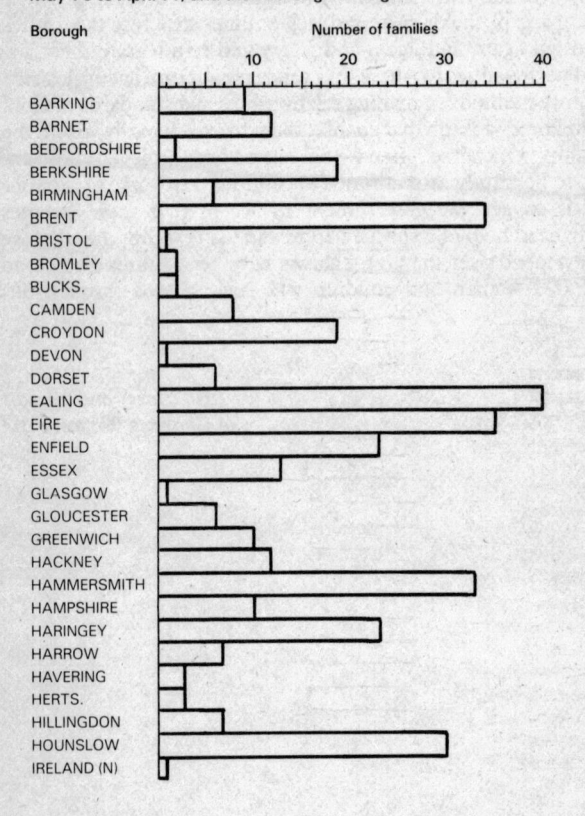

186

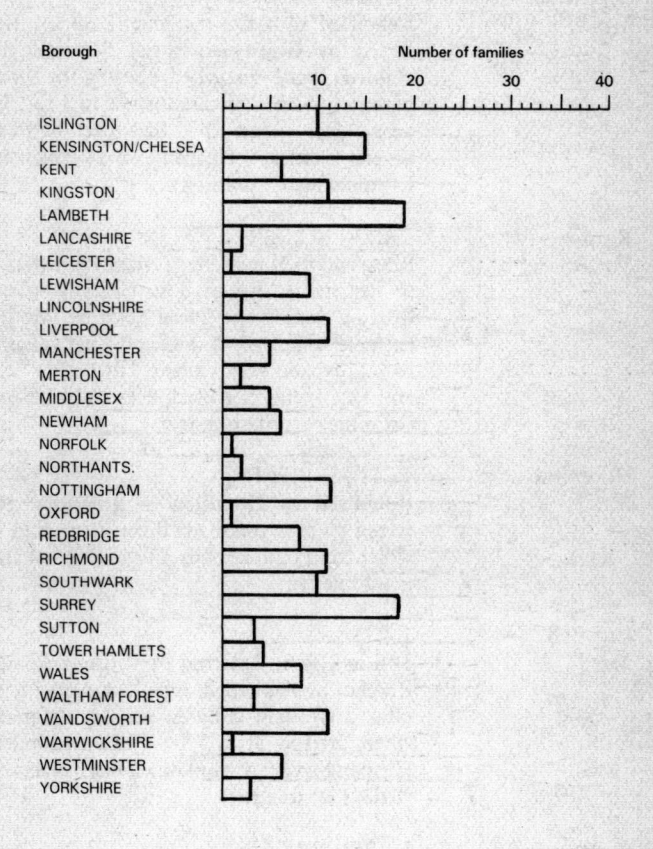

Borough	Number of families
ISLINGTON	
KENSINGTON/CHELSEA	
KENT	
KINGSTON	
LAMBETH	
LANCASHIRE	
LEICESTER	
LEWISHAM	
LINCOLNSHIRE	
LIVERPOOL	
MANCHESTER	
MERTON	
MIDDLESEX	
NEWHAM	
NORFOLK	
NORTHANTS.	
NOTTINGHAM	
OXFORD	
REDBRIDGE	
RICHMOND	
SOUTHWARK	
SURREY	
SUTTON	
TOWER HAMLETS	
WALES	
WALTHAM FOREST	
WANDSWORTH	
WARWICKSHIRE	
WESTMINSTER	
YORKSHIRE	

May 1976-May 1977: 377 Mothers.

The following are details of the families seen during the first three months only of the year covered.

MAY 1976

Greenwich Mrs L + 3	15.10.75 - 29.8.76 Rehoused by GLC in Slough, Bucks. Referred by Greenwich Social Services. All children very disturbed, beaten by both parents. Mother in care for her first sixteen years. Her oldest child has been in care several times. Husband very violent. Criminal record unknown.
Kent Mrs A + 1	3.6.75 - 10.6.76 Returned to Maidstone. Tenancy transferred to her name. Referred to Citizens Advice Bureau, Maidstone Social Services. Mother battered child, was a thief and a pathological liar. Husband very violent. Hit her on head and face giving her black eyes and bruising. Criminal record unknown.
Hounslow Mrs J + 1	17.11.75 - 9.11.76 Rehoused by Hounslow in Brentford. Referred by her probation officer. One child – violent and promiscuous. Mother violent and manipulative.
Croydon Mrs L	1.4.75 Still at CWA. Referred by Citizens Advice Bureau. She has spent time in a mental hospital. Left eight children behind. Pregnant when arrived at CWA – child adopted. Husband's violence unknown but has served 90 days for fraud.
Berks Mrs H + 3	1.1.76 - 28.5.76 Rehoused by Beaconsfield Council. Referred by media. Children very violent and disturbed. Destructive – smashed property and always in trouble with the neighbours. Husband very violent. Used knives, attempted

	strangulation, threw plates, gave frequent black eyes. Criminal record unknown.
Gloucester Mrs McT	8.1.76 - 15.5.76 Went to Palm Court Hotel. Referred by media. Husband very violent − scratches, bites and hits her on the face and chest. Criminal record unknown.
Enfield Mrs C + 2	19.1.75 - 7.6.76 (also 28.8.76 - 13.12.76) First time took a flat from an advertisement. Second time went to Second Stage House − Park Road North. Referred by Edmonton Social Services. Children beaten by both parents. Badly neglected by mother. Husband very violent. Beat her through both pregnancies. She has been in hospital from beatings. Criminal record unknown.
Berkshire Mrs H + 1	20.1.75 - 29.9.76 Rehoused by her council in Slough. Referred by her Social Worker in Slough. Child by another relationship. Shows disturbance. Husband married 3 times − violent in each relationship and pathological liar. Mother violent to child. Criminal record unknown.
Herts Mrs T + 2	23.1.76 − 2.6.76 Went to St. Alban's Women's Aid. Referred by her sister who had been at CWA. One child in voluntary care due to beatings from both parents, another child living with her sister. Two children at CWA very confused, withdrawn and disturbed. Husband violent − gave Mrs T black eyes and bruised both face and body. Criminal record − 3 weeks prison for violence.
Middx Mrs B + 1	29.1.76 - 19.6.76 Went to Second Stage house. Referred by friend. Child not unduly disturbed. Husband punches and throws knives. Criminal record − drunken driving.

Wales Mrs H	5.2.76 - 21.6.76 Rehoused in flat in Acton. Referred by Social Worker in Cardiff hospital. Children all disturbed and violent. The eldest boy has done 6 months in detention for Taking and Driving Away (TDA). Mrs H also violent towards children. Ex-husband — been divorced three years but still living together. Mrs H suffered broken jaw, bruises, black eyes. She is once again living with her ex-husband in her new flat. Husband's criminal record — 12 months for assault.
Ireland Mrs P + 3	5.2.76 - 17.5.76 Went to Palm Court Hotel. Referred by Dublin Women's Aid. All children very disturbed. Oldest child violent and destructive. Husband not physically violent but mentally cruel. Criminal record for breaking and entering, drunk and disorderly.
Southwark Mrs P + 2	1.5.76 - 14.8.76 Went to Palm Court Hotel. Referred by Social Services. Children not beaten by parents but disturbed by scenes. Youngest boy very clinging — changed enormously while at CWA. Mrs P a good mother. Violence was always when husband in drink. Husband in prison for theft.
Gloucestershire Mrs C + 4	19.2.76 - 14.5.76 Went to Palm Court Hotel. Now has own flat in Richmond. Referred by media. Arrived without children but over period of months got all four children from father with his consent. Husband beat her through all pregnancies, broken nose and mental torture. No criminal record.
Manchester Mrs P + 1	4.2.75 - 18.5.76 (Also 21.12.76 - 25.5.77) Been in and out frequently during this period. Always returns to marital home. Referred by health visitor, social worker, probation officer. Has 4 children, various

ones have been in to CWA on different occasions. Most recent visit with 6 month old baby who has been in hospital for over 5 months. Mother has returned to marital home with baby. Have warned Social Services that baby likely to die unless action taken. Mother in care since 6 years old — periods back at home were disastrous. 7 attempted suicides, compulsive liar and very manipulative. 6 miscarriages. Severe marital problems. Actual physical violence unknown. Both have criminal records — theft, assault, receiving stolen goods.

Hampshire
Mrs R

16.3.76 - 15.11.76
Went to Palm Court Hotel. Referred by a friend. Violent woman. 2 children with the father — he has custody. Husband violent when drunk, gets very jealous. Criminal record unknown.

Lambeth
Mrs F

16.3.76 - 21.5.76
Went to Palm Court Hotel. Referred by doctor and Citizens Advice Bureau. 3 children all with father. Oldest child scarred from beatings. Mother has taken 2 overdoses and been in hospital several times due to beatings. Husband very violent — severe bruising to head and arms. Mrs F horrifically bruised on entry to CWA. Husband charged by her, £25 fine and bound over, freed on bail.

Enfield
Mrs R + 2

22.3.76 - 20.8.76 (been in CWA earlier)
Rehoused by transfer. Referred by Probation Officer. Both children have been in care and show disturbance at young age. Husband very violent — severe bruising, stitches in head and eye. Criminal record unknown.

Barnet
Mrs J + 2

26.3.76 - 7.5.76
Returned to marital home. Spent one night in Acton Women's Aid and returned to CWA. Referred by media and Citizens Advice

Bureau. Children witnessed violence but have not been beaten. Husband beaten her with a poker, beats her on head. Criminal record unknown.

Kensington and Chelsea
Mrs B

30.3.76 - 4.6.76
Went to St Alban's Women's Aid. Referred by Probation Officer. 6 children all in care, oldest child because of stealing, the others because of family life. Husband has beaten her very badly but only during the last 4 years. Mother has 28 charges of theft; father's record unknown.

Devon
Mrs J + 1

28.12.75 - 2.3.77
Went to Tower Hamlets Women's Aid. Referred by television. Has 3 children all by different fathers — one with the father, one in care and the youngest with her. All three relationships were violent. Mother was in an approved school. 3 overdoses, one very serious. Many offences of shop lifting and has spent 22 months in prison. Man of second relationship now serving 10 years.

Islington
Mrs W + 2

11.4.76 - 13.10.76
Went to live with friends in Chiswick. Referred by media. Children — father is good with them; mother shows no lasting interest. Not beaten. Husband violent, kicks and punches her. He has no criminal record. Husband now has custody of two children.

Essex
Mrs W + 1

11.4.76 - 15.5.76
Went to Palm Court Hotel. Referred by media. 2 older children with father — oldest child often abused by him. Husband violent — has broken her nose, blacked her eyes and caused extensive bodily bruising. Criminal record unknown.

Croydon
Mrs O + 2

12.4.76 - 25.5.76
Went to hostel in Croydon. Referred by

	Social Worker. Children never hit by father. Husband violent only recently, never drinks. Criminal record unknown.
Lambeth Mrs V + 2	15.4.75 - 10.8.76 Went to Brighton Women's Aid. Referred by friend who had been in CWA. Children not hit by father, but fairly frequently by mother while at CWA. Husband thrown and broken things over her head, sexually assaulted her causing her womb to split, seldom drinks but goes with other women. Criminal record unknown.
Richmond Mrs M + 2	21.4.76 - 23.5.76 also 3.6.76 - 6.7.76 Returned to marital home after tenancy transferred to her name. Referred by police. Oldest child not husband's and is beaten regularly. Very unloved by mother and is withdrawn and disturbed. Husband an alcoholic. Bruising to body and black eyes. Criminal record unknown.
Kilburn Mrs F + 3	2.2.76 - 8.6.76 Rehoused by local council. Referred by Social Services. Children all of different relationships. Beaten by co-habitee who is father of youngest. Violence mutual — she is as violent as he is. She leaves him frequently — she is very provocative. He had long record of prison sentences for assault and theft.
Harrow Mrs B + 1	23.4.76 - 1.8.76 Went to live with friend from CWA. Referred by friend who had been at CWA. 3 children — 2 with the father. He hits all the children and the eldest, due to punches, has had hospital treatment for concussion, his eyesight affected. Husband from violent family — given punches to body and black eyes. Criminal record unknown.
Liverpool Mrs B + 1	24.4.76 - 14.5.76 also 12.6.76 - 15.4.77 After first visit went to Second Stage house.

After second visit went to Liverpool with boyfriend. Referred by media. Child very disturbed, speech retarded. Now in voluntary care. Mother from violent background, was in care at 12 but frequently ran away. She is a violent and extremely manipulative woman. Has formed a second violent relationship while at CWA. Father beat child and broke his arm. Assaulted Mrs B with various objects, pushed her under a car, and has spent one week in hospital due to beatings. Criminal record for violence.

Essex
Mrs H + 3

30.4.76 - 3.5.76
Returned to marital home. Referred by Dagenham Civic Centre. All children by a previous marriage — no information available. When drunk husband smashes plates, chairs, etc; when sober he beats her. Criminal record unknown.

Enfield
Mrs M + 3

30.4.76 - 3.5.76
Went to her mother. Referred by Welfare Officer. Children not beaten by father. Husband violent recently, insanely jealous, threw a knife which stuck in her head, beatings to head and face. Criminal record unknown.

Hammersmith
Mrs M + 5

28.1.76 - 7.6.76
Went to Second Stage House. Referred by police. All children badly disturbed. Oldest child has been in Detention Centre for 6 months for 'Taking and Driving Away'. The children have recently been attacked by the father. Husband has caused heavy bruising, he punches, kicks and uses mental torture. She is a violent woman and admits that she only really feels alive in a potentially violent situation. She has now returned with all her children to her husband in Scotland.

Islington
Mrs D + 2

8.3.76 - 23.3.76 also 5.5.76 - 21.5.76
On both occasions returned to marital home.

Referred by media. Children disturbed – older child bedwets. Husband violent only when drunk – given her black eyes and has had 8 stitches in the head when he hit her with a piece of wood. He is from a violent background and has spent time in homes and hospitals. Men's Aid involved.

Ealing
Mrs B + 2

4.5.76 - 5.5.76
Went to Merton Women's Aid. Referred by Samaritans. Oldest child has been hit by father and marked badly. Husband violent when drunk but regrets it afterwards. Heavy punching to ribs causing hospitalisation. Criminal record unknown.

Hackney
Mrs D + 2

4.5.76 - 6.5.76
Returned to marital home. Referred by friend who had heard of CWA. Both children very young and not hit by father. Husband not physically violent but uses mental torture. Won't let her out of the house day or night. No criminal record.

Hackney
Mrs J + 2

6.5.76 - 10.5.76
Went to Acton Women's Aid. Referred by media. Children by former husband, co-habitee does not hit them but violent towards mother – beats her up regularly, very jealous of other men. He had very little love as a child. Mother comes from very poor background – father left when she was young and mother died when she was 16. Husband has done one year in prison.

Hammersmith
Mrs G

6.5.76 - 7.5.76
Went to Ireland to live with her mother. Has one very young child with her mother in Ireland. Co-habitee violent – serious face and head injuries causing stitches and hospitalisation, body bruising. Criminal record – has been inside for assaulting her.

Wandsworth Mrs H + 1	6.5.76 - 8.5.76 Returned to marital home. Referred by a friend who has been battered. 5 more children at home with father.
Kent Mrs G + 1	6.5.76 - 11.5.76 Went to Sydenham Women's Aid. Referred by media. Child very young, has been hit by father. Husband has been married before, his wife left him due to his beatings. Very violent — blackened eyes and bad bruisings. Criminal record — 1 year in prison for assaulting his former wife.
Ealing Mrs C	10.5.76 - 24.7.76 Went to live with boyfriend. Referred by media. 3 children in care. Children by her husband who was not violent. Co-habitee split her head open several times, severe facial and bodily bruising. She is an alcoholic. Co-habitee in and out of prison for assault and theft.
Lewisham Mrs K + 5	10.5.76 - 14.5.76 Returned to marital home. Referred by Social Services. Violence is mutual. They both come from violent homes. She often leaves him.
Lambeth Mrs A + 1	11.5.76 - 13.5.76 Returned to marital home. Referred by Kennington Social Services. 2 other children by first husband in care. Second husband has hit her with iron bar, metal springs and brooms, extensive bruising to body. He drinks very little. Criminal record unknown.
Leicester Mrs D + 2	11.5.76 - 13.5.76 Went to Chislehurst Women's Aid. Referred by Hendon Social Services. First child, aged 3, is psychologically disturbed, can be aggressive and cries all the time. Has been hit and abused by father. Husband beat up her sister and mother in an attempt to find her.

	Has hit her with bricks. Always taking drugs. Criminal record – has done 2 years for assault and drugs.
Hackney Mrs R + 1	1.12.75 - 20.4.76 – been in many times. Returned to marital home. Referred by Health Visitor at John Scott Health Centre. Child is disturbed, has been hit by father, is used as a go-between with her parents, always gets snatched by father and then mother returns home. Husband violent, drinks seldom. Has caused damaged ribs and black eyes. Has been involved in Men's Aid. Criminal record – 9 months for theft.
Lambeth Mrs C + 1	7.5.76 - 7.6.76 Returned to marital home. Referred by County Hall. Child is ESN and was in a special school but mother took her out when she came to CWA. Husband very violent causing hospitalisation and a hysterectomy due to beatings. Criminal record unknown.
Richmond Mrs H + 5	14.5.76 - 19.5.76 (been in before several times). Returned to marital home. Referred by TV programme on CWA. Children disturbed and confused by mother's frequent travelling from one refuge to another. It is as if her way of taking a holiday is to visit a refuge. Husband has a drink problem, bruising to face and body.
Hackney Mrs A + 2	14.5.76 - 17.5.76 Left one night – no one knows where to. Referred by media. Father doesn't hit children – oldest child not his. Husband not physically violent but mentally cruel. Got into financial difficulty then started drinking and gambling. Criminal record unknown.
Ealing Mrs G + 3	13.5.76 - 18.5.76 Went to Acton Women's Aid so she could continue to work. Referred by Acton Police.

	Children — oldest 2 by another marriage. 2 of his children in a Children's Home. Not very violent — a few black eyes in the past.
Wales Mrs K + 2	14.5.76 - 15.5.76 Went to Cardiff Women's Aid. Referred by Social Services. Children have been in care for short periods, are difficult to control at times, never been beaten but have witnessed violence. Husband from a very violent background. Married young, always violent, bodily bruising, black eyes. Criminal record unknown.
Southwark Mrs B + 5	17.5.76 - 18.5.76 Went to Chislehurst Women's Aid. Referred by local priest. Children — 3 oldest are from a previous marriage which was non-violent but the husband died. Children disliked, beaten and abused by stepfather, very frightened of him. He has broken Mrs B's nose, tried to throw her off 4th floor balcony, caused bodily bruising. Works as Buckingham Palace labourer. Criminal record unknown.
Lewisham Mrs D + 6	15.5.76 - 20.5.76 Went to Bletchley Women's Aid. Referred by media. Children haven't been beaten but witnessed violence. Husband's violence started when the baby died, blamed his wife and started to beat her regularly, threatened her with a knife.
Hounslow Mrs O'T	18.5.76 - 6.12.76 Alcoholic and went to hospital to be 'dried out'. Referred by Chiswick Police. 6 children: 5 grown-up and 1 in care. Mother brought up in a convent when parents split up, was beaten by nuns. Has had 3 relationships and beaten in all of them. Stayed with her mother briefly but beaten by her. 2 nervous breakdowns, an overdose resulting in 6 months in mental hospital. Been an alcoholic for 10 years. Co-habitee violent when

	she is drunk, causing black eyes. Mrs O'T has various charges for being drunk and disorderly.
Lambeth Mrs C + 2	18.5.76 - 20.5.76 Went to live with her brother. Referred by Gingerbread. Children very young, not beaten by father. Husband violent whether drunk or sober, causing black eyes, facial bruising, attempts at strangulation. Criminal record unknown.
Ealing Mrs F + 4	18.5.76 - 20.5.76 Went to Sydenham Women's Aid. Referred by a friend who had heard of CWA. Oldest child got one heavy beating off father when returned home late one day. Has ever since been very frightened of him. Has always beaten mother, heavy into drink and drugs. Never gave her any money. When he started beating the children she left. Mother on 2 year probation for shoplifting.
Bucks Mrs G + 3	19.5.76 - 20.5.76 Went to Bury St Edmund's Women's Aid. Referred by media. Children have not been beaten but witnessed it. Husband from a very violent background and has beaten wife and family. Does not drink. Criminal record – bail and probation for Grievous Bodily Harm and Actual Bodily Harm.
Hammersmith Mrs C + 2	20.5.76 - 26.5.76 also 3.6.76 - 14.8.76 Both times returned to marital home. Referred by Hammersmith Hospital. Children not been beaten by father. Mrs C received regular beatings, black eyes, facial bruising and damage to ribs. Criminal record unknown.
Essex Mrs H	21.5.76 - 26.5.76 Left to get children but never returned. Referred by social worker. 4 children, the oldest 3 have been in care for 2½ years. All are

now with father. Social Services have care and control over 3 eldest (order was not revoked). Oldest child, 7 years, is mentally retarded and is seeing child guidance for paranoia. 2nd oldest has regular nightmares. Husband violent and a drug addict, has attempted strangulation. Mother has attempted suicide after an abortion. Criminal record unknown.

Hammersmith
Mrs McI + 2

23.5.76 - 25.5.76
Went to Wandsworth Women's Aid. Referred by Charing Cross Hospital. Children never been beaten by father but harsh and impatient with eldest child. Worships and spoils younger one. Husband a heavy drinker, causes heavy bodily bruising. Criminal record — fighting in pubs — Grievous Bodily Harm and 3 months for jumping bail.

Middlesex
Mrs L + 2

23.5.76 - 26.5.76
Left leaving no address. Referred by media. Children very young, not beaten by father. Husband uses mental torture rather than physical violence, humiliating her in front of friends and neighbours, accuses her of having affairs. When not drunk he is very apologetic. No criminal record.

Ealing
Mrs E

25.5.76 - 26.5.76
Went to live with her sister. Referred by Social Worker. No children. Husband not violent, hit her once, but has serious alcoholic problem. Since his wife left he has taken 2 overdoses, stabbed himself and split his head open when falling down the stairs.

Enfield
Mrs S + 5

25.5.76 - 4.6.76 also 18.6.76 - 27.7.76
1st time returned to marital home. 2nd time went to Lewisham Women's Aid. Children have all been beaten. Oldest child beaten with a boot so badly she haemorrhaged. All are disturbed. Husband very violent. His

	father beat him. He has got scars from it. Has always beaten his wife — given her 13 stitches to the eye, lacerated ligaments in hand, severe cuts, eyes so often blackened that they are permanently damaged. Criminal record — 2 months in prison for driving offences. History of violent assaults.
Middlesex Mrs W + 1	25.5.76 - 28.5.76 Returned to marital home. Referred by a former mother from CWA. 3 children are with the father. Oldest child attends the doctor for her nerves, gets anxious and has pains in her stomach. Second child wets the bed. He doesn't beat them but plays roughly and makes them anxious. Husband doesn't drink but has given her 2 broken fingers, beatings to the head, cut lip resulting in 9 stitches, many black eyes. Criminal record unknown.
Kent Mrs M + 5	24.5.76 - 29.5.76 Went to Chislehurst Women's Aid. Referred by 'Refuge'. 3 oldest children by first marriage, picked on by stepfather and oldest child once beaten by him. Husband has broken her nose and fingers, given her black eyes. He does not drink but stays out a lot. Mother from violent background, sexually interfered with by father when young. Has taken an overdose. Criminal record unknown.
Essex Mrs G + 2	28.5.76 - 12.7.76 Went to Palm Court Hotel. Referred by social worker and CAB. Children have sometimes been beaten by father. Oldest child very nervous. Husband has caused wife several head injuries, resulting in hospitalisation, and broken ribs. Mother has taken several overdoses and been in psychiatric hospital.
Woolwich Mrs M + 4	30.5.76 - 4.6.76 — been in and out of CWA nine times from 1973.

Returned to marital home. Referred by Health Visitor. Social Services involved but no action taken. Children all disturbed, beaten by father, particularly the eldest but not the youngest. Common-law husband very violent, she received stab wound to shoulders, frequent bodily bruising. Highly provocative woman.

Dublin
Mrs H + 3

20.4.76
Presently care-taking one of CWA properties. Referred by Dublin Women's Aid. Children all very disturbed. 2 other children died in cot deaths. Oldest child (by another relationship) very violent, aggressive and steals — been in trouble with police but no action taken as under age. Second child — loud, aggressive and can be vicious and bad-tempered. Youngest child withdrawn, speech retarded. Husband very violent, severe facial bruising, fractured ribs, broken nose, stitches to head on several occasions, tried to drown her in bath. Has badly beaten oldest child, twice splitting his head open. Mother, a violent woman, has great difficulty in mothering her children. They are often left filthy, and she both physically and mentally lashes out at them, especially the oldest child.

Following entries no details available due to short stay

Barnet
Mrs C

1.5.76 - 2.5.76 Went to friends.

Southall
Mrs M + 2

2.5.76 - 3.5.76 Went to Swindon Women's Aid.

Lewisham
Mrs M

7.5.76 - 8.5.76 Left no address.

Haringey
Mrs C + 3

10.5.76 - 12.5.76 Went to live with parents.

Barking Mrs T + 4	12.5.76 - 14.5.76	Went to Islington Women's Aid.
Birmingham Mrs F + 1	16.5.76 - 17.5.76	Went to Lewisham.
Greenwich Mrs F + 1	15.5.76 - 17.5.76	Went to Lewisham.
Haringey Mrs W + 1	17.5.76 - 18.5.76	Went to Canterbury Women's Aid.
Surrey Mrs R + 2	21.5.76 - 24.5.76	Left, address unknown.
N. London(?) Mrs McH	26.5.76 - 30.5.76	Left, address unknown.
Middlesex Mrs S + 2	30.5.76 - 1.6.76	Went to another Women's Aid.
Islington Mrs Y + 2	30.5.76 - 1.6.76	Returned to marital home.

JUNE 1976

Warwickshire 28.5.76 - 29.6.76
Mrs T + 2   Went to CWA Putney house. Referred by Harrow housing department. Married twice — oldest child is of first marriage. No evidence of violence towards children — but he has been violent in front of them, smashes up the home. Oldest girl very withdrawn and thin. Violent particularly during last year — repeated kicks, punches and abuse. He came from violent background — beaten and farmed out to relatives. No known criminal record.

Kent Mrs O + 3	1.6.76 - 6.6.76 Returned to marital home. Referred by media. Oldest child still with father, he is tired of running even though father beats him. Youngest child is backward — at a special school. Husband extremely violent — has broken her nose, blacked her eyes, bruises all over. He is also violent to other people. He comes from violent background. Criminal record — started in Borstal — prison four times for GBH, has also been in for manslaughter for 3½ years.
Surrey Mrs S + 1	1.6.76 - 5.7.76 (returned 20.7.76 - 26.7.76). Initially returned to marital home, later went to live with her mother. Referred by a friend at Palm Court. No evidence of violence towards child. He is common-law husband — violent for several years — has broken her nose, hit her on breasts, kicked, slashed her wrists with razor. He gets chronically depressed, under treatment. No known criminal record.
Kent Mrs S + 3	3.6.76 - 8.6.76 Returned to marital home (now working in Kent Wa). Referred by Chislehurst refuge. She has been married twice — present relationship with co-habitee. Oldest child by first marriage, one by second and youngest by co-habitee. 2 children have been in care for 3 months. All 3 relationships were violent — she has tried suicide several times, been in mental hospital for 3 months. Co-habitee violent and sexually perverted. No known criminal record.
Wandsworth Mrs B + 1	3.6.76 - 8.6.76 Went to Wandsworth WA. Referred by Wandsworth WA. Child is disturbed, has been beaten by father and has seen mother beaten. He is violent and severely depressed — has been in mental hospitals for paranoia. She drinks heavily. No known criminal record.

Wandsworth Mrs K + 2	5.6.76 - 11.6.76 Went to Wandsworth WA. Referred by Wandsworth Social Services. Children not abused, but have seen violence. Husband violent towards her and her family — he has tried to strangle her several times. Heavy drinker. No known criminal record.
Westminster Mrs C	5.6.76 - 11.6.76 (returned 12.7.76 - 13.7.76). Initially returned to marital home, then went to Kent WA. Referred by media. Child is with husband — has heart murmur, no evidence of violence towards her. He is violent over money mainly — she has got him into a lot of debt and made friends that he dislikes. She agrees that she provokes him unbearably — she comes from disturbed background. No known criminal record.
Kensington and Chelsea Mrs B + 2	7.6.76 - 24.8.76 Rehoused in Chiswick. Referred by media. He is very strict with children, beats and abuses them. He is common-law husband — has beaten her several times. He sleeps around and has given her VD several times — she has been in hospital 8 times because of it. He gambles and drinks heavily. Her mother was married to a very violent man. He has no known criminal record.
Surrey Mrs D + 2	7.6.76 - 22.6.76 Returned to marital home. Referred by media. No evidence of beating of children, but he is not interested in them. Mainly mental torture — he gives her no money for food, has had several affairs with other women, including her sister. Gambles heavily. No known criminal record.
Hackney Mrs W + 1	7.6.76 - 12.6.76 Went to East End Mission. Referred by Gingerbread. Child has not been beaten, has been threatened with drowning — is hyperactive. He is common-law husband — has split

	her head open with a razor, attempted to smother her while pregnant. His former wife divorced him for cruelty. He has criminal record — several periods in prison for theft with violence.
Haringey Mrs A + 2 (4 others with her mother)	8.6.76 - 13.9.76 Went to Palm Court Hotel. Referred by local police. 2 children with her are disturbed by what they have seen — mother is fast with her fists. She has been married twice, four children of first marriage are with her mother as she could not cope. Second husband is from violent home — so is she. He has beaten her unconscious with poker — she was in hospital for months. He has criminal record.
Essex Mrs D + 2	10.6.76 - 14.8.76 Returned to marital home to be rehoused. Referred by media. Children have not been beaten but have witnessed much violence. Children of former marriage. Co-habitee violent, has kicked her about on the street in front of onlookers, has hit her in front of the children's teacher, has hit her mother. Very jealous. Mother's previous marriage also very violent. Criminal record unknown.
Hammersmith Mrs N + 1	10.6.76 - 10.8.76 Went to live with friend. Referred by Welfare Officer, Hammersmith. Child a few months old, and has very bad eczema. Husband violent, brought her from Nigeria to UK after they were married. Hit her first when she was pregnant and has hit her ever since. Husband's child from a former marriage came to visit and he beat her — she went back. Criminal record unknown.
Hackney Mrs S + 1	10.6.76 - 19.6.76 Returned to marital home. Referred by Samaritans, Hackney. Child by previous relationship, has not been beaten but has witnessed mother getting beaten. Child has been

	getting a lot of nervous sicknesses. Husband a heavy drinker, has broken her fingers, hits her with whatever he can get hold of. Criminal record unknown.
Middlesex Mrs W + 2	13.6.76 - 18.6.76 Went to Camden Women's Aid. Referred by friend who had heard of CWA. Children have not been hit except for eldest child when very young. Common-law husband violent, heavy drinker, hits her around head and face. Has a girlfriend and threatens to take the children and go and live with her. Criminal record unknown.
Kensington and Chelsea Mrs L	14.6.76 - 18.6.76 Returned to marital home. Referred by her Social Worker. Five children with the father. Husband gets into bad temper and arguments ensue, but not violent. Mother has left to teach him a lesson. Criminal record unknown.
Hammersmith Mrs N + 1	14.6.76 - 18.6.76 Went to Camden Women's Aid. Referred by Health Visitor. One child at home with father, one at CWA, a few months old. Husband not seriously violent, but very quick-tempered. They quarrel a lot, he has hit her but not badly. Criminal record unknown.
Hammersmith Mrs S + 1	14.6.76 - 21.6.76 Went to Jamaica for a holiday. Referred by family planning doctor. Child not hit by father but noticed at CWA that mother beats him badly. Child disturbed and still not potty-trained at 4 years old. Husband has kicked and punched her, torn her clothes, threatened her with a knife, very jealous. Criminal record – in prison once for Grievous Bodily Harm.

Lincs Mrs W + 4	8.3.76 - 19.7.76 Returned to marital home. Referred by media. All children disturbed, hit by mother. Father hit 3 youngest. He threw second child down the stairs, punched her and held her under a cold tap. Mother neglects the children, goes out frequently and leaves them. One of children had fractured skull when hit by mother at 6 months old. Husband violent, always has been, has given her fractured nose, blackened eyes, attacks her with feet and fists, tries to sexually upset her. Mother is from a broken home, was beaten by her father. Has attempted suicide. All children are now in care. Criminal record unknown.
Camden Mrs L + 1	15.6.76 - 16.6.76 (in and out on several occasions). Went to St Alban's Women's Aid – always moves on to other refuges, but only stays for a few days and then returns to marital home. Referred by media. Child is by another man, but step-father loves the child and has not beaten it. Husband has blackened her eyes, stabbed her hand, smashes her nose, caused bruising to face and body. Drinks heavily and is very jealous. Mother was in care as a child, got pregnant after being raped at 14 years old. Social Services took child into care. Mother purposely got pregnant again to replace that child. Mother appears to be attracted by husband's violent ways. Criminal record – has long prison record of violent offences, assault and robbery, served 3 years. Only out for 6 days before he stabbed a man and went back in again.
Surrey Mrs S	20.6.76 - 28.6.76 Returned home after hearing husband had left. Referred by Samaritans. Child is with mother-in-law, has witnessed beatings. Husband uses her as punching-bag, hitting her in the eye, once causing her glasses to break and cutting her eye. Bruising on stomach, arms

and head. He does not drink. Criminal record unknown.

Ealing
Mrs C + 2

21.6.76 - 23.6.76
Returned to marital home. Husband agreed to seek advice from Men's Aid. Referred by Social Worker. Children not beaten by father. Oldest child disturbed, has terrible crying fits and is nervous. Husband has attempted strangulation, caused bruising to entire body, paranoid and jealous, always accusing her of having affairs, smashes house. Parents fought. Mother had unhappy childhood. Criminal record — drinking and driving, licence removed.

Newham
Mrs D + 2

21.6.76 - 26.6.76
Returned to marital home. Referred by Samaritans. 2 children at home, very disturbed, violent, steal. Have been beaten by father. Husband has given her black eyes, caused bruising to head and body, cuts to head, attempted strangulation and has threatened her with a knife. He is from a violent background, his mother was proud of her bullying husband. Mother's parents are both alcoholics. No criminal record.

Surrey
Mrs M + 1

22.6.76 - 29.6.76
Went to Chislehurst Women's Aid. Referred by Camberley 'Help' Centre. One child is living with grandparents. Child at CWA has witnessed violence, gets hysterical, beats a toy teddy bear, is violent to mother. Husband has thrown mother down stairs, kicked and punched her, has bruised and inflamed cartilage in chest. Husband has attempted strangulation and tried to suffocate her with a pillow. Criminal record unknown.

Ealing
Mrs C + 1

23.6.76 - 26.7.76
Gone to Merton Women's Aid. Referred by Social Services, Ealing. Child very young, been in hospital with malaria and jaundice.

	Husband violent only recently. Sent the baby to Ghana when it was 4 months old to live with his mother, arguments started over this, mostly slapping. Mother went to Ghana and brought baby back. Violence continued and increased. Criminal record unknown.
Waltham Forest Mrs F + 3	25.6.76 - 28.6.76 also 6.7.76 - 11.7.76 Returned both times to marital home. Referred by Vicar, Chingford. Children have not been beaten by father except for second child. Husband violent particularly at beginning of marriage, attempted strangulation, wants her to have sex with other men and for them to have sex with other couples. Criminal record – shot at a policeman with an air rifle. Put on probation, prison 1 year for fraud.
Northamptonshire Mrs P	26.6.76 - 20.7.76 Went to Acton Women's Aid. Referred by media. 2 children grown up. Husband violent through most of 28 years of marriage – punches, kicks, broken her arm. His mother lives with them and she has been in a mental hospital for 6 years. Criminal record unknown.
Richmond Mrs M + 2	7.4.76 - 11.4.76 also 28.6.76 - 10.8.76 First time to marital home. Some time went to Palm Court Hotel. Referred by Health Visitor. Children not beaten by father – doesn't pay much attention to them. Mother takes out aggression on eldest child. Husband violent, but only when drunk. Drinks heavily, and gambles. Caused general bruising to body. Mother has been accused of gossip and malicious behaviour while at Palm Court. No criminal record.
Hampshire Mrs H	28.6.76 - 29.6.76 Returned to collect children and did not come back. Referred by television. 2 children at home, could not get them when she left.

Husband violent, does not drink, gets in bad tempers and throws objects. Criminal record unknown.

Dorset
Mrs R + 2

28.6.76 - 30.6.76
Went home for weekend, never returned. Referred by media. Children not beaten by father but is very strict with them. Husband's violence spasmodic. Has caused blackened eyes, shoves and pushes her a lot, always critical and abusive. He's an only child and very spoilt. No criminal record.

Newham
Mrs P + 1

29.6.76 - 1.7.76
Went to Newham Women's Aid. Referred by Gingerbread. Child not beaten by father, he's always been good with child. Has punched mother, banged her head against the wall, given her black eyes. Has hit her for imaginary things she has done, he always has to be right. Criminal record unknown.

Kent
Mrs C + 4

30.6.76 - 1.7.76
Went to Canterbury Women's Aid. Referred by media. 3 oldest children by another relationship. Youngest child spoilt by father, other children notice this, he's not interested in them though he has not beaten them. Husband beats mother regularly, severe bruising to arms, heavy drink problem. When not drunk he's a loving man. Been married before — marriage broke up because of his drinking. Criminal record unknown.

Ealing
Mrs F + 2

30.6.76 - 9.7.76
Returned to marital home. Referred by media. Children not beaten by father, he's very good with them. Youngest child run over 3 years ago and still needs treatment. Husband has fractured mother's skull and bruised jaw 2 years ago. She left him and came to CWA for 3 weeks. Hasn't really hit her since then but has pushed her several times and threatened her. He lives on his

nerves. Mother has lived in fear for 2 years waiting for him to hit her. Lives on valium, feels he's mentally disturbed. Criminal record unknown.

Following entries no details available due to short stay

Kensington and Chelsea Mrs McC	1.6.76 - 2.6.76 Went to Kent Women's Aid.
Brent Mrs L	4.6.76 - 6.6.76 Went to Springfield Hospital.
Hounslow Mrs W + 3	21.6.76 - 24.6.76 Home after obtaining an injunction.
Oxfordshire Mrs D + 1	25.6.76 - 26.6.76 Went with her brother.

JULY 1976

Richmond Mrs M + 2

1.7.76 - 6.7.76
Returned to marital home. See June figures for details. Came in with new baby — husband had snatched middle child and taken him to Scotland. Case conference recommended that older girls should go into care. This did not happen. Mother caused fight at CWA and again returned home.

Middlesex Mrs K + 1

1.7.76 - 3.8.76
Went to Palm Court Hotel. Referred by friend who had been at CWA. 3 other children staying with her parents. Older child had been run over — 1 year in hospital. Married twice — after first marriage each took 2 children. Second marriage in 1975 —

always violent — she took him to court for assault — later reconciled. He drinks heavily — but hits her drunk or sober. Kicks and punches her in the head, broke her nose. Comes from violent home — beaten by both parents. No criminal record.

Hillingdon
Mrs C + 2

2.7.76 - 6.7.76
Went to live with her mother. Referred by Social Services. Eldest child not his, probability that younger is not either. Threatened to pulverise baby. Violent since marriage 17 years ago — drinks excessively. Matters got worse since she had an affair — he has tried to stifle her, punches to arm. Criminal record unknown.

Richmond
Mrs K + 3

2.7.76 - 12.7.76
Went to Palm Court Hotel. Referred by local police. Middle child under-nourished — under hospital for bronchitis. Co-habitee a 54 year old opera singer. He is father of all the children, she is Hungarian. Mainly mental torture but some physical fighting between them. Very dirty family — she can barely cope with children. Some indication of battering.

Barnet
Mrs F + 3

3.7.76 - 7.7.76
Returned to marital home. Referred by media. All children with husband. No evidence of child abuse. He is Pakistani, she is Danish. Very stormy relationship — he denied paternity of children. Accuses her of poisoning his food, and thinks she is unfaithful. She has had black eyes, bruising, punching. He treats her as his property. Criminal record uknown.

Bristol
Mrs M + 1

5.7.76 - 26.7.76
Went to Bristol Women's Aid. Referred by Weston-super-Mare Women's Aid. 3 children live with her parents. Epileptic daughter at CWA, bad kidney disease, very

nervous — beaten by both parents. Older children left home because of father. Second marriage for her — he has been violent for 10 years, fractured her skull, thrown her downstairs, 2 stillborn children after beatings, sexual perversion. He drinks and gambles, is registered blind after stabbing in fight. Mother is violent too and provokes violent situations.

Hammersmith
Mrs M + 1

6.7.76 - 13.7.76
Returned to marital home. Referred by hospital. Beaten throughout pregnancy — baby nearly died. Common-law wife for 9 months. Both West Indian known each other eight years. He is constantly jealous of her. Denied paternity of child. Both of them beaten as children in West Indies. He has injured her face, blacked her eyes, thrown her across the room — put her in hospital twice. He had police record for violence. Criminal record unknown.

Southwark
Mrs L + 2

6.7.76 - 16.7.76
Went to Suffolk Women's Aid. Referred by Citizens Advice Bureau. Refused by Southwark Refuge. Children withdrawn and frightened. He has set fire to their clothes and smashed up the house. Husband terrorises the household — treats mother like a slave, threatens her with a knife. He cut her off from her family, constantly tells her that he wants to kill her. Beat her badly when pregnant. Denies paternity. He has seen a psychiatrist. Has long prison record for theft.

Berkshire
Mrs McC + 1

8.7.76 - 9.7.76
Went to live with sisters. Referred by hospital social worker. 3 other children with husband. 9 pregnancies altogether. No evidence of child abuse. Violence started because of her excessive domesticity in home and with children. He always hits her where it doesn't

	show. She admits her responsibility for violence – says that she nags a lot. He has no criminal record.
Hounslow Mrs L + 5	8.7.76 - 13.7.76 Returned to marital home. Referred by media. Two marriages – 2 children from each and one from another relationship. Present husband beats children of former marriage – slaps them round the head. He comes from violent family. Started beating her 2 years ago, black eyes, punches her. He used to beat his mother. He drinks heavily. No known police record.
Hammersmith Mrs S + 3	9.7.76 - 18.7.76 Went to Merton Women's Aid. Referred by Citizens Advice Bureau. 2 of children wet their bed regularly, one has nervous eczema. During 7 year relationship beatings have regularly occurred. Both of them have had affairs and drink too much. Husband's mother abandoned him in Jamaica. He was brought up by relatives who beat him. She too was beaten regularly. Criminal record unknown.
Wandsworth Mrs S	10.7.76 - 13.7.76 Disappeared from refuge. Referred by psychiatrist. Violent for 2 years of marriage – particularly bad when drunk, he punches and kicks her. Drinks heavily – beats only when drunk. He comes from adopted family. She was beaten by parents, always violent towards her. He suffers from manic depression, sees psychiatrist. She has been to hospital with beatings. Has also had psychiatric treatment for schizophrenia. Was in mental hospital for a year.
Ealing Mrs O'S + 1	11.7.76 - 18.7.76 Went to Acton Women's Aid. Referred by media. No violence towards child. He is common-law husband – left her a year ago,

keeps returning. Both are Irish. He gambles and drinks heavily — bangs his head against the wall, has thrown her off walls and knocked her out. Accuses her of affairs. No criminal record.

Barnet
Mrs S

15.7.76 - 16.7.76
Went to Islington Women's Aid. Referred by media. Aged 61 — 2 married children. He has been violent for 30 years. Very morose, drinks heavily, well-known novelist. Eldest child attempted suicide then married alcoholic, is on drugs.

Hackney
Mrs M

15.7.76 - 16.7.76
Went to live with mother. Referred by GPO Welfare. During 6 year marriage to Persian he was always critical and jealous of her. Has beaten her on body, split her lip open, broken her teeth. Has threatened to mutilate her pets and to wound her badly. He treats her like dirt, and says that she is his property. No criminal record.

Merton
Mrs D + 1

16.7.76 - 17.7.76
Returned to marital home. Referred by media. Husband denies paternity of child. He has mistress and child who have also been at CWA. He belongs to motorbike gang. She invented whole history of violence and maintained that her brother had been murdered by husband. All untrue. Left to go back to him. Very disturbed and pathological liar from violent background.

Ealing
Mrs H

16.7.76 - 17.7.76
Went to stay with uncle. Referred by legal aid centre. Husband 15 years older — second arriage for him. Violent one year — very dominating, thinks she is his slave. Both are very depressive.

Brent
Mrs D + 2

17.7.76 - 23.8.76
Went to CWA community flat. Referred by

	media. Children not beaten but witnessed violence. Violence since start of marriage — punches, kicks and smashes house up regularly. Mainly violent when drunk. He comes from violent Irish background. She had happy childhood. Petty theft record.
Hammersmith Mrs M + 2	18.7.76 - 24.7.76 Returned to marital home. Been in CWA two years ago. One child in care. She batters the children. Oldest one violent towards her and other children. Middle child beaten with stick. Social Services know of abuse and put him into care for 2 years. She is very violent and manipulative, baby originally came in with facial bruising. She comes from violent home. He was very spoilt. She has been hospitalised with cuts and stab wound. He drinks heavily and is well known to the police.
Eire Mrs W + 2	18.7.76 - 29.3.77 Rehoused in Milton Keynes. Referred by her sister who had been at CWA. Eldest child had suffered fractured skull due to father's beatings — gets severe headaches, very disturbed and hyperactive, steals a lot and was very violent on entry. Baby also had been beaten by father. They married in Ireland at 15 — both from large, violent families. He drinks heavily — in prison most of the time for assault, theft etc. Children scarcely know him.
Westminster Mrs M + 2	19.7.76 - 28.7.76 Returned to marital home. Referred by local police. Children under hospital treatment — non-accidental injury history and parental neglect. Father beats all children — family is Moroccan. One child in care after beatings. Violent towards her as well — punches and insults. She has attempted suicide. Social Services involved with family. No known criminal record.

Merton Mrs A + 2	20.7.76 - 27.7.76 Returned to co-habitee. Referred by Social Services who have been regularly involved. One child beaten by him – police called in after this. He is very violent towards her and children of previous relationship. Children on At Risk register. Much fighting over his ex-wife who he still sees. He is member of motorbike gang. Has criminal record.
Barnet Mrs C + 1	20.7.76 - 23.7.76 Returned home. Referred by Social Services. No violence towards child. He is co-habitee – she has been married before, child is of second marriage. He is 30 years older – chronic alcoholic, regularly in hospital, unemployed. He smashed her nose, attempted strangulation – always when drunk. She comes from insecure background. He has no criminal record.
Southwark Mrs R + 1	22.7.76 - 27.7.76 Returned to marital home. Referred by friend. No violence towards baby. Second marriage for him. Married 3 years – violence started 2 years ago – punching in face, arms and back, threatened to cut her throat. They argue constantly over money. He doesn't drink – comes from good family like her. Both very inadequate. No criminal record.
Enfield Mrs D	23.7.76 - 2.8.76 (returned to CWA in December 1976). Returned to marital home – child with father. Referred by husband's probation officer. She came in with broken arm. No violence towards baby. He has been violent for 2 years – since wedding night. Very jealous of baby. He was very spoilt only child. He has punched, kicked and burnt her with cigarettes – mostly when drunk. Thrown boiling water over her, attempted strangulation. On dole for 2 years. Prison record for theft and Grievous Bodily Harm.

Hillingdon Mrs E + 3	24.7.76 - 29.7.76 Went to Homeless Family Unit in Hillingdon. Referred by Media. Eldest daughter battered by father — case taken to Crown Court. He is in prison now for that. Both of them were badly beaten and neglected as children. Have known each other since early teens. They married at 16. He has beaten her for years — punching, bullying, cutting. Drinks heavily, very jealous. Both have police records for assault.
Brent Mrs S + 2	25.7.76 - 9.8.76 Returned to marital home. Referred by Brent Social Services. Eldest child bronchitic — no violence towards children but younger child violent. Violent situation escalated when he moved his brother in — brother is violent and abusive, treats her like a slave. Husband mean with money. He is very weak and influenced by family. No criminal record.
Islington Mrs McM + 2	27.7.76 - 28.7.76 Went to live with Mother. Referred by Social Worker who visits regularly. Children not beaten by him but both are sickly and nervous. She is deaf and dumb. She lost her first baby after beatings. He is very jealous — gambles and drinks heavily, in and out of work, mean with money. Has thrown her through window, kicked and punched her. He was very spoilt as child. Petty crime record.
Wales Mrs P + 1	28.7.76 - 3.8.76 Returned to relatives in Wales. Referred by N. Wales Women's Aid. Three children at home. Oldest daughter (now 21) was savagely beaten and forced to eat cigarettes as test of love. She is now on probation. Violence started when children were small. He only beats her when drunk, has punched her, dislocated jaw, thorough bully. He is ex-Sergeant Major. Has thrown her naked on to the streets and terrorised the family. No known criminal record.

Birmingham Mrs H + 2	28.7.76 - 7.8.76 Went to live with mother. Referred by Media. He is father of oldest child. She became pregnant at 15. Very violent during pregnancy. Children are violent towards each other. During pregnancy he knocked her to ground, kicked her. Drinks heavily — only beats when drunk. Constant rows over money and other men. No known criminal record.
Islington Mrs W + 5	8.7.76 - 17.7.76 Went to Bristol Community House. Referred by Social Service Unit. Children badly beaten by father. Good mother. Has serious kidney complaint. One daughter aggressive. Criminal record unknown.

Following entries no details available

Hampton Mrs L	1.7.76 - 20.7.76 Went to live with mother.
Westminster Mrs C + 1	12.7.76 - 13.7.76 Kent Women's Aid.
Brent Mrs B + 3	16.7.76 - 17.7.76 Gone home.

APPENDIX B

Observations on Violence-Prone families,
by Erin Pizzey and Jeff Shapiro
(originally published in *New Society*, 23 April 1981)*

Chiswick Women's Aid specialises in the care and rehabilitation of 'violence-prone' women and their children. 'Violence-prone' is the only phrase I can find that defines as accurately as possible, women who experience gross physical and mental abuse but who choose, despite other viable and attractive alternatives, to remain within the confines of their abusive relationship.

It is precisely these women that are the despair of all agencies and caring organisations. These women, seen as the prototype of 'battered women,' condemn to a barrage of prejudice and a wall of unhelpfulness many thousands of women who genuinely do wish to take refuge and create a new life for themselves and their children.

The time has come for a clear distinction to be made between a woman who has accidentally become involved with a violent partner and who now wishes to leave and to never return again, and a woman who, for deep psychological reasons of her own, seeks out a violent relationship or a series of violent relationships, with no intention of leaving.

In the first instance, the woman and her children will need shelter away from the partner, time to think for herself, and support to take whatever action she chooses. Because it was not herself but her partner who was violent and destructive, she soon regains her equilibrium. Once she has recovered from the trauma of leaving, she will need legal advice and an opportunity for rehousing. It may take three to six months for her to gain sufficient confidence to cope in the community on her own with the children, but she does ultimately achieve this confidence. Such women and their children are the most rewarding families that come to a refuge.

An example of one such woman was Jean. Jean came to us from Cornwall with five children. She was referred by the police who

*Copyright *New Society*, London. Reprinted by permission.

knew her locally. They had watched with sympathy her struggles to bring up her five children with a feckless, brutal husband who occasionally fished for a living. Jean was a great help in the refuge. She was like many of the women who wish to break loose from their past. Jean was overwhelmed at first by the numbers in the refuge, but was able to be philosophical about herself and her future. Now that she was with us, she decided to throw herself into the community. For several months she acted as one of the senior mothers, caring particularly for the younger, more helpless members of the community.

During this time, she succeeded in breaking all links with her husband. She had a painful time dealing with her own guilt at abandoning an inadequate dependent man. She could, however, see quite clearly that her own childhood, which consisted of a loving father but a dead mother, left her at an early age to fill the mothering role for her brothers. She now recognised that this same mothering role was the basis of her relationship with her husband.

Even though the children had suffered emotional damage from their father's brutality, they soon responded to the male staff in the refuge. I had little cause to worry about their future development. In Jean's fourth month with us, she replied to a letter offering a home for a little housework. A year later Jean wrote to us from Scotland to say that she was happy and that she had met a nice man who loved her and the children. A few years later, the two were married. I have subsequently heard from her again, and she is still happy.

Jean is typical, in my experience, of a woman who needs initial support from a caring group and is then well able to manage her own life. Another woman who has come to the refuge, Sally, is an example of a different kind of woman — a 'violence-prone' woman.

Sally came to us with her five children in 1975. She was an attractive woman who took great care of herself physically, and her children were immaculately and expensively dressed. Sally settled into the refuge with the astonishing ease that is characteristically exhibited by violence-prone women. She very soon became the house 'heavy,' teaming up with anyone who would collude with her bullying tactics. She intimidated other families and revelled in the house-meetings when she openly dominated the staff with her indictments of other mothers. Anyone who dared complain about Sally's behaviour would risk retaliation after the staff left.

Her children were puppets, used as visual proof of her worth as a meticulous mother. They could never dare to get dirty, because she would beat them. They usually stood together — little husks with no opinions of their own, mere parrotings of their mother's instructions. Sally's social worker saw little of her, except when she wanted support against her husband. She continually took him to court, but then would allow him back into the house.

The school attended by the children considered her an excellent mother because the children were 'clean, tidy, and polite.' However, all the agencies admitted that they knew of the grave physical abuse that occurred in the family. They were aware that both parents hit the children who could be heard screaming at night, and that fights between the mother and father were 'six of one, half-dozen of the other.' The agencies felt helpless and then resentful because Sally, by flitting from one organisation to the next, with various bits of misfortune, managed to manipulate all agencies in order to achieve her own ends. We, however, had the opportunity to work with Sally day by day. Instead of becoming just another target of her manipulation, we were able to make her own part in her violent relationship obvious to her.

It was impossible not to like her. Her wit and her charm (very practised) won her support from almost everyone. She was intelligent enough to eventually realise that her bullying did not endear her to the staff or to the community. She adopted, instead, a far more beneficial relationship with the mothers and staff.

With me she discussed her family history. It was a huge and violent family. She had never known anything else but violence in relationships. She saw relationships as battlegrounds of power and domination. Her husband was a successful thief, who could provide her with the material goods that represented her security. His physical domination satisfied her emotional and sexual needs. She was one of the first women I counselled who fully described her need for violent sexual intercourse. She needed a degree of pain to feel pleasure.

During her time with us, she was in regular provocative contact with her husband. This gave us the chance to talk with him at great lengths about his feelings for her. He was, for the most part, bewildered. He was indeed violent, with no threshold of frustration. He repeated endlessly that Sally knew how to make him 'blow,' and he was concerned that he might kill her. His fears were certainly justified, given the injuries she had sustained in the past. The children were fond of him, and he took them out regularly from the refuge.

Sally seemed to be making progress within herself. She apparently needed fewer and fewer outbursts of aggression and dramatic events to fuel her need for excitement. We moved her to a second stage house nearby. Meanwhile, her husband found a much less provocative woman.

Sally seemed to take this in her stride. She got a job. Then she found herself another violent relationship and we were back to square one. She put the children into care and went off. We heard later on that she had a job and the children had been returned to her. Another mother, who had been equally aggressive, but who had ended all her past behaviour to become a school-governor, a play-group leader, and an organiser of her block of flats' residents committee, kept an eye on Sally. She reported that this was a hopeless task. Sally turned to this woman when the violence was untenable. Sally would swear, 'This is the last time,' but she would go back again and again. She can still be seen in the local supermarkets, wearing her badges of black eyes and bruised legs. She is one of the many women we were unable to rescue. It is these women who most need the understanding help of all caring agencies.

Years ago I realised that violence was a form of addiction and the whole concept of the refuge was built round the idea of a 'de-escalating' station. You cannot take a woman away from the war and give her peace. Her stress levels will be too high, and she will return to the fray.

There is a hormonal side to this. Scientific research by Malcolm Carruthers and his colleagues at the Maudsley Hospital in London points to the possibility that certain individuals may become 'addicted' to the hormones that excitement releases into their bloodstream.

Colloquially, people speak about 'getting the adrenalin flowing,' when they are excited. But this is not strictly correct. Adrenalin is the hormone which is released into the blood by the adrenal glands to help you cope with a frightening or terrifying situation — a first parachute jump, a dangerous walk along a crumbling cliff-path. It is the 'fear-anxiety' hormone. The same glands, however, also release a hormone called noradrenalin at times of excitement, extreme activity and stress. This stimulates pleasure centres in the brain and makes us 'stress-seekers.'

When racing drivers go onto the track or boxers go into the ring, their noradrenalin level rises. The Maudsley group has also shown that a rise in noradrenalin is associated with smoking and with coffee drinking. Among its other effects, noradrenalin helps dull sensitivity to pain. This may be useful in battle. There is the famous anecdote about the man riding away from Waterloo. On being greeted with the remark 'Gad, sir, your leg is shot off,' he looks down, sees it is, and faints.

Noradrenalin is no doubt a mechanism developed to enable the body to rescue itself from a threatened danger. But, in violence-prone families, this 'fight and flight' mechanism is in constant use. There is a psychosomatic link here, according to Carruthers's investigations — a kind of feedback loop. Because the mechanism is more often used, it is more easily tripped into action. In violent families, the children experience innumerable moments of great anxiety, which are followed by a 'noradrenalin high.' They become, so to speak, addicted to this.

As children, and later as adults, they keep trying to recreate the excitement level that violent occasions precipitate. It may be, too, that the noradrenalin has some marginal effect in numbing the pain they receive. It is also more than likely that many of the people we are talking about are heavy smokers — another trip switch for noradrenalin.

This all fits in with studies at Broadmoor, which have tried to pin down the hormonal differences between violent and non-violent inmates. (D.D. Woodman reported on this in *New Society* on 4 September 1980.)

Sally was just such an example on every human level. She could understand her needs and the dire consequences of her behaviour, but her addiction to excitement was such that we were unable to offer anything as satisfying as violence.

Our discussions with her, both in groups and in private, always turned round the need she had to create excitement. 'It is the moment just before I get hit,' she would explain. This made sense. That moment was the ultimate pitch of excitement punctured by the blow that would come. For some women only the edge of possible death is satisfying enough. Some such women we have known have died.

Over the years we have seen so many women that for me a pattern emerges. The violence-prone women who have presented themselves asking for refuge usually had no intention of using the refuge as anything other than another move in their warring relationships, just as they had abused many other caring agencies. The typical violence-prone woman would arrive in the middle of the night with only some of her children, for she had left a hostage or two at home. Usually after getting immediate money to cover her need for cigarettes, she would recount with great relish the appalling violence — mental, physical, and sexual — that she had experienced. The listening children would pretend to occupy themselves, having heard the same stories many times before in many other offices.

The next request would be that she should be accompanied by a member of staff to 'get her clothes from back home.' This usually means a further confrontation with her partner, with the cards stacked in her favour. We would refuse the offer. After all, Daniel did not return to the lions' den to retrieve his hat. If she seriously wished to leave, we could get her belongings later. We then find, checking with every agency possible, that the family has many other problems, and is known to the housing department for arrears, to health visitors for neglect of children, to the social work team for having children on the at risk register, to NSPCC for possible child abuse, to the education and welfare department for non-attendance, to doctors' surgeries for many medical problems, and to the hospital — where mother is treated for overdoses, father sees a psychiatrist spasmodically to appease mother, and the children are referred for nervous illnesses such as asthma, migraine, nervous tics, rashes, diarrhoea, stomach cramps, and suspected epilepsy.

Her arrival at our door is all part of her chaotic lifestyle. She is well used to using any agency as a means of helping her out of her immediate difficulty. Here we have the beginning of the pattern not often realised by other agencies because they do not have residential care for violence-prone families. One unifying factor in all these families is their undoubted ability to extract every possible benefit, both financial and emotional, from everyone surrounding them. This creates a sense of failure and eventual dislike, as everyone attempts to come to grips with their behaviour.

It is necessary for everyone in the caring field to offer some help or remedy to anyone in distress. This fact is well known, most particularly to these women. As soon as a violence-prone woman says she is in distress, she expects certain solutions to be offered. In accepting these attempts to help, she can justifiably also accept money, clothes, shelter.

However, once the solution offered requires her to cooperate in changing her goals, she will very often create a 'hazard' to endanger this. For example, she says, 'I must collect my clothes.' Or, after a social worker has spent hours finding her a place to stay, she says the children don't like it here/want to go home/miss their dad. More simply, she moves into the refuge and rings a 'friend,' who tells her husband where she is. She is then 'forced' to return home. By returning home, she returns to her original satisfying pattern of behaviour and no change has occurred.

Chaotic behaviour is a comfortable and natural state of being for those people who have been brought up in families where they were virtually unable to learn expected social behaviour, or where every rule they learnt was one of sheer survival.

Mary H, after years of therapy with us, married an extremely nice, non-violent man. She was the proud owner of a very beautiful home. One of our staff visited the happy bride, who provided a tour round the house. 'It must be wonderful, Mary, not to have all those bills hanging over you all the time,' the staff member said. Mary paused and then said wistfully, 'Yes, but I don't half miss it sometimes . . . hiding on the floor from the milk . . . fiddling the electric.'

Mary originally arrived on our doorstep like a wild animal. She had three children with her and was about to give birth to another. She was very violent to her children as well as abusive and dominating to others in the community. It took three years to effect a change in Mary. She will never be completely honest, because she finds the thrill of a fiddle too compelling. She now is, however, gentle with her children. She is clean, and is able to communicate with other people without horrifying them. Above all, she is comfortable with her present life. In this case, we replaced her usual pattern of chaos with a goal of harmony.

Anyone in this field should look carefully at what they are offering as a solution. If the offer is realistic, the intervention of the therapists should help the client. If the offer reflects, however, the agency's need to deal quickly with a crisis, or the agency's attempt to buy off a difficult customer with a panic measure, the solution will prove useless and will be turned to the client's advantage. You then get a very high amount of what Americans call 'staff burnout.'

The following diagram shows the violence-prone woman's chaotic pattern of behaviour:

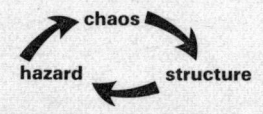

chaos → structure → hazard → chaos (cyclic)

This vicious circle is self-perpetuating and is learned from one generation to the next. The agency must not only see that the solution offered is feasible for the client, but must also be able to forecast and prepare for hazards created by the client if she actually has no wish to change. Sometimes the hazards created by the clients to avoid unwanted pressure can be much more dangerous than the original problem.

Our aim is to change this chaotic pattern. We accept that the families present themselves as being in chaos. We understand that breaking their chaotic lifestyle will take time. The whole concept of our therapeutic community is designed to give women and their children the support they will need to adjust into the community, and then change the pattern of chaos. We offer an alternative to the original pattern of:

chaos ➜ structure ➜ hazard ➜ chaos

The new pattern of the change away from chaos and towards the alternative goal, harmony is:

chaos ➔ therapeutic intervention ➔ intergration (change) ➔ harmony

We feel that, among caring agencies, there needs to be more understanding of these families. Agencies must change their usual procedure in dealings with violence-prone families, which is to dump them in the New Towns in a ghetto, or to ship them very tactfully off to another borough. We need many more residential, therapeutic communities that offer the families a chance to learn a new kind of behaviour that will enable them to live comfortably and harmoniously with their neighbours.

APPENDIX C

CLIENT'S BRIEF FOR AN IDEAL REFUGE FOR PROBLEM FAMILIES *

A battered wife needs short-term sanctuary because she has left her violent relationship and has no wish to return to make further violent relationships. She is resourceful enough to make use of the lawyers, housing services and the self-help support that is found in the refuge, and therefore needs time to rehabilitate herself in order to become a solo parent. However, the majority of women they deal with are violence-prone with long-term multiple problems who frequently either continue violent relationships or return to violent relationships thereby damaging the children. This is where the therapeutic techniques of the staff and the purpose-built accommodation must reflect the needs of the disturbed multi-problem families.

The concept at a time of crisis in the life of these families is to concentrate on the main needs of those seeking refuge.

1. The fear of a violent partner
2. Safety within the confines of the building
3. Rehabilitation through relationships with other mothers in the same situation and the normal contact with daily staffing.

They accept that while these families are in crisis there is a degree of chaos and antisocial behaviour that needs the internal focus of the staff and the self-help element of the older members of the community. The design of the building must therefore reflect both a protective element for the mother and her children and acknowledge the disruptive element of the families within the neighbourhood.

For this reason Chiswick Family Rescue wish to offer to the mothers and to the neighbourhood a building in a quiet cul-de-sac designed to achieve two ends: the concept of holding the community safely within the arms of the house as a shelter and at the same time

---

* Porter-Wright. Reproduced by permission.

offering the neighbourhood no sense of alarm as the exterior of the refuge should be built in the traditional form of a sanctuary like the old convents and other cloistered communities where the entrance is through a door in the wall enclosing the community.

The majority of the families are there because they have turned their backs on society and it is CFR's job to rehabilitate them not only from violence-prone behaviour but from a variety of antisocial behaviour. The building must reflect these intentions by containing the disturbance so that it does not spill out and create the problems that have occurred in the past with the neighbourhood.

For a woman in flight for her life, the concept of the refuge with a facade which is unbreachable, is comforting. It also makes it difficult for a dangerous man to make any sort of gesture where there are no windows or any points of access to get into the building. Furthermore, it protects the neighbours from accumulated rubbish being thrown out of the windows, mothers and children hanging out of windows or irritating the neighbours by unseemly behaviour. CFR have learnt from experience that many of these families need time to be resocialised, and during that time they need the protection, the care and the discipline of a cloistered community.

It is of great importance to the general working of the refuge that all the mothers and children function within and as part of the community. It is essential, therefore, that the layout of the spaces within the building is such that it becomes impossible for a member, or small groups of members, of the community, to mark out and claim areas as their own territory. Thus it would seem desirable that the areas of corridors and the enclosing of spaces be kept to a minimum, and to provide as free a flow of movement and space within the building as possible.

The organisation and layout of the spaces within the new refuge will be greatly influenced by the experience gained from the many years of working with these mothers and their children in the existing refuge in Chiswick High Road. From this experience the basic requirements are to provide a purpose-built refuge to house 70 women and children with communal cooking, eating, sitting, washing and sleeping facilities; adequate interior and exterior play areas, laundry facilities, sufficient lavatories and wash areas, small open office and interview cubicles. To provide also, either within or adjacent to the refuge, adequate space for supervised play/learning activities.

The new refuge must not only be so designed and constructed to withstand the heavy wage demanded of it but also provide a welcoming and secure presence to the mothers and children. The refuge must above all be a place where care and love can flourish and the well-being and resocialisation of the families contained within it be its prime function.

Local Authority Requirements
After full consultation with the officers of the London Borough of Hounslow, it has been agreed that the new purpose-built refuge is in essence a house in multiple occupation and therefore is to comply with the regulations contained within the 6th Schedule of the 1957 Housing Act, Section 15 of the 1961 Housing Act, purpose Group 11 of the Building Regulations and other related local authority regulations and standards.

The relevant points from the above regulations that specifically apply to this building are as follows:

Bedrooms:
No bedroom to accommodate more than 2 persons.
Floor area of double bedrooms to be not less than $10.25m^2$ (110 sq ft). Permitted floor area to exclude area of any built-in cupboards.
Interconnecting doors between bedrooms will be permitted.

Permitted numbers:
The permitted number (PN) of people that can inhabit any particular dwelling is arrived at by adding up the number of habitable rooms, excluding kitchens, bathrooms etc., bearing in mind that no room, regardless of its size, can count for more than 2 people.
Adults and children over 10 years of age count as 1. Children from 1 - 10 years count as ½ and children under 12 months are not counted at all.

Day areas:
Large communal kitchen, dining and living space will be permitted, provided there is adequate cooking and wash-up facilities.
There are no regulations as to the size of the kitchen.
The only regulation with regard to communal rooms such as sitting rooms are from the D of E Circular 170/74, which requires 2 sq metres per person of communal living space.

Fire Regulations:	All habitable rooms to be entered from a common corridor via ½hr. fire doors. All internal staircases to be contained within a 1 hr. fire protected enclosure. No children will be permitted to inhabit any rooms above first floor level. All floors to be compartment floors of at least 1 hr. FR.
Sanitary Requirements:	For every 8 persons, irrespective of age, there shall be provided a fixed bath or shower and one water closet with hand washing facilities. Lavatories and bathrooms to be installed in separate rooms entered from a common passage or hallway. Hand basins are not required within the bedrooms.
Car parking:	Although the regulations require 1 parking space per 10 occupants, it has been agreed with the Borough Engineer that due to the unusual circumstances of this project, parking facilities for 3 cars only will be acceptable.
Play spaces:	There are no regulations related to size of play areas. After discussion with the Planning Department it was agreed that the D of E Circular 79/72 be used as a guide. This Circular requires 3 sq metres of play area per child.

Two main points emerge from the above information. The first is that the average ratio of mothers to children and the proportion of these children that are between 1 and 10 years of age is of prime importance in arriving at the number of 2 person habitable rooms required in order to accommodate the permitted number of 70 mothers and children.

The second point that arises is the conflict between CFR's requirements for dormitory sleeping accommodation and the Housing Acts regulation of allowing a maximum of 2 people per bedroom. It is argued that interconnecting doors between bedrooms are to be allowed, it would therefore seem logical to group the bedrooms together in order to have as many linking doors as possible. It is essential that the building can house 70 persons, so that at no time does it, with regard to the regulations, become overcrowded. It should be pointed out that the refuge functions best when it is full and busy, therefore at times of lower numbers it would be useful if some sleeping areas could be closed off or used for other purposes. It is not contrary to the regulations to sleep as many people to a room as you wish, as long as there are enough rooms to be countable for the permitted numbers. Thus together with the limitations of the site, the number and grouping of countable 2 person rooms is a most important criterion controlling the design of the building.

From the figures supplied by CFR of their numbers over the last year the breakdown of persons contained within their maximum figures of 70 are as follows:

> 23 mothers, 14 children over 10 years, 30 children under 10 and 2 children less than 12 months. This means that although the refuge is housing 70 persons, as regards the regulations on PN the number of people the refuge has to accommodate is 52. Bearing in mind that the sitting-room and other open functional dayrooms are included in the count of 2 person habitable rooms and allowing for three such rooms, the new refuge will require bedroom accommodation for 46 persons — 23 double bedrooms in all.

The sketch of the proposed bedroom layout on page 234 satisfies the requirements of CFR and the Regulations imposed by Hounslow.

1: In order to open up the bedrooms one with another to create a dormitory sleeping arrangement, the bedrooms are of minimum width and maximum length, thus allowing very wide interconnecting doorways.

2: To satisfy CFR requirements for all rooms to face away from the street and on to the space at the rear, the common corridor is positioned around the exterior perimeter of the site, lit by means of clerestory windows.

3: To satisfy CFR's requirements for a free-flowing building with all habitable rooms having access to the rear, all bedrooms will open out onto a linking balcony which leads down to the courtyard.

Planning Information
Stairs — To satisfy the Fire Safety requirements, 2 internal, fully protected stairs will be required, with 1 external stairs leading off the linking balcony.

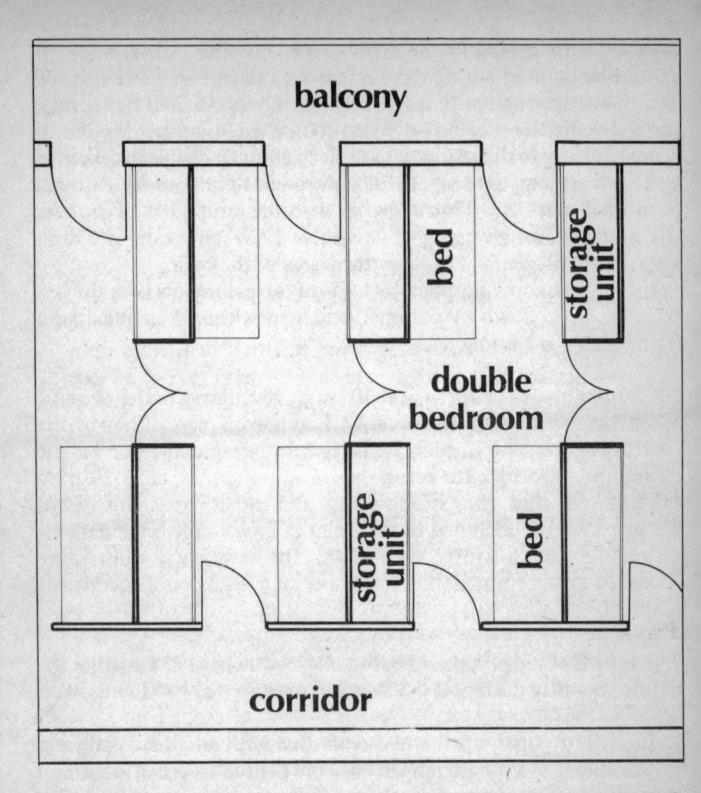

[Floor plan diagram: a double bedroom layout with balcony at top, corridor at bottom, two beds and two storage units labelled.]

Lavatories – A total of 9 lavatories will be required, preferably spread throughout the property.

Bathrooms – A total of 9 bath or shower rooms are required. It is proposed that the majority of these be located on the first floor adjacent to the bedrooms.

Kitchen – The main meals are eaten communally and are prepared by one or two people only. The equipment required within the kitchen area is – 1 large, catering standard, electric oven and hob, large double sinks and drainers, catering size refrigerator, ample worktop area and a fully ventilated lockable food store with space for a deep-freeze.

Communal rooms – Applying the D of E recommendations a total area of 140 sq m. of communal space will be required. It is suggested that the majority of this space form the main eating, living area of the centre of the refuge, with perhaps one or two smaller rooms provided for quieter activities.

Bedrooms — 24 double bedrooms are required. Each bedroom should have ample storage space for personal belongings and where possible be linked to the adjoining bedrooms. It is suggested by CFR that all beds are built-in as double bunks so that children from larger families can sleep together. As the 24 double bedrooms constitute the single largest use of floor area it is inevitable that some of the bedrooms be situated on the ground floor.

Office — A small open general office is required directly off and forming an integral part of the central living space. It is important that the office is not fully enclosed in order to prevent staff or mothers from isolating themselves from the community. It is suggested that it forms part of a reception area adjacent to the front entrance. Although the office should be open during daytime hours, it is important that the area containing the files etc. be lockable at night.

Laundry — A room large enough to accommodate 2 or 3 heavy-duty sinks, boards and tubs. Because of their vulnerability the installation of washing machines and driers is not recommended. The laundry should have direct access to an external drying area.

Play areas — To comply with the D of E requirements a total of 130 sq m. of external play space is required, accommodating one piece of play equipment such as a climbing frame.

CFR also require at least one internal play room for such activities as table tennis, bar billiards etc. This playroom should be directly accessible from the external play area.

Building height — It is a local planning requirement that in a building of this type children shall not be permitted to inhabit rooms above first floor level. CFR's experience also indicates that a three-storey structure becomes unmanageable due to the isolation of the third floor from all the daytime activity and therapy at ground level. The new refuge will therefore be a two storey structure.

Floor usage — In order to produce as busy and therapeutically desirable atmosphere as possible within the refuge, it is proposed that all communal daytime areas be grouped together around the rear courtyard, thus maximising the use of this courtyard as an extension and integral part of the community centre. It is therefore proposed that the first floor be used for sleeping purposes only and the ground-floor accommodate all the daytime activities. As has been previously pointed out, some of the bedrooms will have to be positioned at ground floor level.

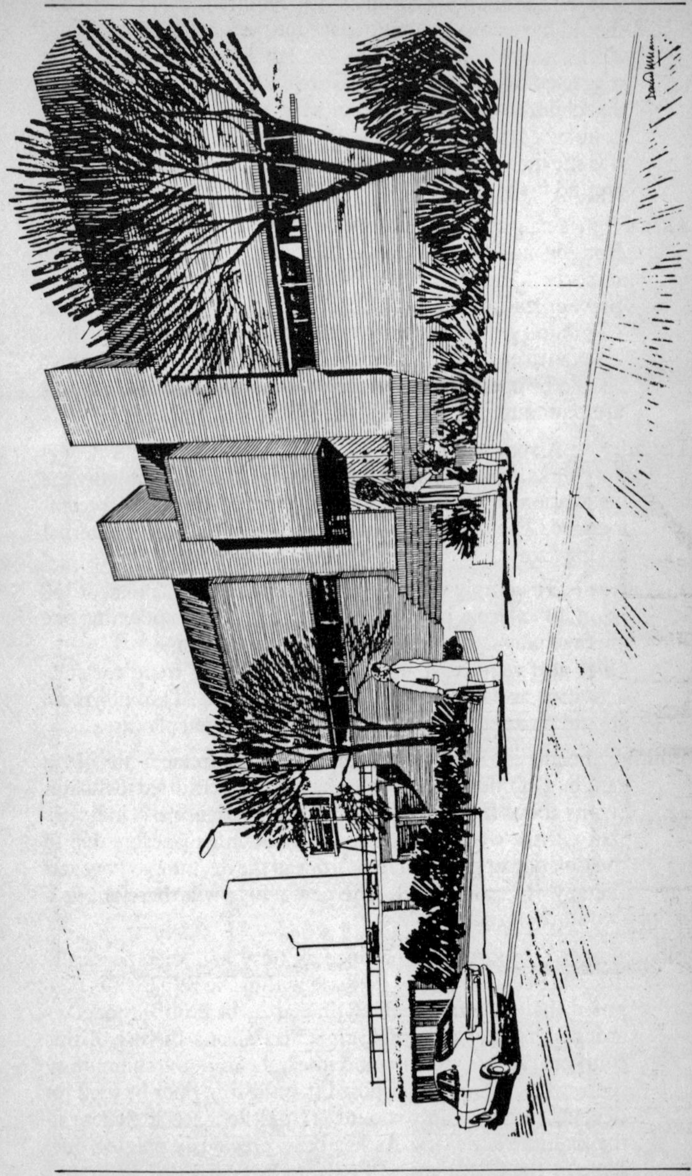

play area

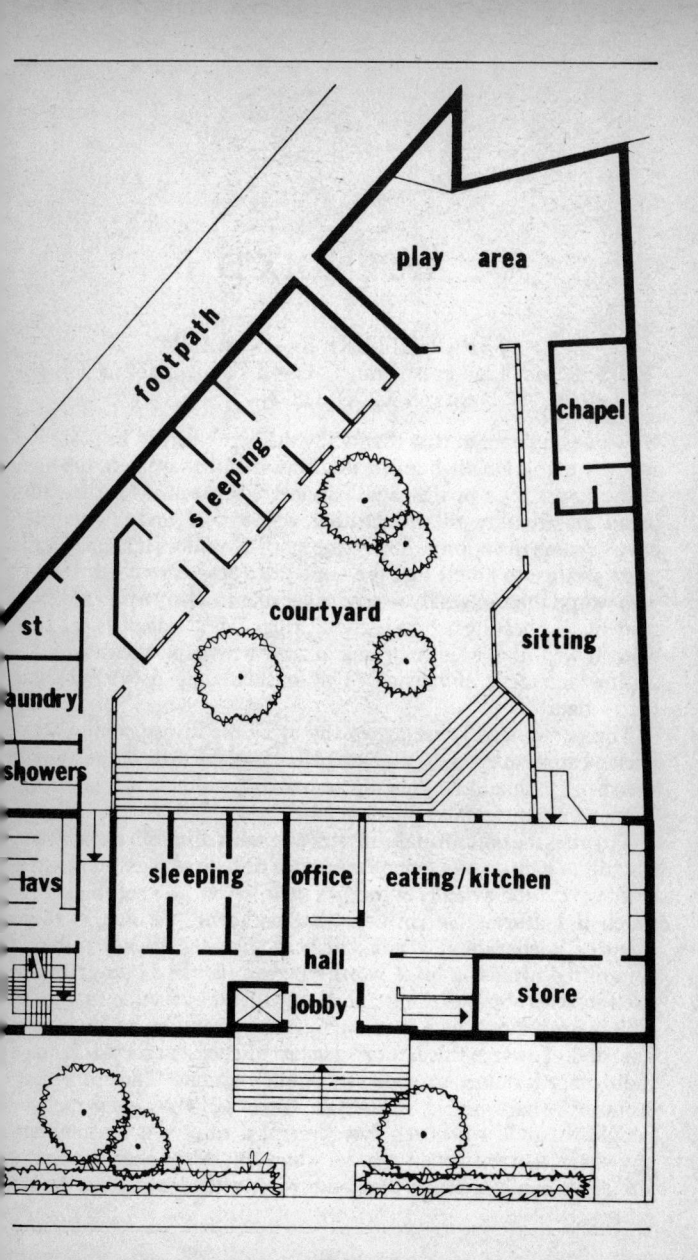

footpath

sleeping

chapel

st

laundry

courtyard

sitting

showers

lavs | sleeping | office | eating/kitchen

hall
lobby | store

APPENDIX D

'WIFE TORTURE IN ENGLAND'
(Extracts from a report by Frances Power Cobbe, published in *The Contemporary Review*, vol. XXXII, 1878)

How does it come to pass that while the better sort of Englishmen are . . . exceptionally humane and considerate to women, the men of the lower class of the same nation are proverbial for their unparalleled brutality, till wife-beating, wife-torture, and wife-murder have become the opprobrium of the land? How does it happen (still more strange to note!) that the same generous-hearted gentlemen, who would themselves fly to render succour to a lady in distress, yet read of the beatings, burnings, kickings, and 'cloggings' of *poor* women well-nigh every morning in their newspapers without once setting their teeth, and saying, 'This must be stopped! We can stand it no longer'?

The paradox truly seems worthy of a little investigation. What reason can be alleged, in the first place, why the male of the human species . . . should be the only animal in creation which maltreats its mate, or any female of its own kind?

To get to the bottom of the mystery we must discriminate between assaults of men on other men; assaults of men on women who are not their wives; and assaults of men on their wives. I do not think I err much if I affirm that, in common sentiment, the first of these offences is considerably more heinous than the second — being committed against a more worthy person (as the Latin grammar itself instructs boys to think); and lastly that the assault on a woman who is *not* a man's wife is worse than the assault on a wife by her husband. Towards this last or *minimum* offence a particular kind of indulgence is indeed extended by public opinion.* The proceeding seems to be surrounded by a certain halo of jealousy, which inclines people to smile whenever they hear of a case of it (terminating anywhere short of actual murder), and causes the mention of the subject to conduce rather than otherwise, to the hilarity of a dinner party . . .

Thus is comes to pass, I suppose, that the abstract idea of a strong man hitting or kicking a weak woman — *per se*, so revolting — has somehow got softened into a jovial kind of domestic lynching, the grosser features of the case being swept out of sight, just as people make endless jests on tipsiness, forgetting how loathsome a thing is a drunkard. A 'jolly companions' chorus seems to accompany both kinds of exploits. This, and the prevalent idea (which I shall analyze by-and-by) that the woman has generally deserved the blows she receives, keep up, I believe, the indifference of the public on the subject.

Probably the sense that they must carry with them a good deal of tacit sympathy on the part of other men has something to do in encouraging wife-beaters, just as the fatal notion of the good fellowship of drink has made thousands of sots. But the immediate causes of the offence of brutal violence are of course very various, and need to be better understood than they commonly are if we would find a remedy for them. First, there are to be considered the class of people and the conditions of life wherein the practice prevails; then the character of the men who beat their wives; next that of the wives who are beaten and kicked; and finally, the possible remedy.

Wife-beating exists in the upper and middle classes rather more, I fear, than is generally recognised; but it rarely extends to anything

---

*Not universally I am glad to hear. In Yorkshire and several other countries a very old custom exists, or did exist as late as 1862, called 'Riding the Stang' or 'Rough Music,' which consists in giving a serenade with cows' horns, and warming-pans, and tea-kettles to a man known to have beaten his wife or been unfaithful to her. See a very curious account of it, and of its good effects, in Chambers' Book of Days, vol. ii. p.510. A correspondent kindly sends further details, from which it appears that there is always a sort of herald or orator on the occasion, who, when the procession halts before the delinquent's house, recites verses in this style :—

(*piano*)
fortissimo)

> 'There is a man in this place,
> Has beat his wife (a pause)
> Has beat his wife!!
>
> ' 'Tis a very great shame and disgrace
> To all who live in the place,' & c.

The custom derives its name from the old Scottish 'Strange' — a long pole on which the culprit is sometimes made to take a very disagreeable ride.

beyond an occasional blow or two of a not dangerous kind. In his apparently most ungovernable rage, the gentleman or tradesman somehow manages to bear in mind the disgrace he will incur if his outbreak be betrayed by his wife's black eye or broken arm, and he regulates his cuffs or kicks accordingly. The dangerous wife-beater belongs almost exclusively to the artisan and labouring classes. Colliers, 'puddlers,' and weavers have long earned for themselves in this matter a bad reputation, and among a long list of cases before me, I reckon shoemakers, stonemasons, butchers, smiths, tailors, a printer, a clerk, a bird-catcher, and a large number of labourers. In the worst districts of London (as I have been informed by one of the most experienced magistrates) four-fifths of the wife-beating cases are among the lowest class of Irish labourers — a fact worthy of more than passing notice, had we time to bestow upon it, seeing that in their own country Irishmen of all classes are proverbially kind and even chivalrous towards women.

There are also various degrees of wife-beating in the different localities. In London it seldom goes beyond a severe 'thrashing' with the fist — a sufficiently dreadful punishment, it is true, when inflicted by a strong man on a woman; but mild in comparison of the kickings and tramplings and 'purrings' with hob-nailed shoes and clogs of what we can scarcely, in this connection, call the 'dark and true and *tender* North.' As Mr Serjeant Pulling remarks,* 'Nowhere is the ill-usage of woman so systematic as in Liverpool, and so little hindered by the strong arm of the law; making the lot of a married woman, whose locality is the 'kicking district' of Liverpool, simply a duration of suffering and subjection to injury and savage treatment, far worse than that to which the wives of mere savages are used.' It is in the centres of dense mercantile and manufacturing populations that this offence reaches its climax. In London the largest return for one year (in the Parliamentary Report on Brutal Assaults) of brutal assaults on women was 351. In Lancashire, with a population of almost two millions and a-half, the largest number was 194. In Stafford, with a population of three-quarters of a million, there were 113 cases. In the West Riding, with a million and a-half, 152; and in Durham, with 508,666, no less than 267. Thus, roughly speaking, there are nearly five times as many wife-beaters of the more brutal kind, in proportion to the population, in Durham as in London. What are the conditions of life among the working classes in those great 'hives of industry' of which we talk so proudly? It is but justice that we should picture the existence of the men and women in such places before we pass to discuss the deeds which darken it.

*Transactions Social Science Associations, 1876, p.345.

They are lives out of which almost every softening and ennobling element has been withdrawn, and into which enter brutalizing influences almost unknown elsewhere. They are lives of hard, ugly, mechanical toil in dark pits and hideous factories, amid the grinding and clanging of engines and the fierce heat of furnaces, in that Black Country where the green sod of earth is replaced by mounds of slag and shale, where no flower grows, no fruit ripens, scarcely a bird sings; where the morning has no freshness, the evening no dews; where the spring sunshine cannot pierce the foul curtain of smoke which overhangs these modern Cities of the Plain, and where the very streams and rivers run discoloured and steaming with stench, like Styx and Phlegethon, through their banks of ashes . . .

These, then, are the localities wherein Wife-torture flourishes in England; where a dense population is crowded into a hideous manufacturing or mining or mercantile district. Wages are usually high though fluctuating. Facilities for drink and vice abound, but those for cleanliness and decency are scarcely attainable. The men are rude, coarse, and brutal in their manners and habits, and the women devoid, in an extraordinary degree, of all the higher natural attractions and influences of their sex. Poor drudges of the factory, or of the crowded and sordid lodging-house, they lose, before youth is past, the freshness, neatness, and gentleness, perhaps even the modesty of a woman, and present, when their miserable cases come up before the magistrate, an aspect so sordid and forbidding that it is no doubt with difficulty he affords his sympathy to them rather than to the husband chained to so wretched a consort. Throughout the whole of this inquiry I think it is very necessary, in justice to all parties, and in mitigation of too vehement judgment of cases only known from printed reports, to bear in mind that the women of the class concerned are, some of them wofully unwomanly, slatternly, coarse, foul-mouthed — sometimes loose in behaviour, sometimes madly addicted to drink. There ought to be no idealizing of them, *as a class*, into refined and suffering angels if we wish to be just. The home of a Lancashire operative, alas! is not a garden wherein the plants of refinement or sensitiveness are very likely to spring up or thrive.

Given this direful *milieu*, and its population, male and female, we next ask, what are the immediate incitements to the men to maltreat the women? They are two kinds, I think, — general and particular.

First, the whole relation between the sexes in the class we are considering is very little better than one of master and slave. I have always abjured the use of this familiar comparison in speaking generally of English husbands and wives, because as regards the upper orders of society it is ridiculously overstrained and untrue.

But in the 'kicking districts,' among the lowest labouring classes, Legree himself might find a dozen prototypes, and the condition of the women be most accurately matched by that of the negroes on a Southern plantation before the war struck off their fetters. To a certain extent this marital tyrannny among the lower classes is beyond the reach of law, and can only be remedied by the slow elevation and civilization of both sexes. But it is also in an appreciable degree, I am convinced, enhanced by the law even as it now stands, and was still more so by the law as it stood before the Married Women's Property Act put a stop to the chartered robbery by husbands of their wives' earnings. At the present time, though things are improving year by year, thanks to the generous and far-seeing statesmen who are contending for justice to women inside and out of the House of Commons, the position of a woman before the law as wife, mother, and citizen, remains so much below that of a man as husband, father, and citizen, that it is a matter of course that she must be regarded by him as an inferior, and fail to obtain from him such a modicum of respect as her mental and moral qualities might win did he see her placed by the State on an equal footing . . .

Of course the ideas of the suffering wives are cast in the same mould as those of their companions. They take it for granted that a Husband is a Beating Animal, and may be heard to remark when extraordinarily ill-treated by a stranger, — that they 'never were so badly used, no not by their own 'usbands.' Their wretched proverbial similarity to spaniels and walnut-trees, the readiness with which they sometimes turn round and snap at a bystander who has interfered on their behalf, of course affords to cowardly people a welcome excuse for the 'policy of non-intervention,' and forms the culminating proof of how far the iron of their fetters has eaten into their souls. A specially experienced gentleman writes from Liverpool: 'The women of Lancashire are *awfully fond* of bad husbands. It has become quite a truism that our women are like dogs, the more you beat them the more they love you.' Surely if a bruised and trampled woman be a pitiful object, a woman who has been brought down by fear, or by her own gross passions, so low as to fawn on the beast who strikes her, is one to make angels weep?

To close this part of the subject, I conceive then, that the common idea of the inferiority of women, and the special notion of the rights of husbands, form the undercurrent of feeling which induces a man, when for any reason he is infuriated, to wreak his violence on his wife. She is, in his opinion, his natural *souffre-douleur*.

It remains to be noted what are the principal incitements to such outbursts of savage fury among the classes wherein Wife-beating prevails. They are not far to seek. The first is undoubtedly *Drink* — poisoned drink. The seas of brandy and gin, and the oceans of beer, imbibed annually in England, would be bad enough, if taken pure and simple, but it is the vile adulterations introduced into them which make them the infuriating poisons which they are — which literally *sting* the wretched drinkers into cruelty, perhaps quite foreign to their natural temperaments. As an experienced minister in these districts writes to me, 'I have known men almost as bad as those you quote (a dozen wife-murderers) made into most kind and considerate husbands by total abstinence.' If the English people will go on swallowing millions' worth yearly of brain poison, what can we expect but brutality the most hideous and grotesque? . . .

2. Next to drunkeness as a casue of violence to women, follows the other 'great sin of great cities,' of which it is unnecessary here to speak. The storms of jealousy thence arising, the hideous alternative *possession* of the man by the twin demons of cruelty and lust — one of whom is never very far from the other — are familiar elements in the police-court tragedies.

3. Another source of the evil may be found in that terrible, though little recognized passion, which rude men and savages share with many animals, and which is the precise converse of sympathy, for it consists in anger and cruelty, excited by the signs of pain; an impulse to hurt and destroy any suffering creature, rather than to relieve or help it. Of the widespread influence of this passion (which I have ventured elsewhere to name *Heteropathy*), a passion only slowly dying out as civilization advances, there can, I think, be no doubt at all. It is a hideous mystery of human nature that such feelings should lie latent in it, and that cruelty should grow by what it feeds on; that the more the tyrant causes the victim to suffer the more he hates him, and desires to heap on him fresh sufferings. Among the lower classes the emotion of Heteropathy unmistakably finds vent in the cruelty of parents and step-parents to unfortunate children who happen to be weaker or more stupid than others, or to have been once excessively punished, and whose joyless little faces and timid crouching demeanour, instead of appeals for pity, prove provocations to fresh outrage. The group of his shivering and starving children and weeping wife is the sad sight which, greeting the eyes of the husband and father reeling home from the gin-shop, somehow kindles his fury. If the baby cry in the cradle, he stamps on it. If his wife wrings her hands in despair, he fells her to the ground.

4. After these I should be inclined to reckon, as a cause of brutal outbreaks, the impatience and irritation which must often be caused in the homes of the working classes by sheer *friction*. While rich

people, when they get tired of each other or feel irritable, are enabled to recover their tempers in the ample space afforded by a comfortable house, the poor are huddled together in such close quarters that the sweetest tempers and most tender affections must sometimes feel the trial . . .

It is their interminable, inevitable propinquity which in the lower classes makes the nagging, wrangling, worrying women so intolerably trying. As millers get accustomed, it is said, to the clapping of their mill, so the preliminary experience must be severe indeed.

These, then, are the incentives to Wife-beating and Wife-torture. What are the men on whom they exert their evil influence?

Obviously, by the hypothesis, they are chiefly the drunken, idle, ruffianly fellows who lounge about the public-houses instead of working for their families. Without pretending to affirm that there are no sober, industrious husbands goaded to strike their wives through jealousy or irritation, the presumption is enormous against the character of any man convicted of such an assault. The cases in which the police reports of them add, 'He had been bound over to keep the peace several times previously,' or 'He had been often fined for drunkenness and disorderly behaviour,' are quite countless. Sometimes it approaches the ludicrous to read how helplessly the law has been attempting to deal with the scoundrel, as, for example, in the case of William Owen, whom his wife said she 'met for the first time beside Ned Wright's Bible-barrow,' and who told the poor fool he had been 'converted.' He was known to Constable 47 K as having been convicted *over sixty times* for drunkenness and violent assaults; and the moment he left the church he began to abuse his wife.

The pitilessness and ferocity of these men sometimes looks like madness. Alfred Stone, for example, coming home in a bad temper, took his wife's parrot out of its cage, stamped on it, and threw it on the fire, observing, 'Jane! it is the last thing you have got belonging to your father!' In the hands of such a man a woman's heart must be crushed, like the poor bird under his heel.

Turn we now from the beaters to the beaten. I have already said that we must not idealize the women of the 'kicking districts.' They are, mostly, poor souls, very coarse, very unwomanly. Some of them drink whenever (we cannot forget the awful stories of the Burial Clubs); many are hopelessly depraved, and lead as loose lives as their male companions. Many keep their houses in a miserable state of dirt and disorder, neglect their children, and sell their clothes and furniture for gin. Not seldom will one of these reckless creatures pursue her husband in the streets with screams of abuse and jeers. The man knows not where to turn to escape from the fury. When he comes home at night, he probably finds her lying dead drunk on the bed, and his children crying for their supper. Again, in a lesser degree, women make their homes into purgatories by their bad tempers. There was in old times a creature recognised by law as a 'Common Scold,' for whom the punishment of ducking in the village horse-pond was formally provided. It is to be feared her species is by no means to be reckoned among the 'Extinct Mammalia.' Then comes the 'nagging' wife, immortalized as 'Mrs Caudle;' the worrying, peevish kill-joy, whose presence is a wet blanket — nay, a wet blanket stuck full of pins; the argumentative woman, with a voice like a file and a face like a ferret, who bores on, night and day, till life is a burden.

These are terrible harpies. But it is scarcely fair to assume that every woman who is accused of 'nagging' necessarily belongs to their order. I have no doubt that every husband who comes home with empty pockets, and from whom his wife needs to beg repeatedly for money to feed herself and her children, considers that she 'nags' him. I have no doubt that when a wife reproaches such a husband with squandering his wages in the public-house, or on some wretched rival, while she and her children are starving, he accuses her to all his friends of intolerable 'nagging,' and that, not seldom having acquired from him the reputation of this kind of thing, the verdict of 'Serve her Right' is generally passed upon her by public opinion when her 'nagging' is capitally punished by a broken head.

But *all* women of the humblest class are not those terrible creatures, drunken, depraved, or ill-tempered; or even addicted to 'nagging.' On the contrary, I can affirm from my own experience, as well, I believe as that of all who have had much to do with the poor of great cities, there are among them at least as many good women as bad — as many who are sober, honest, chaste, and industrious, as are the contrary. There is a type which every clergyman, and magistrate, and district visitor will recognize in a moment as very common: a woman generally small and slight of person, but alert, intelligent, active morning, noon, and night, doing the best her strength allows to keep her home tidy, and her children neat and well fed, and to supply her husband's wants. Her face was, perhaps, pretty at eighteen: by the time she is eight-and-twenty, toil and drudgery and many children have reduced her to a mere rag, and only her eyes retain a little pathetic relic of beauty. This woman expresses herself well and simply: it is a special 'note' of her character that she uses no violent words, even in describing the worst injuries. There is nothing 'loud' about her in voice, dress, or manners. She is emphatically a '*decent*,' respectable woman. Her only fault, if fault it be, is that she will insist on obtaining food and clothing for her children, and that when she is refused them she becomes that depressed, broken-spirited creature whose mute, reproachful looks act as a goad, as I have said, to the passions of her oppressor. We shall see presently what part this class of woman plays in the horrible domestic tragedies of England.

We have now glanced at the conditions under which Wife-beating takes place, at the incentives immediately leading to it, the men who beat, and the women who are beaten. Turn we now to examine more closely the thing itself.

There are two kinds of Wife-beating which I am anxious the reader should keep clearly apart in his mind. There is what may be called *Wife-beating by Combat*, and there is Wife-beating properly so called, which is only wife, and not wife-and-husband beating. In the first, both parties have an equal share. Bad words are exchanged, then blows. The man hits, the woman perhaps scratches and tears. If the woman generally gets much the worst of it, it is simply because cats are weaker than dogs. The man cannot so justly be said to have 'beaten' his wife as to have vanquished her in a boxing-match. Almost without exception in these cases it is mentioned that 'both parties were the worse for liquor.' It is in this way the drunken woman is beaten, *by the drunken man*, not by the ideal sober and industrious husband, who has a right to be disgusted by her intoxication. It is nearly exclusively, I think, in such drunken quarrels that the hateful virago gets beaten at all. As a general rule she commands too much fear, and is so ready to give back curse for curse and blow for blow, that, in cold blood, nobody meddles with her. Such a termagant is often the tyrant of her husband, nay, of the whole court or lane in which she lives; and the sentiments she excites are the reverse of those which bring down the fist and the clogs of the ruffian husband on the timid and meek-faced woman who tries, too often unsuccessfully, the supposed magic of a soft answer to turn away the wrath of such a wild beast as he . . .

The second kind of Wife-beating is when the man alone is the striker and the woman, the stricken. These are the cases which specially challenge our attention, and for which it may be hoped some palliative may be found. In these, the husband usually comes home 'the worse for liquor,' and commences, sometimes without any provocation at all, to attack his wife, or drag her out of the bed where she is asleep, or has just been confined. Sometimes there is preliminary altercation, the wife imploring him to give her some money to buy necessaries, or reproaching him for drinking all he has earned. In either case the wife is passive so far as blows are concerned, unless at the last, in self-defence, she lays her hand on some weapon to protect her life — a fact which is always cited against her as a terrible delinquency*. . .

Such are the two orders of Wife-beating with which a tolerably extensive study of the subject has made me familiar. It will be observed that neither includes that ideal Wife-beater of whom we hear so much, the sober, industrious man goaded to frenzy by his wife's temper or drunkenness. I will not venture to affirm that that Ideal Wife-beater is as mythical as the griffin or the sphinx, but I will affirm that in all my inquiries I have never yet come on his track . . . Regarding the extent of the evil it is difficult to arrive at a just calculation. Speaking of those cases only which come before the courts, – probably, of course, not a third of the whole number – the elements for forming an opinion are the following: –

In the Judicial Statistics for England and Wales, issued in 1877 for 1876, we find that of Aggravated Assaults on Women and Children, of the class which since 1853 have been brought under Summary Jurisdiction there were reported.

In 1876 - - - - - 2,737
In 1875 - - - - - 3,106
In 1874 - - - - - 2,841

How many of these were assaults made by husbands on wives there is no means of distinguishing, but, judging from other sources, I should imagine they formed about four-fifths of the whole.

Among the worst cases, when the accused persons were committed for trial or bailed for appearance at Assizes or Sessions (coming under the head of Criminal Proceedings), the classification adopted in the Parliamentary Return does not permit of identifying the cases which concerned women only. Some rough guess on the matter may perhaps be formed from the preponderance of male criminals in all classes of violent crime. Out of 67 persons charged with Murder in 1876, 49 were men. Of 41 charged with Attempt to Murder, 35 were males. Of 157 charged with Shooting, Stabbing, &c., 146 were men. Of 232 charged with Manslaughter, 185 were men; and of 1,020 charged with Assault inflicting bodily harm, 857 were men. In short, out of 1,517 persons charged

---

*Such was the case of Susannah Palmer, a few years ago, whose husband had beaten her, and sold up her furniture again and again, blackened her eyes, and knocked out her five front teeth. At last on one occasion, with the knife with which she was cutting her children's supper, she somehow inflicted a slight cut on the man while he was knocking her about the head. He immediately summoned her for 'cutting and wounding him,' and she was sent to Newgate . . .

with crimes of cruelty and violence, more than five-sixths were males, and only 235 females. Of course the men's offences include a variety of crimes besides Wife-beating and Wife-torture.

The details of the crimes for which twenty-two men who were capitally convicted in 1876 suffered death are noteworthy on this head. (Criminal Statistics p.xxix.) Of these:—

> Edward Deacon, shoemaker, murdered his wife by cutting her head with a chopper.
> John Thomas Green, painter, shot his wife with a pistol.
> John Eblethrift, labourer, murdered his wife by beating.
> Charles O'Donnell, labourer, murdered his wife by cutting her throat.

Besides these, five others murdered women with whom they were living in vicious relations, and three others (including the monster William Fish) murdered children. In all, more than half the convicted persons executed that year were guilty of wife-murder, — or of what we may term *quasi*-wife-murder.

A source of more accurate information is to be found in the abstracts of the Reports of Chief Constables for the years 1870-1-2-3-4, presented to the Home Secretary, and published in the 'Report on Brutal Assaults' (p. 169, et seq.). In this instructive table Brutal Assaults on Women are discriminated from those on men, and the total number of convictions for such assaults for the whole five years is 6,029; or at the average of 1,205 per annum. This is, however, obviously an imperfect return. (*Explains.*) Thus I conceive that we may fairly estimate the number of brutal assaults (*brutal* be it remembered, not ordinary) committed on women in England and Wales and actually brought to justice at about 1,500 a year, or more than four per diem; and out of these the great majority are of husbands and wives.

Let us now proceed from the number to the nature of the offences in question. I have called this paper English *Wife-torture* because I wish to impress my readers with the fact that the familiar term 'wife-beating' conveys about as remote a notion of the extremity of the cruelty indicated as when candid and ingenuous vivisectors talk of 'scratching a newt's tail' when they refer to burning alive, or dissecting out the nerves of living dogs, or torturing ninety cats in one series of experiments.

Wife-*beating* is the mere preliminary canter before the race, — the preface to the serious matter which is to follow. Sometimes, it is true, there are men of comparatively mild dispositions who are content to go on beating their wives year after year, giving them occasional black-eyes and bruises, or tearing out a few locks of their hair and spitting in their faces, or bestowing an ugly print of their iron fingers on the woman's soft arm, but not proceeding beyond these minor injuries to anything perilous. Among the lower classes, unhappily, this rude treatment is understood to mean very little more than that the man uses his weapon – the fists – as the woman uses hers – the tongue – and neither are very much hurt or offended by what is either done by one or said by the other . . . But the unendurable mischief, the discovery of which has driven me to try to call public attention to the whole matter, is this Wife-*beating* in process of time, and in numberless cases, advances to Wife-*torture*, and the Wife-torture usually ends in Wife-maiming, Wife-blinding, or Wife-murder. A man who has 'thrashed' his wife with his fists half-a-dozen times, becomes satiated with such enjoyment as that performance brings, and next time he is angry he kicks her with his hob-nailed shoes. When he has kicked her a few times standing or sitting, he kicks her down and stamps on her stomach, her breast, or her face. If he does not wear clogs or hob-nailed shoes, he takes up some other weapon, a knife, a poker, a hammer, a bottle of vitriol, or a lighted lamp, and strikes her with it, or sets her on fire; – and then, and then only, the hapless creature's sufferings are at an end.

I desire specially to avoid making this paper more painful than can be helped, but it is indispensable that some specimens of the tortures to which I refer should be brought before the reader's eye. I shall take them exclusively from cases reported during the last three or four months. Were I to go further back for a year or two, it would be easy to find some more 'sensational,' as, for example, of Michael Copeland, who threw his wife on a blazing fire; of George Ellis, who murdered his wife by pitching her out of window; of Ashton Keefe, who beat his wife and thrust a box of lighted matches into his little daughter's breast when she was too slow in bringing his beer; and of Charles Bradley, who, according to the report in the *Manchester Examiner*, 'came home, and after locking the door, told his wife he would murder her. He immediately set a large bulldog at her, and the dog, after flying at the upper part of her body, seized hold of the woman's right arm, which she lifted to protect herself, and tore pieces out. The prisoner in the meantime kept striking her in the face, and inciting the brute to worry her. The dog dragged her up and down, biting pieces out of her arms, and the prisoner then got on the sofa and hit and kicked her on the breast.' . . .

But the instances of the last three or four months – from September to the end of January – are more than enough to establish all I want to prove; and I beg here to return my thanks for a collection of them, and for many very useful observations and tabulations of them, to Miss A. Shore, who has been good enough to place them at my disposal.

It is needful to bear in mind in reading them, that the reports of such cases which appear in newspapers are by no means always reliable . . .

> James Mills cut his wife's throat as she lay in bed. He was quite sober at the time. On a previous occasion he had nearly torn away her left breast.
>
> J. Coleman returned home early in the morning, and finding his wife asleep, took up a heavy piece of wood and struck her on the head and arm, bruising her arm. On a previous occasion he had fractured her ribs.
>
> John Mills poured out vitriol deliberately, and threw it in his wife's face, because she asked him to give her some of his wages. He had said previously that he would blind her.
>
> James Lawrence, who had been frequently bound over to keep the peace, and who had been supported by his wife's industry for years, struck her on the face with a poker, leaving traces of the most dreadful kind when she appeared in court.
>
> Frederick Knight jumped on the face of his wife (who had only been confined for a month) with a pair of boots studded with hobnails.
>
> Richard Mountain beat his wife on the back and mouth, and turned her out of her bed and out of their room one hour after she had been confined.
>
> Alfred Roberts felled his wife to the floor, with a child in her arms; knelt on her, and grasped her throat. She had previously taken out three summonses against him, but had never attended.
>
> John Harris, a shoemaker, at Sheffield, found his wife and children in bed; dragged her out, and, after vainly attempting to force her into the oven, tore off her night-dress and turned her round before the fire 'like a piece of beef,' while the children stood on the stairs listening to their mother's agonized screams.
>
> Richard Scully knocked in the frontal bone of his wife's forehead.
>
> William White, stonemason, threw a burning paraffin lamp at his wife, and stood quietly watching her enveloped in flames, from the effects of which she died.
>
> William Hussell, a butcher, ran a knife into his wife several times and killed her. Had threatened to do so often before.

Robert Kelly, engine-driver, bit a piece out of his wife's cheek.

William James, an operative boilermaker, 'I am sorry I did not kill both' (his wife and her mother).

Thomas Richards, a smith, threw his wife down a flight of fourteen steps, when she came to entreat him to give her some money for her maintenance. He was living with another woman — the nurse at a hospital where he had been ill.

James Frickett, a ratcatcher. His wife was found dying with broken ribs and cut and bruised face, a walking-stick with blood on it lying by. Frickett remarked, 'If I am going to be hanged for you, I love you.'

James Styles beat his wife about the head when he met her in the City Road. She had supported him for years by char-work, and during the whole time he had been in the habit of beating her, and on one occasion so assaulted her that the sight of one of her eyes was destroyed. He got drunk habitually with the money she earned.

John Harley, a compositor, committed for trial for cutting and wounding his wife with intent to murder.

Joseph Moore, labourer, committed for trial for causing the death of his wife by striking her with an iron instrument on the head.

George Ralph Smith, oilman, cut his wife, as the doctor expressed it, 'to pieces,' with a hatchet, in their back parlour. She died afterwards, but he was found Not Guilty, as it was not certain that her death resulted from the wounds.

I think I may now safely ask the reader to draw breath after all these horrors, and agree with me that they cannot, *must* not, be allowed to go on unchecked, without some effort to stop them, and save these perishing and miserable creatures. Poor, stupid, ignorant women as most of them are, worn out with life-long drudgery, burdened with all the pangs and cares of many children, poorly fed and poorly clothed, with no pleasures and many pains, there is an enormous excuse to be made for them even if they do sometimes seek in drink the oblivion of their misery — a brief dream of unreal joy, where real natural happiness is so far away. But for those who rise above these temptations, who are sober where intoxication holds out their only chance of pleasure; chaste in the midst of foulness; tender mothers when their devotion calls for toilsome days and sleepless nights, — for these good, industrious, struggling women who, I have shown, are the chief victims of all this cruelty, — is it to be borne that we should sit patiently by and allow their lives to be trampled out in agony?

What ought to be done?

(There follows a long plea for public action.)

I entreat my readers not to turn away and forget this wretched subject. I entreat the gentlemen of England — the bravest, humanest, and most generous in the world, — not to leave these helpless women to be trampled to death under their very eyes. I entreat English ladies, who, like myself, have never received from the men with whom we associate anything but kindness and consideration, and who are prone to think that the lot of others is smooth and happy as our own, to take to heart the wrongs and agonies of our miserable sisters, and to lift up on their behalf a cry which must make Parliament either hasten to deal with the matter, or renounce for very shame the vain pretence that it takes care of the interests of women.

FRANCES POWER COBBE.

NON-FICTION

GENERAL
- ☐ The Chinese Mafia — Fenton Bresler — £1.50
- ☐ The Piracy Business — Barbara Conway — £1.50
- ☐ Strange Deaths — John Dunning — £1.35
- ☐ Shocktrauma — John Franklin & Alan Doelp — £1.50
- ☐ The War Machine — James Avery Joyce — £1.50

BIOGRAPHY/AUTOBIOGRAPHY
- ☐ All You Needed Was Love — John Blake — £1.50
- ☐ Clues to the Unknown — Robert Cracknell — £1.50
- ☐ William Wordsworth — Hunter Davies — £1.95
- ☐ The Family Story — Lord Denning — £1.95
- ☐ The Borgias — Harry Edgington — £1.50
- ☐ Rachman — Shirley Green — £1.50
- ☐ Nancy Astor — John Grigg — £2.95
- ☐ Monty: The Making of a General 1887-1942 — Nigel Hamilton — £4.95
- ☐ The Windsors in Exile — Michael Pye — £1.50
- ☐ 50 Years with Mountbatten — Charles Smith — £1.25
- ☐ Maria Callas — Arianna Stassinopoulos — £1.75
- ☐ Swanson on Swanson — Gloria Swanson — £2.50

HEALTH/SELF-HELP
- ☐ The Hamlyn Family First Aid Book — Dr Robert Andrew — £1.50
- ☐ Girl! — Brandenburger & Curry — £1.25
- ☐ The Good Health Guide for Women — Cooke & Dworkin — £2.95
- ☐ The Babysitter Book — Curry & Cunningham — £1.25
- ☐ Living Together — Dyer & Berlins — £1.50
- ☑ The Pick of Woman's Own Diets — Jo Foley — 95p
- ☐ Coping With Redundancy — Fred Kemp — £1.50
- ☐ Cystitis: A Complete Self-help Guide — Angela Kilmartin — £1.00
- ☐ Fit for Life — Donald Norfolk — £1.35
- ☐ The Stress Factor — Donald Norfolk — £1.25
- ☐ Fat is a Feminist Issue — Susie Orbach — £1.25
- ☐ Fat is a Feminist Issue II — Susie Orbach — £3.50
- ☐ Living With Your New Baby — Rakowitz & Rubin — £1.50
- ☐ Related to Sex — Claire Rayner — £1.50
- ☐ Natural Sex — Mary Shivanandan — £1.25
- ☐ Woman's Own Birth Control — Dr Michael Smith — £1.25
- ☐ Overcoming Depression — Dr Andrew Stanway — £1.50
- ☐ Health Shock — Martin Weitz — £1.75

POCKET HEALTH GUIDES
- ☐ Depression and Anxiety — Dr Arthur Graham — 85p
- ☐ Diabetes — Dr Alex D. G. Gunn — 85p
- ☐ Heart Trouble — Dr Simon Joseph — 85p
- ☐ High Blood Pressure — Dr James Knapton — 85p
- ☐ The Menopause — Studd & Thom — 85p
- ☐ Children's Illnesses — Dr Luke Zander — 85p

TRAVEL
- ☐ The Complete Traveller — Joan Bakewell — £1.95
- ☐ Time Out London Shopping Guide — Lindsey Bareham — £1.50
- ☐ A Walk Around the Lakes — Hunter Davies — £1.75
- ☐ Britain By Train — Patrick Goldring — £1.75
- ☐ England By Bus — Elizabeth Gundrey — £1.25
- ☐ Staying Off the Beaten Track — Elizabeth Gundrey — £2.95
- ☐ Britain at Your Feet — Wickers & Pedersen — £1.75

HUMOUR
- ☐ Don't Quote Me — Atyeo & Green — £1.00
- ☐ Ireland Strikes Back! — Seamus B. Gorrah — 85p
- ☐ Pun Fun — Paul Jennings — 95p
- ☐ 1001 Logical Laws — John Peers — 95p
- ☐ The Devil's Bedside Book — Leonard Rossiter — 85p

REFERENCE

- ☐ The Sunday Times Guide to Movies on Television — Angela & Elkan Allan — £1.50
- ☐ The Cheiro Book of Fate and Fortune — £1.50
- ☐ Hunter Davies's Book of British Lists — £1.25
- ☐ NME Guide to Rock Cinema — Fred Dellar — £1.50
- ☐ What's Wrong With Your Pet? — Hugo Kerr — 95p
- ☐ The Drinker's Companion — Derek Nimmo — £1.25
- ☐ The Complete Book of Cleaning — Barty Phillips — £1.50
- ☐ The Oscar Movies from A-Z — Roy Pickard — £1.25
- ☐ Collecting For Profit — Sam Richards — £1.25
- ☐ Islam — D. S. Roberts — £1.50
- ☐ Questions of Motoring Law — John Spencer — £1.25
- ☐ Questions of Law — Bill Thomas — £1.25

GAMES AND PASTIMES

- ☐ The Hamlyn Book of Wordways 1 — 75p
- ☐ The Hamlyn Family Quiz Book — 85p

WAR

- ☐ The Battle of Malta — Joseph Attard — £1.50
- ☐ World War 3 — Edited by Shelford Bidwell — £1.50
- ☐ The Black Angels — Rupert Butler — £1.35
- ☐ Gestapo — Rupert Butler — £1.50
- ☐ Hand of Steel — Rupert Butler — £1.35
- ☐ The Flight of the Mew Gull — Alex Henshaw — £1.75
- ☐ Sigh for a Merlin — Alex Henshaw — £1.50
- ☐ Hitler's Secret Life — Glenn B. Infield — £1.25

GARDENING

- ☐ 'Jock' Davidson's House Plant Book — £1.50
- ☐ A Vegetable Plot for Two — or More — D. B. Clay Jones — £1.00
- ☐ Salads the Year Round — Joy Larkcom — £1.50
- ☐ Gardening Tips of A Lifetime — Fred Loads — £1.50
- ☐ Sunday Telegraph Patio Gardening — Robert Pearson — £1.00
- ☐ Greenhouse Gardening — Sue Phillips — £1.25

COOKERY

- ☐ A-Z of Health Foods — Carol Bowen — £1.50
- ☐ The Giant Sandwich Book — Carol Bowen — £1.50
- ☐ Vegetarian Cookbook — Dave Dutton — £1.50
- ☐ Jewish Cookbook — Florence Greenberg — £1.50
- ☐ Know Your Onions — Kate Hastrop — 95p
- ☐ Indian Cooking — Attia Hosain and Sita Pasricha — £1.50
- ☐ Home Preserving and Bottling — Gladys Mann — 80p
- ☐ Home Baked Breads & Cakes — Mary Norwak — 75p
- ☐ Easy Icing — Marguerite Patten — 85p
- ☐ Wine Making At Home — Francis Pinnegar — 80p
- ☐ Cooking for Christmas — Shona Crawford Poole — £1.50
- ☐ Microwave Cookbook — Jill Spencer — £1.25
- ☐ Mixer and Blender Cookbook — Myra Street — 80p
- ☐ Diabetic Cookbook — Elisabeth Russell Taylor — £1.50
- ☐ The Hamlyn Pressure Cookbook — Jane Todd — 85p

HUMOUR

- ☐ Don't Quote Me — Atyeo & Green — £1.00
- ☐ Ireland Strikes Back! — Seamus B. Gorrah — 85p
- ☐ Pun Fun — Paul Jennings — 95p
- ☐ 1001 Logical Laws — John Peers — 95p
- ☐ The Devil's Bedside Book — Leonard Rossiter — 85p

FICTION

GENERAL

☐ The Free Fishers	John Buchan	£1.50
☐ Huntingtower	John Buchan	£1.50
☐ Midwinter	John Buchan	£1.25
☐ A Prince of the Captivity	John Buchan	£1.25
☐ The Eve of St Venus	Anthony Burgess	£1.10
☐ Nothing Like the Sun	Anthony Burgess	£1.50
☐ The Memoirs of Maria Brown	John Cleland	£1.25
☐ A Man	Oriana Fallaci	£1.95
☐ Savannah Blue	William Harrison	£1.50
☐ Duncton Wood	William Horwood	£1.95
☐ The Good Listener	Pamela Hansford Johnson	£1.50
☐ The Honours Board	Pamela Hansford Johnson	£1.50
☐ Buccaneer	Dudley Pope	£1.50
☐ An Inch of Fortune	Simon Raven	£1.25

HAMLYN WHODUNNITS

☐ Some Die Eloquent	Catherine Aird	£1.25
☐ The Case of the Abominable Snowman	Nicholas Blake	£1.10
☐ The Widow's Cruise	Nicholas Blake	£1.25
☐ The Worm of Death	Nicholas Blake	95p
☐ Thou Shell of Death	Nicholas Blake	£1.25
☐ Tour de Force	Christianna Brand	£1.10
☐ King and Joker	Peter Dickinson	£1.25
☐ A Lonely Place to Die	Wessel Ebersohn	£1.10
☐ Gold From Gemini	Jonathan Gash	£1.10
☐ The Grail Tree	Jonathan Gash	£1.25
☐ The Judas Pair	Jonathan Gash	95p
☐ Spend Game	Jonathan Gash	£1.25
☐ Blood and Judgment	Michael Gilbert	£1.10
☐ Close Quarters	Michael Gilbert	£1.10
☐ The Etruscan Net	Michael Gilbert	£1.25
☐ Hare Sitting Up	Michael Innes	£1.10
☐ Silence Observed	Michael Innes	£1.25
☐ The Weight of the Evidence	Michael Innes	£1.10
☐ There Came Both Mist and Snow	Michael Innes	95p
☐ The Howard Hughes Affair	Stuart Kaminsky	£1.10
☐ Inspector Ghote Draws a Line	H. R. F. Keating	£1.10
☐ Inspector Ghote Plays a Joker	H. R. F. Keating	£1.25
☐ The Murder of the Maharajah	H. R. F. Keating	£1.25
☐ The Perfect Murder	H. R. F. Keating	£1.10
☐ A Fine and Private Place	Ellery Queen	£1.25
☐ The French Powder Mystery	Ellery Queen	£1.25
☐ The Siamese Twin Mystery	Ellery Queen	95p
☐ The Spanish Cape Mystery	Ellery Queen	£1.10

NAME ....

ADDRESS ....

....

Write to Hamlyn Paperbacks Cash Sales, PO Box 11, Falmouth, Cornwall TR10 9EN.

Please indicate order and enclose remittance to the value of the cover price plus:

U.K.: Please allow 45p for the first book plus 20p for the second book and 14p for each additional book ordered, to a maximum charge of £1.63.

B.F.P.O. & EIRE: Please allow 45p for the first book plus 20p for the second book and 14p per copy for the next 7 books, thereafter 8p per book.

OVERSEAS: Please allow 75p for the first book and 21p per copy for each additional book.

Whilst every effort is made to keep prices low it is sometimes necessary to increase cover prices and also postage and packing rates at short notice. Hamlyn Paperbacks reserve the right to show new retail prices on covers which may differ from those previously advertised in the text or elsewhere.